# Arab Women in the Field

 *Contemporary Issues in the Middle East*

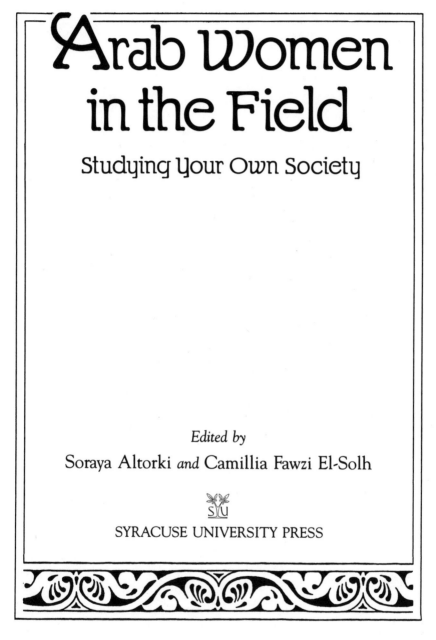

# Arab Women in the Field

## Studying Your Own Society

*Edited by*

Soraya Altorki *and* Camillia Fawzi El-Solh

SYRACUSE UNIVERSITY PRESS

FIRST EDITION 1988
91  92  93  94  95  96  97  98  99          6  5  4  3  2

The paper used in this publication meets the minimum requirements of American National
Standard for Information Sciences—Permanence of Paper for Printed Library Materials, ANSI
Z39.48–1984. ∞™

"The Library of Congress has cataloged the first printing of this title as follows":

**Library of Congress Cataloging-in-Publication Data**

Arab women in the field : studying your own society / edited
by Soraya Altorki and Camillia Fawzi El-Solh. — 1st ed.
    p.  cm. — (Modern Arab studies)
    Bibliography: p.
    Includes index.
    ISBN 0–8156–2449–2 (alk. paper).  ISBN 0–8156–2450–6
(pbk. : alk. paper)
    1. Ethnology—Arab countries—Fieldwork.  2. Women
anthropologists—Arab countries.  3. Women—Research—
Arab countries.  I. Altorki, Soraya.  II. El-Solh, Camillia
Fawzi. III. Series.
GN346.A7  1988
306'.0917'4927—dc19                          88–20018
                                                    CIP

Manufactured in the United States of America

*To the memory of Ali Mokhtar, in recognition of his contribution to a wider understanding of Arab society, and to the cause of Arab women.*

# Contents

# A Note on References

Multiple references to authors in the text are not given alphabetically but chronologically, i.e., according to date of publication.

Bibliographies of individual contributions have been combined at the end of the manuscript in order to avoid repetition.

# Contributors

**Lila Abu-Lughod** is a Palestinian-American. She received her Ph.D. in anthropology from Harvard University and was on the faculty of Williams College for several years. She is currently Associate Professor, Department of Religion, Princeton University. Author of a book, *Veiled Sentiments: Honor and Poetry in a Bedouin Society,* and several articles on the Awlad Ali Bedouins of Egypt and on Middle East anthropology, she is now at work on a book that explores the implications of feminist theory for ethnography.

**Soraya Altorki** is a Saudi Arabian who received her Ph.D. in anthropology from the University of California, Berkeley. She is currently Professor of Anthropology at the American University in Cairo. Her publications include *Women in Saudi Arabia: Ideology and Behavior Among the Elite.* Her research focus is on ideology, social change, and community development. She is currently engaged in research on the involvement of Saudi Arabian women in the post-oil economy.

**Camillia Fawzi El-Solh** is of Egyptian/Irish parentage. She received her master's degree in economics/sociology from the University of Cologne, West Germany, and her Ph.D. in sociology from Bedford College, University of London. She is currently Research Associate at the Centre for Cross Cultural Research on Women, Queen Elizabeth House, University of Oxford, and is involved in post-doctoral research on Arab immigrant communities in Britain.

**Suad Joseph** is an Associate Professor of Anthropology at the University of California, Davis. She was born in Lebanon. Educated in the U.S., she received her Ph.D. from Columbia University. Her initial work was on the politicization of religious sects in Lebanon. More recent work has focused on the connections between women, family, local community and the state in the Middle East.

**Soheir Morsy** is an Egyptian who received her Ph.D. in medical anthropology from Michigan State University. Her research and publications have been in the area of the political economy of health, peasantry and agrarian transformation, Third World underdevelopment, and gender in cross-cultural perspective.

**Seteney Shami,** a Jordanian, received her B.A. in anthropology from the American University of Beirut and her M.A. and Ph.D. from the University of California, Berkeley. She is currently Assistant Professor and Head of the Anthropology Section at the Institute of Archaeology and Anthropology at Yarmouk University, Irbid, Jordan. Her research interests are ethnicity and politics, urban anthropology, and migration studies. She is currently writing up the results of her research in a squatter area in Amman, Jordan.

Arab Women in the Field

# 1

# Introduction

SORAYA ALTORKI and CAMILLIA FAWZI EL-SOLH

$A$ *rab Women in the Field* addresses a hotly debated issue in the social sciences, namely, the constraints on fieldwork that result from the fact that social scientists themselves are cultural beings whose backgrounds greatly influence the data they gather. It attempts to do this on the basis of two particularly important manifestations: the issue of being female and the issue of being indigenous in Arab society, which—among other things—is characterized by a pervasive segregation of the sexes.

This task is now possible owing to the availability of relevant studies. Although the work of Arab female social scientists did not begin in earnest until the 1960s, their number has since grown significantly. This is evidenced, for example, by the substantial enrollment of Arab women in the social science departments of the various Arab universities (see Massialas and Jarrar 1983). More specifically, the involvement of Arab women in the study of other women in their own societies parallels the period of cultural and political awakening that occurred throughout that region following World War II (Nelson 1986:8). This was a period of national struggle for independence, of mounting demands for decolonization, and of calls for serious attempts at development. This era is also characterized by an upsurge of feminism in the West and the attendant interest in the condition of women in Arab societies. Such interest was reflected in the growing number of studies on women by women that began to appear during the 1960s and 1970s. Although most of these studies were carried out by Western women (e.g., Sweet 1960; Fernea 1965), a number of Arab women were already becoming engaged in the study of Arab society and of women in these societies (e.g., Mohsen 1967; El-Hamamsy 1972, n.d.; Abu Zahra 1982).

It was, however, in the wake of the humiliating defeat of Arab countries by Israel in 1967—commonly referred to as the *naksah* (setback)—that a period of more serious questioning began. For many Arab intellectuals, male and female alike, the *naksah* initiated a long and painful process of examining their own societies, their values and institutions. It also meant a deeper questioning of their relationship with the West and a more vehement rejection of imperialism and what was diagnosed as its cultural manifestations (see Dessouki 1977). Underscoring the role of scientific knowledge in reproducing structures of social inequality, some Arab scholars challenged the models and theories developed in Western society and which have been integrated into the body of social science (e.g., Khalifa et al., 1984). Amid this intellectual, political, and social climate, Arab women have become more involved in the production of knowledge about their own societies and about women in these societies (e.g., Farrag 1971; Rassam 1974, 1980; Mohsen 1974, 1985; Mernissi 1975; Baffoun 1977; El-Messiri 1978; Sabbah 1984).

*Arab Women in the Field* records for the first time the field experiences of a number of women of Arab descent and illustrates their attempt to deal with epistemological issues of relevance in the study of their own society. Our task will involve the examination of the role that gender and indigenous status may play in structuring knowledge about others in Arab society. More specifically, we shall be looking at the experiences of Arab female researchers in order to assess the range of variables that may interact with gender and indigenous status to affect their access to and construction of knowledge.

## Studying One's Own Society

The study of one's own society using fieldwork methods—that is, the collection of data firsthand and primarily through the technique of participant observation—is of course not new. Sociologists by tradition study population segments within their own complex societies. Even anthropologists, who traditionally studied "the other," attempted the study of

American minorities as early as the 1920s (see Lynd and Lynd 1929; Warner 1949). It is not our purpose here to present a detailed account of such field research, but rather to note that interest in the study of one's own society increased in the 1960s (see Gans 1962; Liebow 1967; Keiser 1969), becoming progressively popular both in the Third World (e.g., Srinivas et al. 1979; Fahim 1982a) and in North America (e.g., Spradley 1970; Agar 1973; Messerschmidt 1981).

The reasons for this are complex. They are related, among other issues, to the crisis in Western social sciences, where the validity of hitherto accepted theories and methodologies began increasingly to be questioned. This trend, reflecting a growing concern with questions of relevance and authenticity, challenged the basic premises upon which objectivity in the social sciences had been based. The increasing preoccupation with social, political and economic conditions in Western society—e.g., discrimination on the basis of race and class, environmental issues, inflation, crime, and urban unrest—also forced the recognition that anthropology is the study of the human condition in general and not exclusively of a particular segment in society. Thus, involvement with issues at home brought these anthropologists back to their own societies, where they applied methods and perspectives gained from the study of other cultures (Messerschmidt 1981:5; cf. Nader and Maretzki 1973). In fact, some went so far as to claim that although cross-cultural research was important for the anthropologist, "ethnographic research carried out in one's own society may be the *sine qua non* for anthropology itself" (Wolcott 1981:265).

A related and integral question has to do with the relationship of scientific knowledge to its historical, cultural, and social context. Since the middle of the nineteenth century, if not before, there has been a growing understanding among philosophers that the form and substance of knowledge—being a social product—is historically conditioned. The type and content of knowledge is subject to the continuing development of humanity, both socially and intellectually.

Following the development and refinement of the sociology of knowledge, inspired by the works of Marx (1859), Durkheim (1915), and Lukacs (1922), and established by Mannheim (1936),[1] the past few decades have witnessed a wider acceptance of the view that the production of knowledge and the validity of its content are intimately connected with the social position of its producer. Recognizing that knowledge is historically, culturally, and socially conditioned, contemporary fieldwork accounts have begun to reflect an increasing awareness of the difficulties inherent in overlooking the subjective elements affecting field research (Scheper-Hughes 1983c:157–159; Clifford 1986:13).

Social scientists are now drawing attention to the fact that both researcher and researched participate in structuring "reality," which is objectified for us in the ethnographies we read (see Dwyer 1982). Their content is influenced by the social scientists and the questions they ask. These works are also affected by the informants and the interpretation that they place on their experience, for informants may express their own subjective concerns which do not necessarily reflect those of the wider community or society (cf. Abbott 1983; Scheper-Hughes 1983a). As Rabinow observes, we are now forcefully aware that the "data we collect is doubly mediated, first by our own presence and then by the second-order self-reflection we demand from our informants" (1977:119). To deny that there is a necessary tie between the field-worker and those she or he studies is to overlook that subjectivity is an inherent part of the fieldwork experience. Hence it is necessary to uncover the role that the self plays in the construction of our knowledge of the other (Murphy 1972:102–3). However, it is important to note that the self here goes beyond the focus on the individual. It also extends to include "the cultural and social interests that those individuals carry with them, deliberately or in spite of themselves" (Dwyer 1982:xvii).

## Implications of Gender and Foreign Status

One essential component of this social and cultural repertoire is gender, which is defined as the socially imposed division between the sexes. Feminist research has played a crucial part in our understanding of the role of gender in society (cf. Archer and Lloyd 1982; Cesara 1982). Moreover, it is female social scientists in particular who have underlined the relevance of the researcher's sex and gender to the process of fieldwork and who have uncovered the problem of bias and its significance with regard to access to data (cf. Oakley 1981; Abbott 1983; Morgan 1983). Gender-related bias has been shown to have at least three distinct dimensions: the selective perception of those studied; limitations on access to specific information; and the possibility that the researcher may overlook important variations in gender roles in different situational contexts (Clark 1983:118).

The question of access to knowledge is of particular relevance in sex-segregated societies, where the separation of men from women is paralleled by a separation in their cultural and social knowledge. But it is important to bear in mind that when we refer here to sex segregation in society, we acknowledge that it both varies in intensity and also fluctuates between, on the one hand, the isolation of women from public life and the exclusion of men from female activities, and, on the other hand, a less stringent bifurcation of social life, whereby women venture into public space and participate in numerous "male" spheres but must nevertheless observe real or decorous distance from men.[2] What is significant for our purpose is the observation that female researchers working in sex-segregated societies have to contend with the relevance of their gender to the field experience itself. This raises the question of whether gender limits their mobility to the extent of confining them to the study of female population groups in these societies. In other words, does gender confine the explorations of female researchers to narrow ranges in the study of human society, which consequently affects their theorizing about it?

The available published literature strongly suggests that gender may be a potentially limiting factor in the female researcher's efforts to work in societies characterized by a high degree of sex segregation. Thus, female social scientists who have done fieldwork in purdah societies such as Pakistan report that their gender imposed limited access to the research community and restricted exploration mainly to the world of women (see Papanek 1964; Pettigrew 1981; Pastner 1982). Even in societies with a less dramatic separation between the sexes, such as Taiwan, a woman anthropologist observes that being "a young woman closed off from me certain kinds of information and experiences" (Diamond 1970:126). This appears to be also true of relatively less sex-segregated societies like rural Greece, where the gender of the researcher limited her work predominantly to female population groups (see Friedl 1970; Du Boulay 1974).

Similar problems are echoed in many studies carried out by women scholars investigating aspects of Arab societies where sex segregation exhibits a great variation. Though early studies hardly mention the fieldwork experience, we may conclude from the subjects they explored and the type of data gathered that female field-workers worked primarily with women (see Blackman 1927; Granqvist 1935). More recent studies carried out by Western women in Arab societies indicate a similar influence. Thus, Van Spijk (1982c) found that being a woman was significant in her study of women's health care in an Upper Egyptian village. Fuller (1961) and Fernea (1965) report similar conditions some two decades earlier during fieldwork in rural Syria and Iraq respectively. Studies by Arab women researchers also provide some evidence that gender structured their access to data. For example, in a study of several villages in the

Kharga Oasis in Egypt, Husain (1970) found that her access to these communities was influenced by the latter's perceptions of her gender role (cf. Mohsen 1967; Ibrahim 1979).

However, the role of gender is neither completely rigid nor absolute. In the first instance, gender role can be modified when the society under examination lacks a rigid definition of such roles. In the second place, gender interacts with other factors that may override and minimize its constraining effects even in societies with high sex segregation.

Research suggests, for example, the importance of a researcher's foreign status in this respect. Thus, Papanek asserts that the Western woman researcher in a society such as Pakistan can, in fact, escape the gender role commonly ascribed to native women. Furthermore, she can participate in the definition of her role in the community and thereby attain more "role flexibility" (1964:160). Working in the same society as Papanek, Pastner confirms the latter's hypothesis but adds that not only can its applicability be limited in specific circumstances, but definitions of the foreign woman's researcher role may vary within the same society, thereby offering a range of accommodations (1982:124).

Studies carried out in Arab societies also suggest, either directly or implicitly, that the status of foreigner will tend to permit more flexibility and mobility for the foreign female researcher than would be possible for local women. For example, Krieger indicates that though she had to negotiate a mutually acceptable definition of gender role with the people she studied in a low-income urban district in Cairo, she managed to "find ways around gender role expectations" by also stressing her "identity as a Western woman" (1986:124). Similarly, Fluehr-Lobban illustrates that being a female Western researcher in the Sudan implied the option of sitting with men even if her husband (also an anthropologist carrying out his own fieldwork) was not present (1986:188). Eickelman reports how her foreign status in a highly sex-segregated village in Oman enabled her to venture into the market, a freedom not readily accorded to the women in this community (1984:35). Similar observations have been made by Fernea in Iraq (1965), Nader in rural Lebanon (1970), and Dwyer in Morocco (1978). However, it should be noted that it is not always clear whether their relative mobility is due to their role as researchers or to their status as foreigners.

But research experiences of female social scientists also suggest that apart from foreign status, there are other factors that interact with gender and structure the researcher's knowledge of reality. For example, education is a variable that interacts with gender and may in fact override its limiting influence. Similarly, the particular stage of a woman's life cycle is important in availing her of access to and rapport with the research community, as well as providing her with a specific cultural niche (Diamond 1970:126; Gonzalez 1986:85).

## Fieldwork and Indigenous Status

The examples that refer to the interaction between gender and foreign status underscore the possible relevance of indigenous status to the construction of sociological knowledge. Before exploring this issue, it should be noted that, apart from a plethora of terms to designate research in one's own society (Messerschmidt 1981:13), there is no agreement on the criteria defining this entity. Sometimes, the term "indigenous" is used to indicate a researcher belonging to a specific nation-state. At other times, its use denotes membership in a cultural area or in a specific community. In addition, language, religion, ethnicity, and class at times define the specificity of indigenous status. In this volume, the term denotes the researchers' membership in a cultural area with which they identify or are identified. However, it should be noted that our contributors at times use the term "indigenous" synonymously with the term "insider." At other times, the term "outsider" is used to denote a person of indigenous status but who is not a member of the specific sub-culture under study.

Furthermore, there appears to be no consensus in the literature about the relevance of indigenous status to the scope of the data collected. Even a cursory glance at the published material directly or indirectly concerned with this issue underlines the fact that this debate is far from being resolved in the social sciences.

On the one hand, it is held that the indigenous field-worker has the indisputable advantage of being able to attach meanings to patterns that he or she uncovers much faster than the non-indigenous researcher who is unfamiliar with the culture of the wider society (Stephenson and Greer 1981). Being part of the same cognitive world implies that subject and object share a similar body of knowledge. To quote Wax: "Secondary socialization (or resocialization) does not supply the fieldworker with the same authority as the native" (1971:14). This advantage may also be understood in terms of the difference between a passive understanding and the active mastering of a language (Schuetz 1944). Language is in this sense not just a crucial tool for comprehending those we seek to study (Owusu 1978). It is above all a means of building rapport and a symbol of closeness (Pelto and Pelto 1973). Being indigenous also implies the advantage of being able to understand a social reality on the basis of minimal clues; i.e., the meanings of cultural patterns are more readily understood (Stephenson and Greer 1981:125). Indigenous field-workers are believed to be able to avoid the problem of culture shock or anomie (Nash 1963). They are expected to be less likely to experience "cultural fatigue," namely, the strain of being a stranger in an unfamiliar cultural setting, and the demands this places on their role as researcher (Jones 1973).

On the other hand, there are those who suggest that indigenous status implies a greater potential for value conflict. Language and cultural differences cease to constitute "safety barriers," in the sense that the indigenous researcher will find it more difficult to maintain the kind of social distance that the outsider/stranger in his or her role of researcher may be able to (Ablon 1977:70). Indigenous field-workers may well have a problem of keeping emotional distance when researching in their own community of discourse (Cassell 1977). This is in turn related to the assumption that the more divergence there is between subject and object, the less difficult it is for the field-worker to distinguish between his or her own values and the experiential world of the research community (Colfax 1966; Aguilar 1981). Furthermore, it is suggested in the literature that the insider may experience some difficulty in recognizing patterns in which he or she has been socialized (Stephenson and Greer 1981). Some Third World anthropologists contend that because their position in their own society is not politically or ethically neutral, indigenous field-workers may also find it difficult to be objective in the study of their own communities (Madan 1982:265). The possibility that they may not be able to "step in and out" of society, that is, to step into the roles of those studied while at the same time being socially distant (Powdermaker 1967:19), brings into question their ability to maintain a detached involvement with those studied. While language is undoubtedly an invaluable research tool, it is believed that the indigenous field-worker is not necessarily immune from the danger of overlooking the nuances of semantic units (Spradley 1979).

## Comparison and Analysis

Some preliminary remarks concerning the contributions to this volume are perhaps relevant at this point before we proceed to examine the validity of the views presented above.

All six contributors are women of Arab descent who have been trained as social scientists in Western academic institutions. However, from the point of view of their background, they can be divided into two groups: those who were raised and socialized in the Arab world (Altorki, El-Solh, Morsy, and Shami) and those who have spent their formative years in the West (Abu-Lughod and Joseph).

Contributors in the former group have an urban upper-middle-class background in common. But this factor is to some extent counterbalanced by a number of dissimilarities, which are reflected in the manner in which components of their role and status have tended to interact during the process of their research endeavors. Such dissimilarities are indicative of the particular cultural and socioeconomic characteristics of their countries of origin in the Arab world.

While contributors in the second group share a number of characteristics with the former, they in addition have a bicultural background. This dimension surfaces in numerous ways in their work and has had some impact on aspects of their self-identity as researchers. However, the relationship between the bicultural experience and identity is in some ways dissimilar. To begin with, it appears to relate to the status that these two contributors elect to adopt upon their return to the Arab world. Joseph moves back to Lebanon as a *mughtaribi*, a status readily available for Lebanese migrants who return to their country of origin. Being more or less a blend of two cultures, this status permits a certain role flexibility, a fact which Joseph manages to bend to her advantage. Abu-Lughod, by contrast, does not move back to her father's country of origin, but to a specific subculture: the Awlad Ali, a sedentarized Bedouin tribe in the Western Desert in Egypt. Although her transient status as a student becomes submerged in the category of a "dutiful daughter," the niche she manages to establish in the research community remains temporary, however much she may have been accorded the freedom to return. For her part, Joseph did not have to seek out or establish a niche, but found it available within the circle of her parents' kin in Lebanon. Even though she too moves back temporarily to the Arab world, these relatives remain a constant factor in her life.

Another difference between Abu-Lughod and Joseph pertains to the construction of identity in the field. For Joseph, this particular issue is predominant during the process of fieldwork and in fact develops into a major research concern. Learning about her parents' country of origin enables her to better comprehend aspects of her own socialization in the country to which they had migrated. With Abu-Lughod, the bicultural experience is symbolically represented in an oscillation between her Pal-

estinian father and American mother as a source for understanding the
reality she chose to study.

Two among the other contributors who have been socialized in the
Arab world also have a bicultural background, although its implications
differ somewhat from those that have affected Abu-Lughod and Joseph.
But again there is a difference in which this attribute manifests itself.
Shami's family are Circassians, an ethnic minority within the dominant
Jordanian Arab society. Though she too grapples with the issue of identity as an important component of her role as researcher, this does not
entail the soul-searching and oscillation apparent in the cases of Joseph
and Abu-Lughod respectively. For El-Solh, the cultural conflict between
the Western world of her mother and the Arab world of her father were
resolved before she embarked upon her fieldwork. The implications of
roots and identity for her "researcher self" were therefore not dominant
issues.

For the following comparative analysis, we propose to view the construction of sociological knowledge as composed of three stages: choice of
topic, acquisition of data, and analysis and interpretation of data. Each of
these stages will constitute an important basis for comparison between
the contributors as well as with the published literature.

*Choice of Topic*

The contributions in this volume suggest that although the choice of
topic may be encouraged by trends in the social science discipline and
influenced by ethical considerations, indigenous status in correlation
with gender role appear to have some bearing on the focus of research.
Thus, both Altorki and Morsy indicate that their motivation to study
their own society had been fed by their personal anguish over social and
political conditions in the Arab world. But while Altorki's gender role
almost inevitably implied that, apart from specific exceptions, she could
not include the world of Arab men in her study of the urban elite in
Saudi Arabia, Morsy was similarly not compelled to restrict her research
to the social world of village women in Egypt. El-Solh's decision to study
the impact of migration was inspired by an interest in the possibilities of
regional cooperation within the Arab world, a focus that involved both
male and female respondents in the Egyptian peasant community she
studied in Iraq. Joseph's study of sectarian identity as a political tool in
Lebanon was intimately related to an interest in her parents' country of
origin and her own search for identity. Similarly, Shami's research on
questions of ethnicity and national cohesiveness among Circassians was

to some extent fed by an interest in her family's ethnic roots. Though Abu-Lughod makes no explicit reference to this point, one may infer from her contribution that the Arab origin of her father inspired an interest in Bedouin culture and society.

*Acquisition of Data*

One way of analyzing the acquisition of data is by focusing on the definition of the status and the accompanying role of the researchers among the people they are studying. We propose that the researcher's role will to a great extent structure access to the field and knowledge of the social reality at hand.

For our purpose, the concept of role may be defined in relational terms; i.e., the field-worker's notions of expected behavior and its implicit and explicit role prescriptions, and the way in which the research community defines this role (see Schwartz and Schwartz 1955).[3] Ideally, the greater the compatibility between home and host cultures, the less potential there would be for role conflict (see Ablon 1977).

Clearly, a diversity of variables affects the role of the researcher and by implication the acquisition of data. To begin with, class origin and education are variables that interact significantly with gender role and indigenous status. However, as the research experiences presented in this volume stress, such interaction is not uniform. Nor does the individual manner in which these particular four variables interact with one another, alone explain the diversity of these experiences. There is, in addition, further possible interaction with the following variables: the field-worker's age, marital status, religious affiliation and ethnic/minority status; the focus and topic of research; the geographical location and ecology of the research community (rural, urban, pastoral); the degree to which sex segregation may or may not be pervasive in the research community; the extent of the historical influence of the central government; the prevalent national and regional political realities; and finally, personality attributes.

With regard to the contributors in this volume, education and class were sometimes equally critical for role definition. In the case of Morsy, for example, the flexibility of her role during fieldwork was primarily a function of her upper-class origin and her education. But such flexibility became even more pronounced by her ability to add to this role the status of "professional woman," which the villagers ascribed to her because of the focus of her research (medical anthropology). This status enabled Morsy to manipulate the traditional social barriers that exist between male and female. Moreover, she managed to overcome the vulnerability traditionally attributed to the female gender role by stressing both her professional status and her role as wife and mother.[4] Her access to the research community was facilitated by the latter's familiarity with female researchers and professional women, as well as the contacts that she as an Egyptian of upper-class origin was able to exploit. Yet it is interesting that these contacts did not adversely affect her rapport with the villagers, who traditionally mistrust external authority.

In Abu-Lughod's case, by contrast, education and class proved to be less significant compared with the influence of origin, religion, age, and marital status.[5] The latter are variables of crucial importance in the status hierarchy adhered to by the Bedouins she studied. Presenting herself in the research community as the daughter of a non-Egyptian Arab Moslem father facilitated her access, since the community attributed impeccable credentials to such an origin. This fact had a profound impact on the process of Abu-Lughod's fieldwork. The expectation that she fit into the category of daughter,[6] a role she willingly assumed, implied her acceptance of a number of consequences that "sex role training" imposes on females in this community (Golde 1970a:3). The adoption of this role eventually led to a loss of flexibility and to the reorientation of Abu-Lughod's research focus. But significantly, being incorporated into the women's world led her to discover the importance of a genre of personal poetry that is important for interpersonal relations and which has not been described before in studies of Bedouin society.

During her fieldwork in an urban squatter settlement in the Jordanian capital, Amman, a subculture with which she was unfamiliar, Shami found that education and class were important factors in the definition of her role. She discovered that these particular variables served to delineate the social distance between the research community and herself. Nonetheless, her social background and respectability as an unmarried woman required some authentication, a hurdle that she overcame by introducing her mother to the research community.[7] On the other hand, during Shami's fieldwork among Circassians like herself, education and class were apparently less relevant in structuring her relationships with her respondents. This was partly due to the fact that a female researcher was not a novelty, since the research community was already familiar with the role category of scholarly woman. Although the female gender role is clearly defined in this Circassian community, the flexibility of its boundaries is to some extent also influenced by marital status. In contrast to many traditional communities in the Arab world, it is the unmarried rather than the married Circassian woman who apparently enjoys a higher degree of physical mobility. Shami was able to take advantage of the implications of this fact for the flexibility of her role in the field, even though she found herself compelled to acknowledge many of the social conventions governing relations between members of this community. Since her family is ethnically Circassian, Shami did not encounter any impediment in securing her entry into the community.

Altorki's access to the field was assured by virtue of her membership in the research community. As such, she was not confronted by the problems of adapting to the role of outsider or stranger,[8] and the implications this entails in Saudi Arabian society. But this membership, together with her gender role, had important consequences for her fieldwork among families of the same class as her own in Saudi Arabia. Being an insider in the fullest meaning of the term implied that Altorki could not avoid the implications of her "personal visibility" in the field (Ablon 1977:70), in the sense that she was personally known to the research community. This status led to expectations that she would conform to a number of rigidly defined conventions, a fact she could not afford to ignore. At the same time, it availed her of information that male researchers could not have attained. But she had to remain aware of the danger that complete incorporation can imply for the role of researcher.[9] Since it was assumed that she must be familiar with her respondents' way of life, Altorki had to define her researcher role in a manner that did not jeopardize her standing in the community and would at the same time allow her to render that world problematic.[10] She managed to attain some flexibility by virtue of her education and lengthy residence outside Saudi Arabia. In a number of instances this was accepted as a valid explanation for the type of questions she posed.

The working-class background of Joseph's parents prior to their migration from Lebanon to the U.S. proved to be a crucial factor for the definition of her role in the field. Though she herself had moved into the American middle class by virtue of her education, her parents' class origin in Lebanon was significant for securing her access to and establishing an affinity with the predominantly working-class neighborhood in which she carried out her fieldwork in Beirut. Such affinity was to some extent also fed by her parents' sectarian affiliation, for Joseph quickly came to realize the multitude of attributes inherent in family name in Lebanese society. Thus, she was essentially regarded as the daughter of Maronite emigrants, rather than as a married American woman of Arab descent. Such identification entailed behavioral expectations that she had to take into consideration.[11] Nevertheless, her education and *mughtaribi* status enabled her to escape such categorization and thus secure some role flexibility in the field. At the same time, to be "in" and "of" a family, and to be involved in a reciprocal network of rights and duties with relatives, revealed to her the strength of maternal family ties in Arab culture. It led Joseph to emphasize the bilateral nature of kinship, which stands in contrast to the anthropological texts emphasizing the importance of patrilineal descent in Arab society.

In the case of El-Solh, both education and class proved significant for the structuring of her relations with the Egyptian migrant peasant community she studied in Iraq. Although these two variables were in some instances superceded by expectations that some of her respondents associated with her Arab descent and religious affiliation,[12] the latter also facilitated her access to and rapport with the research community. However, El-Solh's research experiences were also affected by the attitudes of the bureaucracies in her native Egypt and the host country, Iraq. In Iraq, education, class, and marital status were of secondary importance compared with her gender role and Arab origin. The authorities felt compelled to protect her to the extent of curtailing her freedom to live in the peasant settlement community she was studying. On the other hand, gender, class, and education were not as crucial in El-Solh's dealings with the Egyptian bureaucracy. Rather, it was the political sensitivity of her research focus that proved to be significant.[13] Her role as researcher had therefore to be adapted to the demands and expectations of the different field situations she happened to be in.[14]

Another important factor that influences the role of researchers in Arab society is sex segregation. While the bonds of history, culture, and language uniting the Arab world have a far-reaching impact, these bonds do not preclude diversity in the social and ethnic composition of Arab societies (see Eickelman 1981). Such heterogeneity is reflected in the social stratification within an Arab country. As mentioned earlier, communities in the Arab world will therefore differ with regard to the degree of pervasiveness of sex segregation (see Fernea 1985).

The veil symbolizes the extreme form of such segregation. However, as the contributions of Altorki and Abu-Lughod illustrate, the type of veil and the social situations in which it is mandatory, as well as the meanings attached to its use, may vary from one Arab community to another. A certain degree of sex segregation may also exist without the veil, as the reports of El-Solh and Morsy indicate. Female modesty is in this case circumscribed by socially appropriate behavior and attire and by the avoidance of male strangers (cf. Dwyer 1978; Makhlouf 1979; Tillion 1983).

A relatively extreme case of sex segregation is reported by Altorki in her research among elite urban families in Saudi Arabia. But even here there exists a certain flexibility not readily apparent to the outsider. Altorki illustrates how she was able to take advantage of this fact, even though she was judged as a member of the research community.

Abu-Lughod also reports a comparatively rigidly defined sex segregation in the Bedouin community she studied. She found herself confronted with the necessity of publicly proclaiming her allegiance either to the men's or to the women's social world. She opted for the latter in spite of the restrictions on the flexibility of her researcher role this choice implied. But her choice was more than compensated for by the fact that it did not preclude the possibility of obtaining information about the male social world, for while men may be inclined to talk freely in front of their womenfolk, the women will tend to impart to the men only that knowledge about their social world that they want them to have.

The Egyptian peasant community studied by El-Solh was also characterized by the adherence to the ideal of sex segregation, a factor that the settler families' post-migratory way of life appears to have intensified. Although she did not transcend her status as temporary guest, El-Solh was nevertheless confronted with the expectation that she, as an Arab woman, would conform to some of the behavioral norms prescribed for women in public.

Sex segregation appears to be relatively muted in the Lower Egyptian rural community studied by Morsy, even though its actual extent differs from one social class to another. The flexibility of the boundaries separating the social world of men and women is in this case largely due to the district's contacts with urban centers.

Similarly, Shami reports relatively little sex segregation in the Circassian community at large as compared with the urban squatter settlement she studied in Jordan. Its incidence is circumscribed by specific behavioral patterns indicative of the relatively flexible social boundaries separating both sexes.

Finally, sex segregation was found to be largely absent in the Lebanese urban community studied by Joseph. She reports that the crowded housing conditions in these neighborhoods have served as an effective (if not crucial) means for dismantling the spatial barriers between the sexes (cf. Rugh 1985).

What are the implications of the arguments presented here with respect to the decisive advantage non-indigenous female field-workers are purported to enjoy in sex-segregated societies?

If data is perceived not only as a collection of information about a particular social group or situation, but also as an "understanding of the values and norms, of intentions and consequences and, ultimately, of implication and significance" (Madan 1982:268), then the papers in this volume suggest that female indigenous field-workers may in this respect enjoy a relative advantage over their female non-indigenous counterparts. The conscious or unconscious knowledge, however partial, that researchers can be expected to have of their own wider society, constitutes a particular asset in the sense that they may require relatively fewer cues to grasp how the participants view their own culture.[15] Indigenous field-workers may also be quicker in comprehending the implications of the social situation under study. Regardless of the effects that gender as well as other variables may have on role flexibility, the indigenous field-workers' socialization experiences as well as their linguistic abilities can be expected to provide them with a head start.[16] Time—a crucial cost factor that no researcher can afford to ignore—will generally be on their side.

However, we do not wish to suggest that, given time, the non-indigenous field-worker is not as capable of grasping an emic perspective of society. The actual length of time required to attain it is obviously dependent on a host of factors, not the least of which are the field-worker's personality attributes, such as the potential for adaptation, capacity for rapport, and endurance. Nor do we overlook the possibility that in specific research situations the foreign field-worker may be able to recognize the wider implications of a social reality, the significance of which the indigenous field-worker may not be fully conscious of.[17] We do, however, argue that familiarity with the wider social setting is an asset. The value of such insight is not discounted by the possible subjectivity of the insider's view of his or her own society, since subjectivity could also be the peril of the non-indigenous researcher.

These arguments regarding the relative advantages of being indigenous are, however, subject to some qualification. The contributions in this volume suggest that while familiarity with the basic culture is invaluable, it is the actual extent to which field-workers have firsthand knowledge of the research community that is perhaps a more significant aspect of their indigenous status.[18] However, given the heterogeneity of the social, political, and economic structures in the Arab world, as well as the social scientists' tendency to "study down" (see Nader 1969), it can be assumed that indigenous field-workers will encounter a host of unfamiliar aspects in a research community with which they may not have had much previous contact. In this case, they too will assume or will be ascribed the role of outsiders, or what Freilich (1977) refers to as "marginal natives," a term that denotes those who are on the social fringe of the research community. But even here we would argue that this would not necessarily put them on an equal footing with non-indigenous female field-workers because of their familiarity with the wider society of which they are members and of which their research communities are a part. A further qualification pertains to the fact that indigenous field-workers may, by virtue of their status, be sometimes more readily identified with dominant groups or classes in their own society (see Fahim 1977). This may have far-reaching consequences with regard to their relationship with research communities situated in a less powerful position in the social hierarchy.

To sum up, contributions in this volume confirm that gender influences the acquisition of data. Specifically with regard to the Arab world, they indicate that variables, which can modify or even neutralize the effect of gender in structuring the researcher role, do not interact in a uniform manner. More important, the contributions demonstrate that foreign female researchers are not necessarily at an advantage with regard to access to knowledge in sex-segregated societies. In fact, it may well be the indigenous female field-worker who in specific research situations enjoys a relative advantage in this respect.

*Data Analysis and Interpretation*

Although there appears to be no consensus in the literature on the relevance of all aspects of the situational background of a social scientist to the development and application of paradigms, concepts, and theoretical frameworks, the evidence from this volume underscores the relevance of gender in this context.

Gender appears to be an important variable that influences analysis and interpretation of data by way of its effect on the acquisition of data and on the development of a specific perspective. Joseph, for example, elaborates on how gender role encourages an engendered perspective. Also recognizing a situated perspective, Abu-Lughod indicates how the female view affected her analysis of Bedouin society. Similarly, Altorki argues that paradigms about male/female relations in Arab society were constructed by male ethnographers on the basis of hearsay and unverifiable inferences rather than on firsthand data. For her part, El-Solh found that the model of the "powerless" Egyptian peasant woman did not conform to the reality encountered in the field.

These findings are consonant with the general body of feminist literature, which has pointed to the relevance of gender in structuring knowledge and which has uncovered the androcentric bias embedded in the paradigms and theories of social science. For example, looking at the evolution of humankind, women scholars have uncovered the bias inherent in the conceptual frameworks that perceived this evolution as being predominantly that of males to the exclusion of females. Studies of hunting and gathering societies had overemphasized the role of hunting in these economies. Feminist scholars have revealed and documented the significance of women's gathering activities in the routine diet and in the economy of these societies (see Goodale 1971). Other research carried out by feminists has challenged the earlier claims that band organization was universally patrilineal and patrilocal (see Leacock 1981). The belief in universal male domination and female subordination has been questioned by feminist social scientists who demonstrated that this power asymmetry is contingent upon specific historic conditions associated with relations of distribution, with the rise of private ownership and the formation of classes, the transformation of relationships of production, and the emergence of the state (cf. Sacks 1974; Friedl 1975; Nash 1978; Caufield 1981). Furthermore, anthropological/sociological models of power, which conventionally defined the latter in terms of formal power structures, have largely ignored informal expressions of power in society. Female scholars who study women have revealed the relevance of such informal expressions to a more balanced understanding of the distribution of power in society (see Rogers 1975). Morgan (1983) demonstrates how studies on political action and social movements reflect a male bias in that they have tended to associate rationality/thought/objectivity with male and emotionality/feelings with female. They have discounted the latter in their research and have consequently failed to explain the articulation of feelings and actions in political activity. There has thus been a tendency to perceive men as the main social actors while relegating women to the fringes of social reality (see Etienne and Leacock 1980). These and similar preconceptions, which have been taken as frameworks for the acquisition of data, have consequently limited the validity of the social models and theories seeking to explain human behavior. But these facts should not lead one to overlook the danger pointed out by some feminists, namely that in attempting to correct such bias, feminist analysis may itself be subject to bias (see Scheper-Hughes 1983c).

These examples are not exhaustive, but they indicate that the development of hypotheses and their verification depend on several factors, not all of which are within the realm of science. Theory construction may also be affected by other systems of knowledge (scientific, philosophical, or theological) and thereby be open to bias (see Mulkay 1980). Theories constructed in certain historical and cultural contexts may be specific to those contexts but this does not necessarily mean that they are not objective. The validity of a theory is confirmed by its application. Herein lies the test of its objectivity and its historical and cultural limitation. A theory may be valid for one particular historical period and in one specific cultural tradition. Alternatively, it may span more than one historical period and be cross-culturally valid. But this point does not relate to the objectivity of a theory as much as it relates to attempts to adapt, modify or discard it due to its difficult or impossible application (see Mokhtar 1984). The universal applicability of a theory is thus not a prerequisite for its acceptance. Although theories are culturally and historically bound, their construction of course depends on the kind of data collected in the field. If data is collected from a particular perspective, it follows that the concepts, paradigms, and theories developed to interpret them will be equally bound. By the same logic, as evidence in this volume confirms, data collected in sex-segregated societies may be subject to an engendered perspective. This suggests that theories constructed to explain social phenomena in these societies would be equally structured.

With regard to the influence of indigenous status on the construction of theories, the literature does not point to the immediate or direct relevance of this variable (see Asad 1982). This stand is adhered to by some of the contributors to this volume. For example, both Altorki and Shami stress that with regard to the theoretical examination of data, what matters is the intellectual rigor and the quality of the data, rather than the insider/outsider distinction. Morsy believes that indigenous research provides insights into the workings of society, but does not generate indigenous theories.

However, essays in this volume also suggest that indigenous status may have some bearing on the acquisition of data. Thus, inasmuch as indigenous social scientists may in specific cases have better access to data, they may be in a better position to make a theoretical contribution to understanding social phenomena in their societies. But this is conditional on the limited access of a non-indigenous social scientist to the relevant data. We do not claim that foreign social scientists are unable to generate theories valid for the understanding of societies other than their own. Whatever their national origin, social scientists are subject to the danger of bias—be it racial, religious, ethnic, class, political—though obviously to varying degrees. This can affect the acquisition of data and, by implication, the construction of theoretical frameworks.

### Fieldwork and Ethics

There is, finally, one particular aspect of the field-worker's indigenous status in the Arab world that we deem to be relevant, namely, the ethical implications of the choice of topic and the publication of research findings. Such ethical dimensions undoubtedly are, or should be, of major concern to any social scientist, native or otherwise (cf. Barnes 1967; Weaver 1973; Rynkewich and Spradley 1976). However, as El-Solh points out, the ethical implications of indigenous status in the Arab world may involve a number of dimensions with which Western field-workers in particular may not necessarily be confronted in their own society, or at least not to the same extent.

There is, for example, the issue of the relevance of the research topic for the socioeconomic development needs in the Arab world. The pressure for "action-oriented" research is by no means a prerogative of the Arab field-worker or, for that matter, of researchers in the Third World (cf. Pelto and Pelto 1973; Srinivas et al. 1979; Madan 1982). However, we would argue that its disregard can be more costly in a society where optimal resource allocation is a major problem (see Fahim 1977). None of the contributors to the present volume were financially dependent on the governmental authorities in the countries in which they carried out their studies, a fact that has undoubtedly provided them with some leeway with regard to choice of topic. Most, however, were conscious of the need for the unity of theory and praxis and of the usefulness of their research for better understanding and perhaps changing their society.

The manner in which the field-worker presents her or his "self" to the research community is a further aspect of the ethical implications of fieldwork. Similar to their non-indigenous colleagues, Arab field-workers are not only held accountable by those who constitute their academic frame of reference, but may also be expected to be conscious of their moral obligation to the subject of their study. Hence the moral dilemma faced by Abu-Lughod and El-Solh in defining their identity and divulging information about themselves.

Research carried out by indigenous field-workers in the Arab world implies a further factor, namely their subjection to the authorities under whose jurisdiction they live, however temporary the duration of their stay (see Fahim and Helman 1980). This requirement will weigh heavily in defining priorities in research agendas as well as in decisions regarding the contents of research publications. It is obviously easier to publish findings about a society in which one may never set foot again and whose members are unlikely to obtain copies of what has been written about them. Even though Westerners are being increasingly confronted with the possibility that the "natives" are in a position to challenge their research findings, we suggest that they are to some extent able to escape the political implications of what they choose to publish. By contrast, indigenous field-workers in the Arab world may not easily be able to evade the social and political responsibilities directly or indirectly emanating from their research findings (see Nakhleh 1979).

In conclusion, the contributions in this volume illustrate clearly the role that gender and indigenous status play in the construction of sociological knowledge. In availing women of access to some domains of culture rather than others, gender and indigenous status—in interaction with a host of other variables—illustrate how our view of "reality" may in fact be historically and socially situated.

The resultant view of culture is, by implication, only partial. While studies carried out by men may also be partial, we stress that there is no single complete view of society. The contributors, by illuminating aspects of Arab society hitherto not included in research carried out by men, aptly illustrate that reality is multidimensional. Each perspective expresses one aspect of reality. The "knowledge" generated from these various perspectives according to the canons of the discourse at hand is complementary. Hence the advantage of male over female and indigenous over non-indigenous, or vice versa, will to a large extent depend on the situational context in which the respective researcher finds her- or himself.

The many insights revealed in the following contributions should be of interest not only to social scientists interested in methodological and theoretical aspects of the fieldwork experience and the general area of the sociology of knowledge. Since the volume documents the field experiences of women social scientists, its findings are also of special relevance to feminist studies. Last, but not least, the contributions are an apt portrayal of perhaps the most mystifying aspect of fieldwork, namely the intangibles that render each research experience so uniquely personal.

## Notes

1. According to Marx, man interacts with nature in the process of labor; he not only changes nature, but it changes him as well. More importantly, man interacts with other men, none of whom are exactly like any other, and this human interaction changes man as surely and as constantly as his relationship with nature. Man's consciousness is thus the product of his social being, which is continually developing (1859). These views were in reality the beginnings of what we today know as the sociology of knowledge. Lukacs, following the Marxist tradition, argued that there is no reason to exempt any form of knowledge, even natural science, from being subject to the phenomenon of reification (1922). Durkheim diverged from the general Marxian historicism by insisting on a purely social component to the categories and rules of social life (1915). Mannheim too demonstrated that, with the exception of the natural sciences, knowledge is not merely historically but also socially conditioned. Although influenced by Marx, Mannheim was critical of his ideas. He developed a wider perspective than that of Marx in that he denied the

proletariat the privilege of being the only class that can attain objective knowledge. Instead, he proposed that knowledge is conditioned by the situation of its producer, be it an individual or a class or a group of any sort. This, in turn, led to the idea of the absolute relativity of knowledge. Mannheim is notable for his early attempts to resolve the paradox that arose out of the work of Marx and others; namely, if all knowledge is contingent on history, then even science must be seen as ideology. His answer, simply put, is that scientific canons put the researcher in a different, if not necessarily privileged, position with regard to accurate observation (1936).

2. However, although the distribution of power and authority between men and women in society is generally related to the prevalent pattern of segregation between them, one must not assume that sexual segregation correlates with an asymmetrical power relationship. Thus, there may be a separate but equal existence of the sexes (see Nelson and Olesen 1977:8).

3. Peter Kloos adds a third reference group, namely the scientific community, as being important for the definition of the researcher role (1969:509).

4. This is similar to Ernestine Friedl's experience in rural Greece, where her marital status enabled her to de-emphasize her professional role as researcher, thus facilitating her access to the women's social world without, however, necessarily excluding her from that of the men (1970:212).

5. However, Veena Dua, who studied temple politics in her native Punjab (India), found that caste, education, and class, as well as her unmarried status, were important in structuring her mobility and access to data in the field (1979).

6. Jean Briggs describes the progression of her incorporation into the Eskimo family she lived with during her fieldwork, which began with the status of white person, progressing to that of daughter, and finally to that of offender. All of these roles were assigned to the anthropologist by the research community according to their cultural repertoire. The discrepancy between the field-worker's conception of behavior appropriate to the role of daughter and those held by the community, led to misunderstandings and to her classification as an offender. It is in the light of this experience that Briggs raises methodological questions regarding the selection (or imposition) of roles for the anthropologist in the field, and the congruence or the lack thereof in the definition of these roles (1970:41–43).

7. Khadija A. Gupta's work on small town politics in India is further evidence of the importance of kinship ties in making the field-worker respectable in the eyes of the research community (1979).

8. Alfred Schuetz defines the stranger as one who does not share the "of-course" assumptions or the "thinking as usual" of insiders in a social group. This "thinking as usual" is dependent on four assumptions: (1) social life continues unchanged and previous experiences are a sufficient basis through which future happenings can be mastered; (2) the insider relies on the knowledge handed down to him by previous generations; (3) knowledge about some aspect of an event will facilitate its management and control; and (4) the "schemes of interpretation and expression" are known to others in the social group. Since the stranger does not share these basic assumptions, he will have to question that which is taken for granted by the social group he approaches (1944).

Dennison Nash argues that the ethnographer's role is that of stranger who views the other culture as problematic, who has to overcome problems of cultural differences between himself and the approached group, and who must basically maintain a balance between participation and detachment (1963).

9. As Norris B. Johnson stresses, although it is desirable to become part of the research community, complete incorporation logically eliminates the researcher role (1984:118).

10.  Carroll Pastner also points to the importance of not compromising one's standing in the research community by neglecting to observe the subtleties of situations of purdah (1982).

11.  Similarly, Gloria Marshall describes how her identity as a Black American influenced her researcher role during her study of a Yoruba community in Nigeria. Her hosts regarded her as "a child who has come home," a fact that transformed her status from privileged guest to accepted insider. But this acceptance entailed behavioral expectations associated with her status as a young, unmarried woman, some aspects of which Marshall felt compelled to adhere to (1970:176).

12.  This is in some respects similar to the research experiences of Khalil Nakhleh. He describes how during his study of intersectarian relationships in his native village in Palestine, his status as the son of a prominent Christian family entailed behavioral expectations to which he was expected to conform (1979:344, 348).

13.  Similarly, Frances Henry, researching political development in Trinidad, highlights the vulnerability of research in Third World countries where politically unstable conditions obtain (1966).

14.  In her study of a village community in Greece, Mari H. Clark emphasizes that perspectives of gender role will vary not only cross-culturally, but also situationally within each society (1983).

15.  P. E. De Josselin de Jong underscores the importance of recording the emic in addition to the etic view of culture. He illustrates how in his own fieldwork in Malaya, he checked the anthropologist's structural model against the people's own view of their society. He points out how and why participants may have a wrong impression of some elements of their culture and how especially under conditions of conflict the ideal comes to stand out. It is particularly in relation to the ideal that participants demonstrate an awareness of the structural principles in their society (1967).

16.  This is a point also stressed by Hussain Fahim in his discussion of some of the advantages of being an indigenous researcher (1982a:xix). Khalil Nakhleh also refers to this aspect when he underlines the possible advantages of being an insider (1979:346).

17.  During their study in South Appalachia (U.S.), John B. Stephenson and L. Sue Greer discovered that certain cultural patterns may be so familiar to the field-worker that extra caution must be exercised in order not to overlook them (1981:124).

18.  John B. Stephenson and L. Sue Greer have also drawn attention to the difference between prior knowledge of the culture at large and specific knowledge of the research community (1981:126).

# 2

# Feminization, Familism, Self, and Politics

## Research as a Mughtaribi

━━━━━━ SUAD JOSEPH

The heart of my Middle Eastern research has been in Lebanon. I lived in Lebanon for two and a half years in 1971–1973, investigating the politicization of religious sects in Borj Hammoud, an urban working-class municipality of Greater Beirut. During subsequent trips (1974, 1976, 1978, 1980), I moved toward studying the relationships between women, family, and the polity. The transformations in the scientific project were as much a cause as a consequence of changes within me. The twenty years (since 1967) during which I have focused on the Middle East have taken me on an intellectual journey that has become personal as I have increasingly come to understand the relationships between my professional and personal commitments.

This chapter offers me the luxury of bringing those journeys together for the first time in a professional context. Growing up as an Arab-American has meant becoming a person of two worlds that have often been in conflict. To use the title of a recent conference, many are now "breaking the silence" to address a range of issues between the West and the Middle East. Among these, Arab-American women are beginning to investigate the nature and implications of their bicultural socialization. In this context, it feels special to have an opportunity to write, academically, about the experience of returning to the land of my birth to do research.

25

## Going Home

In 1968 I visited Lebanon on a YWCA exchange camp counselor program. I was the first of my family to return since our immigration to the U.S. in 1949. This first return to Lebanon was, on the surface, like that of many *mughtaribi* (those who have gone abroad). It was high romance. I fell in love with the country, the people, the culture.

However, there was a difference. A graduate student in anthropology at Columbia University, I was laying the groundwork for my doctoral research. I had come not only to be with the Lebanese, but also to study them. From the beginning, I was an insider/outsider. Without knowing it then, I was also a subject/object.

I had a deep sense of having returned to my home. So many things were familiar that after the first couple of months, I lost sight of them. Common events became less visible. I felt a sense of history. I learned about my parents' childhood and the early history of my family in Lebanon. I learned on a personal level the importance of identifying with family and village origins. At an emotional level, familiar feelings were stirred up: feelings of inclusion, of rightness, of morality, as well as sensibilities of politeness.

I felt an awakening of an old knowledge learned at an early age, but rarely applicable in the American context. It surfaced spontaneously around the rituals of kinship, speech, respect. I relished the deference I could give to uncles and aunts about whom I had heard so many stories. There was a pleasure in the certainty of roles.

These people were not alien to me. I knew their mentality, and their methods of reasoning had a familiar logicality. I was persuaded by their thinking on the basis of a rationality that was not directly accessible to my conscious rationality, but was nevertheless inside me. I found myself using the same rationality, even though I was not always able to articulate it in a way that was consonant with my Western-trained thinking.

Having been inundated with American society's stereotyping of Arabs, I found myself, particularly on my first return in 1968, filled with stirrings of an ethnic pride. Images imbued from school textbooks, the media, and conversations of ordinary and educated Americans contrasted with the scenic beauty, the political and social openness, the worldliness, and the high culture I found in the Lebanon of the 1960s and 1970s. The sense of the region's civilization, negated in the West, was evident—as was the West's historic indebtedness to the Middle East.

I was particularly moved by the openness with which people expressed feelings. Raised in a family that felt things deeply, I often felt passion a bit out of place in the U.S. In Lebanon men and women expressed feelings and expected me to do the same. At a layer deeper than I understood, I was reclaiming something of myself. A part of me was finding its way home.

## Conflicting Roles

As someone with roots in the society, my relationships with people and my identities were multifaceted. This both facilitated my work and made it more complex.

I was a member of a local family with relatives from both parents who expected me to be with them, carry out the host of familial obligations, and be a proper Lebanese woman. This conflicted with carrying out fieldwork, which required time, mobility, and occasional unconventional behavior.

To my friends I was a scholar and a poet. They expected intellectual dialogue, mobility, and a cosmopolitan style of interaction.

To the Palestinian and Lebanese progressive friends I was a political activist. They expected participation, political action in the camps, and other support activities. I was also a target of political organizing from some of the young men in Borj Hammoud. One tried to recruit me into the Syrian Social Nationalist Party and several made my apartment a place of ongoing political discussion. In the highly charged political atmosphere of Lebanon during the early 1970s, I found tension between the requirements of fieldwork and political activism. My progressive friends dressed casually, visited each other almost daily, debated Middle Eastern politics, took strong stands on issues, and actively engaged in political work. To present myself in this manner in Borj Hammoud would have alienated the majority of my neighbors. I walked a tightrope between taking stands I felt strongly about (the Palestinian cause) and maintaining the trust of as many as I could of my neighbors.

The scholarly community at the American University in Beirut regarded me as a graduate student fulfilling the requirements of a Ph.D. Treated as a scholar-in-training, I was an unknown who had yet to be proven.

In the neighborhood, I was a friend, a daughter, a mother, a sister. To some I remained the suspected outsider. Minimally, I was a *mughtaribi*, a Lebanese who had returned home. This status gave me a certain legitimacy and access to people in the neighborhood.

It was understandable that I would want to return to Lebanon to learn about my own culture. I was a returning daughter of the land. I had a history. I had a right to the land and a right to be welcomed. That my family was from a nearby suburb of Beirut and came to visit me regularly added to my claims. The visit of my parents to Lebanon during my research further elevated my status as several people from the neighborhood paid them their respects and were in turn received with grace, hospitality, and the familiarity of people who know each other in advance. While to some neighbors I was a passport to America, to others my coming from there meant that I would look down on them. They were surprised that I behaved like an "ordinary" person. For others yet, Arab-Americans were as suspect as any Americans and had to prove themselves trustworthy.

Moving between the various circles required many transformations, externally and internally. I felt torn between the conflicting demands. All wanted more of me than I could give. I was always apologizing. As a result, I frequently put in eighteen- to twenty-hour days. At the time I thought this was normal.


### Sectarian Identities and Choices


The question of identities was central to me in the field, professionally and personally. I had gone to test the hypothesis that leaders in the social and political institutions were pressuring people to use their sectarian identities as political tools to gain access to services and resources. At a personal level, I had for years engaged in a struggle over religious, class, and ethnic/national identities, connected to my upbringing as an immigrant Arab-American.

Raised as a devout Catholic, I had begun to question the Church in my early teens and had left it by my early twenties. Of working-class origins, I was moving into the middle class by virtue of my education. Having been schooled in America in the 1950s when there was a strong sense of Americanizing the masses, particularly the immigrant masses, I had taken on, with some lack of clarity, an American identity. Coming from an apolitical to a conservative environment, I had been "radicalized" in the 1960s. All these transitions entailed transformations of identity.

In America these identities were optional. I could leave the Church and I was no longer a Catholic. My "white-skin" privilege allowed me to identify with the Arab-American community or "pass" as a white American. I could leave the working class and integrate into the middle class. Political labels seemed changeable. The possibility of choices did not diminish (and may have intensified) the tension I experienced over these issues. Nevertheless, there was some apparent choice concerning identities.

In Lebanon, identities did not seem as optional. I was a Maronite, regardless of whether or not I practiced. I was a *mughtaribi*, a woman of local origin who had left and returned. I was from the suburb of Antilias, from the Awwad family, from a working-class background. All of these categories gave me an a priori definition in the eyes of others apart from the meaning they held for me. Although I came to experience some of the comforts of the certainty this gave, I was thrown more deeply into professional and personal questioning over identity.

I wanted to demonstrate that people could and did have choices about their identities. It felt essential to political freedom to have options. I wanted to believe that, given an opportunity, individuals would not be parochial and prejudicial. My posture toward the politicization of sectarian identities allowed me to see that the Lebanese system could not work as it was structured. My focus on institutions and the ruling elite also allowed me to see, before the civil war, that segments of the ruling elite would take the initiative in intensifying religious conflicts and sentiments.

On the other hand, my need to create a secular identity made it difficult for me to accept and understand the emotional organization of prejudice. That I could be judged on the basis of my religion, family, ethnic membership, or any other category boggled my imagination. Intense energy was focused on documenting the coercive pressure of institutions on individuals to use their religious/ethnic identities. I contrasted this with the freedom to make choices that individuals experienced in the more informal settings of the mixed working-class neighborhoods.

In the neighborhood in which I did my fieldwork, I found both confirmation and challenge to my hypotheses and assumptions. The working-class individuals were fluid in their use of and feelings toward identities. They formed deep bonds with neighbors across religious lines and made economic, political, and social use of people regardless of religious, ethnic, class, or national identities. They also, particularly in times of national crises, called up sectarian categories and feelings.

I was caught unaware by this fluidity at times. I mixed openly with people of all sects and nationalities in the neighborhood. I became close friends with Muslim, Armenian, and Christian individuals. I was known to be a supporter of the Palestinian cause and of the rights of underprivileged Muslims and Christians. The visiting networks of women and families with which I was most closely connected were also mixed, although mainly Christian. This was primarily due to the fact that I was pulled into the network of my immediate neighbor, Um Hanna, who was a Palestinian Catholic, and also because I did not have time to keep up with as many as I would have liked of the other invitations to socialize. Despite my public stance and behavior, I found that individuals had preconceptions about my loyalties that had little to do with me. I was expected to act categorically. Other behavior was suspect.

My neighbors' preconceptions emerged in May of 1973 during the two-week conflict between the Lebanese army and the Palestinians. Having just returned from Palestinian friends in the Tel al-Za'tar Camp, I was called up to the roof of my building by Christian friends to watch the Lebanese military bomb the camp in which I had just been. I criticized the Lebanese government. That criticism, made at another moment, would probably have had less impact on my friends. In the anxieties of the moment, my words had a strong effect on several people with whom I had been very close. One was understandable. A strong supporter of the Kataeb (Phalanges Libanaises), Victorine rejected out of hand any sympathy with the Palestinians. But the other was more surprising. A Greek Christian born in Palestine, Abu Fadi and his wife, a Lebanese Greek Orthodox, had appeared to be supportive of the Palestinians prior to the conflict. I sensed in both of them that my criticism, minimal as it was, was experienced as a betrayal. It took several visits and extensive discussions with both families before the relationships were reconciled. For their part, some of the Palestinians pulled in protectively and became more cautious with me. It seemed that both sides in the neighborhood had trouble dealing with an individual who did not act according to a category, particularly in a national crisis.

My questioning of identities probably sensitized me to the social construction of religious/ethnic categories and the situations in which choice-making is possible. However, because of my focus on demonstrating the institutional coercion in the use of identities, I initially did not take in, as much as I could have, the ways in which people enjoyed and felt comforted by prescriptive identities. Given my own rejection of religious faith, I did not see some of the connections between the sociopolitical and the personal. I saw identity, rather than faith, and considered it politically imposed. I was able to anticipate the rise in political tension around religious identities but saw it as externally created. My materialist training at Columbia University combined with rejection of religious faith to create a view that religion was at base economic and political. Seeing the internal as externally created, I felt reluctant to see such individuals as acting from personal conviction and thus did not see their responsibility for their sectarian behavior. It was difficult for me to accept, and therefore see, that some individuals might "choose" parochial identities. "Coerced" or not, the identities were internalized so that individuals came to act, from an inner impulse, on the codes by which people were categorized. Thus the power of these identities to mobilize people into action.

Sectarianism increased in Lebanon after the outbreak of the civil war in 1975. I am convinced that it was not as prevalent prior to the conflict. However, I am also aware that my focus on demonstrating the basis of choice-making of identities may have made me less willing to recognize the prefiguring of the emotional construction of ethnic prejudice. Some basis for it had to exist before the war, otherwise it could not have developed to the extent that it did during the conflict. I still believe that emotions in Lebanon have been reconstructed and inflamed by the politicization of religion during the war, and that emotions and identities are enmeshed in economics and politics. I now also recognize that there was an emotional ground on which this was built. Perhaps someone for whom these identities were not problematical, or who was not as personally invested in the culture, might have seen the prefiguring of emotions.

## Crossing Class Boundaries

I transcended my social class origins during my fieldwork experience. My parents were of mixed rural and urban working-class background when they were in Lebanon and of small town working-class background in the U.S. Because of higher education, my siblings and I had moved into the middle class layers of American society. Returning to Lebanon, I found that both education and American citizenship were passports into the intelligentsia and middle- and upper-class Lebanese society. I became intimate with people with whom I would have had little in common had I stayed in Lebanon. Ironically, my experience with Arab-Americans in New York had been that they determined class position in terms of social origin in Lebanon. To be welcomed into upper- and middle-class circles in Lebanon was at times fascinating, at times confusing, at times painful, and at times ironically amusing.

Since I was in the process of changing class positions, I was highly attuned to social relationships organized around class. I was particularly aware of the processes of inclusion and exclusion and the socialization that was required to make membership in a social class possible. In awe of this inclusion, I was often aware of the differences in class-based patterns of behavior. At times, I experienced an anxiety of being "found out."

There were numerous aspects of social behavior that were culturally assumed but which I had not acquired and around which I felt "declassed." All that I learned from my parents about proper behavior was evoked as I tried to live up to the credentials of membership. My friends occasionally teased me that I was more proper than the Pope. I thought I was being a good middle-class lady. Later I came to think that I was emulating the cultural model of a proper village woman trying to be sophisticated.

I was probably more sensitive to social class differences because of my own class and cultural experience than someone for whom class was not a personal question. In particular, I was aware of inter-class interactions. Watching some of my working-class neighbors and my family interact with my middle- and upper-class friends brought up a range of emotions and observations. My more privileged friends graciously offered respect and hospitality, which was reciprocated with respect and deference. Highly ritualized, the rules of the interactions were well practiced. Knowing and identifying with both sets of friends intimately, I felt that I was on both sides of the interaction.

My class background also gave me an ease with the working-class people who were the focus of my fieldwork. They were not strangers to me. They were familiar in their speech patterns, their behavior, and some of their social mores. I could see my parents and their generation of Lebanese in the faces of Borj Hammoud. Perhaps this gave me some insight or at least the ability to identify with them and understand their struggles in a more personal way than someone for whom these people were strangers.

Indeed some of them were not strangers. In the street on which I lived, I found two families from the same village and family as my brother-in-law. This gave us an immediate familial connection. I saw myself in them and wanted to give them a voice, to speak for them. I sometimes wondered whether I was not speaking for myself through them. This kinship of class created a fundamental bonding between me and my neighbors.

The precariousness of chance must have made me feel at times that I could be delivered back to these conditions. I became extremely close to several individuals in the neighborhood. Occasionally, I felt a sense of jeopardy as their expectations escalated with our increasing intimacy. They treated me as an equal. I both welcomed and resented the concomitant responsibilities and implications. I particularly felt this during my first trip to Lebanon in 1968 when, as a single woman in my mid-twenties, I found myself barraged by marriage proposals from men from rural working-class to urban middle-class backgrounds. Since it was uncommon for a woman to marry below her class position, I saw the proposals as an expression of the still fluid character of my class position. Ego aside, I was sure that for many of them I was a passport to America.

### Bint Al-Jiran: Expectations of the Neighbors

Living in the Borj Hammoud neighborhood, I was caught between the neighbors' expectations that I be both like them and different from them. There was a delicate balance between the intimacy and the social distance that they seemed to want from me.

As an educated American woman, I was supposed to behave with a certain class decorum. They both approved and disapproved of the fact that I only partly did so. They thought of me as *sha'biyyi* (an ordinary folk) or *bint al-jiran* (the neighbors' daughter). They liked the fact that it was easy for them to talk and be at ease with me. But at the same time, they wanted me to have some social distance from them. The women expressed this in terms of my attire and household. I was expected to dress much better than they. Although I thought my clothes were fine, I had a new wardrobe made to meet their standards. While my apartment was clean and orderly, it was not enough for my neighbors. One day, a few of them took matters in their own hands. Descending unannounced unto my apartment, they cleaned everything to their satisfaction.

Because I was from America and educated, I was expected to be a patron to some people. I helped when I could. I intervened with the local and national government, helped some make contacts in the U.S. for emigration, put my car at their disposal, helped in times of illness and crises. The social expectations of patronage, however, were less manageable than the service aspects. A number of people for whom I had done favors began visiting me regularly. It was awkward with one Armenian couple whom I had befriended and lent a not small amount of money. I had expected that they would return it. When I found them visiting me every Monday night, I realized my payment was the status of patron. It was a delicate matter to gently let them know that they need not visit me so frequently. For others, it was simply a matter of doing what I could for them. I was humbled by the recognition that the little I had or knew could make some difference in their comfort.

I was in the anomalous position of being a married middle-class woman living alone in a poor neighborhood that was predominantly family-based. There was a single woman living alone on the same street.

Several married women lived with their parents while their husbands worked abroad. However, most married women lived with their husbands. When my husband joined me in Lebanon, I set up another apartment in a middle-class neighborhood (to meet some of the social requirements of his job). That seemed to satisfy my neighbors. While they were curious about him, they had experienced enough variability in the living arrangements of married women so that I was not incomprehensible to them.

They could not, however, understand why I did not have children, particularly since I so obviously loved and got along with the neighborhood children. Raised in a large nuclear family, I had had nieces and nephews while I was still young and was thus well trained in caring for children. I spent a considerable amount of time with the neighborhood children, who became accustomed to the hospitality of my home and regularly visited me. I had a particularly close relationship with Fadi, the five-year-old son of my neighbor, Um Hanna. My involvement with Fadi and his family seemed quite natural to me. I was considered one of the family and I took the familial responsibilities seriously. The relationship did not feel like fieldwork. Since these family-like relationships were part of my upbringing and culture, I played this role spontaneously. As a result, both my research and my personal life were deeply enriched by coming to know this family so well. My relationship with children may have done more to humanize me to my neighbors than any other aspect of my behavior and was one of the richest aspects of my stay in Borj Hammoud.

The special family relationships were part of and parallel to a number of special friendships. My neighbors, the young men of the street, the *mukhtar* (mayor) and his daughter, the director who was a member of the Dashnak (Armenian Party), the Blind School social worker, and others became a part of my intimate life.

My most demanding friendships were with the women. I felt a lot of pressure from them to immerse myself in their lives. They wanted me to visit on a regular basis and felt insulted if I did not visit as often as they did. Um Hanna often covered up for me by telling them that I asked about them and would visit them soon.

At times, the demands of the women were overwhelming. As I increasingly came to see my relationships with them as personal, I reacted to their demands somewhat as I had to the demands of my own family. I saw the immersion in their relations alternately as suffocating and soothing. I longed for privacy. I felt trapped by their expectations, which I felt obligated to meet, maybe more than a non-native would have felt. Perhaps unlike the latter, my sense of obligation came not from a sense of "this is what one has to do to do fieldwork," but rather from a sense that they had a right to make those demands. They were tapping into deep-seated values that were as much a part of my culture and socialization as theirs. Well trained to perform the socially necessary tasks, I played the culturally appropriate role, fulfilling the obligations, pleasantries and so forth. While I resented the hold they had on me, at the time I could only act in the socially correct manner.

At the same time, the demands enmeshed me in an ocean of relationships. There was a warm, deep, secure feeling in fulfilling the obligations. I felt that I was being a good person in the way in which I had been raised and had not been able to play out fully in the American context. My mother had always said to me: "Do good and throw in the ocean." The good deeds were returned in tidal waves. The reciprocity overwhelmed me. I had never experienced so many people willing to give, to include me, to go out of their way in such a spontaneous, unreflective way. I became enmeshed in a large network of people with intense exchanges of gifts, services, support, and sociability.

The women and their families became so much a part of my personal life that I found it difficult to think of my relationship with them as a source of research data. They became active subjects, rather than objects of research. I enjoyed visiting with them enormously. As time went on, I thought of my time with them as personal. I felt, and was, accepted. I learned in depth about neighborhood life and personal relationships. But the closer I became to the individuals, the harder I found it to treat information they offered as field data and so often did not record valuable information.

### Feminization in the Field

In Lebanon, I became much more aware of my femininity. The expectations of neighbors, family and friends to behave as a proper married woman brought out old and new behaviors. Externally, some changes were easy. I dressed more fashionably and regularly had my hair done. My hand gestures, posture and style of walking transformed to suit the tastes of local men and women. The principles (not the specifics) of these ways of being feminine had been part of my upbringing. Rebelling against my mother and brothers' pressure on me to fit into their image of being female, I thought I had rejected these masks. In Lebanon, I found their inner face. My mother was quite pleased when she visited me. So successfully had I taken on some of these externals of being a Middle Eastern woman, that when I returned to New York I was a mild, but I think pleasant, surprise to my family and friends.

More subtle and less easy to grasp were the internal changes. Foremost among these was a heightened sexuality. It was unlike anything I had felt with Americans; but it was close to what I had experienced within the Arab-American community. As Kandiyoti (1984), Sabbah (1984), and others have pointed out, in the Middle East a woman's sexuality is given, assumed. A man's is achieved and must be continually demonstrated, partly by sexual accomplishments.

I was aware of myself as a woman and as a sexual prey. In part this was because, like most local and foreign women, I was the object of ongoing sexual advances from many quarters. But the heightened sexuality was not only a result of such advances. It was also due to the attitude of men and women toward each other. I was aware of being regarded, observed, evaluated in sexual terms by both men and women. With many men it seemed to be the spontaneous response to a new contact. My coming from America probably meant that I was sexually free and available. It came as a shock to me and to them to learn that I had been raised even more conservatively than some of the Lebanese women of my age group and in many matters was as naive as some local women. My parents had raised their daughters according to the standards of female modesty in Lebanon at the time they had left in 1949. Lebanon had changed, but their image of it had remained the same. Many of my cousins had had a more liberal upbringing in Lebanon than I had had in the U.S.

My response to the heightened sexuality and to my feminization was a spontaneous shyness that I recognized from my childhood and my adolescence but had not experienced in some time. I found I could not communicate how I managed sexuality. My shyness was part of my shield and when that did not work, I was vulnerable. This emotional quality was coming from a source deep within me that was not accessible to rational will. It was, for the most part, a culturally appropriate response. That is, the people around me thought my response was understandable, but were surprised that a woman raised in America would respond in a manner expected of a conservatively raised Lebanese woman.

Mostly the shyness pleased me. I felt safe and protected. It was a cultural shield that indicated that I was an honorable woman. It did not keep all men from making advances, but it brought out a culturally appropriate response that they could understand and that would make some of them back off. The shyness was so spontaneous that it was like a danger signal warning me to protect myself.

The shyness, however, was connected not only to sexual behavior. Generosity, hospitality, praise, kindness at times elicited shyness as did rowdy behavior. It was a response I often could not anticipate or control.

Observing myself, I could see the instrumentality of shyness as a cultural mechanism for controling behavior.

## Family, Personhood and Self

### To Be of a Family:

In 1968, while I was doing research in the southern town of Marja 'yun, I was confronted by a townsman suspicious of my work. He asked about my family. When I answered, he responded: "Oh yes, I had heard that bint 'amm (father's brother's daughter) As'ad Awwad was coming." I felt I became a social (human) being when I identified myself from a known family background.

This event lingered with me on my return trips, reminding me that I was nothing if not a member of a family. While my family in the U.S. had constituted almost my entire personal universe, I had never belonged to a family in such a socially powerful way. However, my enmeshment in my own family helped me to understand the compelling force of group membership in Lebanon.

Accepting the family identity meant taking on the responsibility of protecting family honor. Mostly I was concerned about my parents, who were to make their first trip to Lebanon in twenty-three years during the second year of my fieldwork. I wanted to offer them impeccable creden-tials for their return. I maintained all the reciprocities and activities that would have been expected of me if my family were there—and even more, since I was the sole representative of my family. I did the rounds of visiting on holidays and at deaths, weddings, and other rituals. I was made aware, as a result of my concern for my parents, how the notion of family honor operates to control behavior, particularly the behavior of women. Fulfilling the ever-present, time-consuming obligations further wove me into the family tapestry, leaving few spaces for straying.

### To Be in a Family:

Being in a local family meant dealing with their demands. On my first trip to Lebanon in 1968, I had been cautioned that I should guard my time because the family would consume me. I remembered this when I longed for the anonymity of the anthropologist going off to a strange culture. My cousins and uncles and aunts felt responsible for me. Mainly this took the form of insisting that I spend enormous amounts of time with them. Some of this was wonderful and some was a burden. Since I did not see my family as part of my fieldwork, I experienced the time with them as personal. In retrospect, I learned much about the culture from them.

Among the most interesting cultural behaviors I learned by being in a local family was the manipulation of the bilateral aspects of the kinship system. The anthropological texts of that period spoke little of the maternal side of Middle Eastern families, emphasizing the three p's: patriarchy, patrilineality, and patrilocality. This emphasis coincided with my personal experience since I had had only members of my father's family in the U.S.

I learned, at a rich personal level, the importance of maternal relatives. I spontaneously developed a closer relationship with my mother's family, which was warm and loving. Appearing to have few expectations, they seemed to accept me and respond to time I spent with them as a gift. Being with them felt like a choice and therefore free and joyful.

My father's side of the family appeared to be more judgmental and formal. There was a greater sense of distance. They seemed to respond to my time with them more as obligation. I was expected to be with them and they expected to have to have me. I felt I had to be serious, correct, and always adult with them.

At first, it seemed simply a matter of family styles and personalities. However, in retrospect I see that both sides of my family had a range of personalities. The experience helped me to understand at a personal level the impact of authority on relationships and personas, for even I felt like a different person with the two sets of relatives. My father's family needed to maintain distance to exercise their authority over me. In feeling closer to my maternal relatives, I was living out a cultural norm. Bilaterality was so fundamental that it had an emotional expression.

I also learned to play my *walad al-'amm* (paternal uncles' children) against my *walad al-khaal* (maternal uncles' children). If I did not want to be pulled by one, I could use the other as an excuse. While my insider/ outsider position might have given me more leverage than the cultural norm, I learned from this play that the kinship system was far more bilateral than most texts proclaimed.

### Personhood and Self:

Doing fieldwork in Lebanon raised the question of the difference in the Western and Middle Eastern constructions of personhood and self. I had internalized components of both cultures, although at the time of my first trip to Lebanon, I was, in my sense of self, probably more Middle Eastern than Western. By American middle-class standards, I probably did not have a well-developed sense of myself as an individual. In Lebanon, this was not a handicap, but rather an advantage. I experienced an embeddedness in the family and the social fabric to which I might not have had access had I had a clearer sense of self.

I experienced this sense of self in terms of what I now would call a powerful desire to merge. I felt little sense of my own boundaries and seemed to dive into relationships with people. I wanted to be part of them. This was acted out, in part, in the expectations and willingness to share almost totally, materially and emotionally. The primary mechanism for sharing was the constant attention to the needs and desires of others, for which I had been well trained in my family, and acceptance of the constant involvement of others in matters of personal relevance.

It was dizzying and wondrous. It seemed that I had finally found the kind of relationships I had been seeking. I thought of it then as the difference in the ways Middle Eastern and American people offered friendship.

But there were other signals. I at times felt a sense of danger. Feeling drained and exhausted, I periodically withdrew or balked at the demands for total involvement, total sharing, total presence. The absolute sense of belonging to others was overwhelming. It seemed I could be nothing other than the definition of me prevalent among my family and friends. When I tried to put up boundaries, I found that I was ill equipped. Family and friends had a power over me because I was trained to give over power. I was so much part of the culture that I was overtaken; yet I was socialized enough in the American culture to feel occasionally ill at ease.

At that time, I was more aware of myself as a member of a family than as an individual. I had been struggling with questions of personhood without having a name for them. My bicultural experience gave me the occasional ability both to merge and to separate. It was a vantage point I only partially understood.

## Western Training and Middle Eastern Socialization

### Culture of Indirection:

The experience with merger led me into another critical aspect of Middle Eastern culture. I had been trained in my family to state my needs indirectly and to respond to the indirect statements of others. In the

American context, beyond my own immediate family, my indirect statements were either resented or misunderstood. I was expected to be more direct. In Lebanon, my indirection was responded to readily, and I learned to be more careful in my statements.

Undoubtedly, there is a connection between merger and indirection. My relatively undifferentiated persona and my training in indirection attuned me to a dynamic of relationship and interaction that might have been missed by someone not so trained. I was aware of the use of indirection as sarcasm, as seduction, as demand, and as social control. I found myself fine-tuning an old skill I had learned at my mother's side.

### Active and Passive Modes:

Fieldwork brought up tensions between my scientific training in male-dominated Western academia and my socialization as a Middle Eastern woman. A part of me wanted to remain silent, to observe, to let things and people come to me, to merge, to weave myself into the social web. Another part thought it necessary to direct, to act, to shape, to make events happen.

In interviews, I often set the agenda of the discussion. I felt I was doing good fieldwork when I directed the discussion along planned lines of inquiry. I could be assertive in getting access to people and records. I created social activity around myself and was often the center of activity when I was in a group.

When I was a quiet observer, I was more comfortable and learned an enormous amount. These moments occurred generally when I thought of myself as a woman rather than as a researcher. I often silently receded into the background. The data I gathered in this mode was perhaps richer in emotional and social detail than that gathered in my active researcher mode.

When I was in the active mode, I felt professional, powerful. I was doing my work. The more passive stance did not feel intellectually legitimate.

### Formal and Informal, Structure and Non-Structure:

In traditional anthropological style, I used both structured and un-structured methods. In the structured interviews, I collected and recorded reams of data. In the un-structured, I absorbed and assimilated, often not recording. While I knew that the un-structured interviews and observations were as valuable as the structured, I found it more difficult to record the former systematically. It was not a lack of intellectual awareness of the limits of structured methods, but rather the difficulty of grasping the informal that led me to value the apparently greater "clarity" and "certainty" of the data gathered through structured methods. As a result, I relied more than I had anticipated on a kind of data and method of which I was critical.

Reinforcing this orientation, however, was an aspect of my training that valued information on formal institutions and agencies more highly than information on individuals, everyday life, feelings, and attitudes. Since I saw the formal institutions as the culprits in pressuring people to use their sectarian identities politically, I did extensive formal interviews on local government, schools, service and charity agencies, and social and cultural clubs. I threw myself into the formal interviews with the intensity of the culture addict. Even when I realized, as I did in the field, that it was important to gather data on individuals and daily life, I felt more confident collecting that data formally. To capture the intersectarian relationships in the neighborhood, for example, I did extensive formal interviews on social networks. While that information has become invaluable to me, I now regret that I did not as systematically record what I observed and experienced informally.

Even more elusive were emotions and attitudes. Given how attuned I was, by virtue of my socialization as a Middle Eastern woman, to people's feelings and ways of thinking, it is now remarkable to me that I did not record my observations of them as systematically as I recorded responses to formal inquiries. I think I felt too enmeshed in the emotions, and insufficiently confident of naming what parts of it belonged to someone else, to treat it as data. When I returned from the field, I saw more clearly both the richness of daily life in the street and the wealth of insight I had gained into the inner lives of those people.

*Access of Males and Females:*

Lebanon in the 1960s and 1970s was a relatively open society. I shared in the mobility of native women, although my status as a married woman and an insider/outsider probably added to my freedom. I came and went at all hours of the day and night with no difficulty. I had unlimited access to women, as would be expected. But I also had enormous access to men. The only places that did not feel comfortable were the cafés frequented primarily by men in the urban working-class areas. Since a few neighborhood women did go to cafés, it was not clear to me whether the discomfort came mainly from within me. However, this was not much of an issue because few of the local men frequented cafés and indeed there were only a few of them in Borj Hammoud.

There was also relatively little sex segregation in Lebanon during this period, even among the working classes. Given that most families in Borj Hammoud lived in one- to three-room apartments, sex segregation would have been difficult or impossible to achieve, even if it had been socially desired. I had no difficulty speaking to men alone or with their families. A number of the neighborhood men with whom I had become quite friendly often visited me on their own.

While access was not a significant problem, how to behave was. When I was with men alone, I felt safer in my active scholarly mode. I was businesslike and the boundaries were clear. Yet, I sometimes felt that I learned more—or a different kind of information—in my passive Middle Eastern mode. It was also the behavior that was expected of me. I unconsciously alternated between the two styles. I experienced conflict between them but did not know how to name it.

*Households of Invisible Women:*

I was interested in showing the class basis for the politicization of religion and was focusing on institutions that contributed to this politicization. The materialist training I had had at Columbia coincided with my own tendencies to discount feelings if they did not conform to logic. I tended to intellectualize, abstract, to look for patterns and principles rather than the concrete and particular. Considerations of the irrational, of emotions and particularities were vested in my poetry and essays. As a result of these orientations, I did not make the best use of the enormous access I had to neighborhood women. While I was with them, I felt myself a woman rather than a researcher.

Most of my household interviews were with the female heads of households. But given my own enmeshment in family identity, which was enhanced in the field, I did not tend to see the women as separate individuals. Of course, neither did they. Seeing them as representatives of their households, I did not realize that I was recording a principally female experience. Thinking in household terms, I had devised my questionnaires in a manner to elicit information on the household as a unit. As I analyzed my data, I had to tease out of them information on men and women and reinterpret information solicited from a single person as if he or she spoke for the whole.

*Female as Observer:*

There were some ways in which my socialization as a Middle Eastern woman provided me with culturally specific methodological skills. As I was growing up, my mother constantly admonished me that I may have two eyes, but there were a thousand eyes looking at me. Given that I was raised as a Catholic, this was reinforced by the Church's teaching of the omnipresence of God. I was aware that I would be observed no matter what I did and where I did it. I was also aware that I was expected to be similarly observant, an early training that assisted me as a field-worker. It gave me a pointed insight into the sensitivities of Arab people.

I could see the connection between the sense that one is constantly being observed and cultural patterns that I experienced: heightened sexuality, shyness, willingness to conform to social standards. This sensibility is closely connected with another aspect of my socialization as a Middle Eastern woman that also offered me a culturally specific methodology, but one I was not aware of at the time.

*Merger as a Female Methodology:*

I was not able to distinguish between merger and immersion while I was doing research. Indeed, I did not even know about the distinction. I think that I merged with many of my informants, friends, and family and thought that I was immersing myself in fieldwork. My ability to merge with people allowed me to figuratively "get inside" people in a way anthropologists not so socialized might not have. There was a loss of "objectivity," but given that the latter is subjectively experienced, I am not sure how to evaluate what that loss did to my work.

Merger brought with it an intense focus on "the other." I understood myself through others. My needs, desires, and opinions were reactive, shaped in response to others. Given this sense of self, the cultural training to observe others became a personal imperative. I had to know them to know myself. So I dove in and watched.

I did not think of merger as a research tool at the time. I was not conscious enough of the process to employ it rationally. My not recording information on relationships that I came to regard as personal might in part be because I was too merged to see the difference between self and other. As feminist works have recently made me aware of possible differences in male and female scientific and moral behavior (Gilligan 1982; Keller 1983), I find myself reflecting on the use of merger as a female methodology.

Having somewhat resocialized myself into a sense of boundaries, I considered the possibility of merging and separating by choice. There is no doubt that my unreflective merging with individuals allowed me to experience and learn about the nature of relationships and self from a specialized vantage point. I would think that the more conscious control of self in this matter would be even more revealing.

## Research as Politicization

### Women as Subjects:

As I began analyzing my data after my return to the U.S., I realized that much of it was about women. When I entertained the proposition that the phenomenon I was looking for at the household level—intersectarian relationships—was principally female behavior, I became increasingly interested in questions concerning women. This interest was triggered by attending a panel on women at the Middle Eastern Studies Association Meetings in 1974 and at the meetings agreeing to write papers for two volumes on Middle Eastern women (Fernea and Bezirgan 1977; Beck and Keddie 1978). Later that academic year, I taught my first sex roles course. Using the Rosaldo and Lamphere (1974) reader, I was provoked by the universalist public/private domains argument into a critique in which I argued that the distinction was inapplicable to male and female relationships in Borj Hammoud (Joseph 1975). To pursue the argument, I looked into the significant domains of female activity and found the neighborhood street a critical social arena dominated by women (Joseph 1976a, b; 1977, 1978a). Discovering significant intersectarian relationships in the urban working-class street unlike those in other social arenas, I began to see the neighborhood street as important in the development of a new political culture. Since activity within the street was primarily female activity, it became increasingly clear to me that these women had an impact on politics and the state (Joseph 1978b, c; 1979a, b, c). I began to see them as political actors who shared the same political culture as the men but who, because of their location in the structure, acted differently—they had more intersectarian relationships. The new political culture emerging out of primarily female activity in these urban working-class neighborhoods, I came to argue, was perceived and responded to as a political danger by sections of the ruling elite (Joseph 1983).

The development of my thinking on the Borj Hammoud women coincided with the beginning of my involvement in the women's movement and women's studies in the mid-1970s. Participating in numerous feminist and Marxist-feminist reading groups transformed my research interests as well as the way I looked at theory and method. As feminist and Marxist-feminist anthropology and social theory rapidly evolved from the mid-1970s into the 1980s, I became aware that there is no unengendered perspective.

*Engendered Perspective:*

I was not a feminist when I did my research in the early 1970s, at least not self-consciously. I thought that the sex of the researcher was primarily a matter of the kinds of access women would have versus men. Since I had unlimited access to women and vast access to men in Lebanon, the matter was not problematical. What I did not see was that my perspective and training were engendered.

Recent feminist research seems to be revealing differences between male and female styles that affect scientific method and moral behavior. Carol Gilligan (1982) has argued that men and women in the U.S. have different moral development. Men are more individuated, separated, assertive, aggressive; women are more embedded, attached, relational, nurturing. Along similar lines, Evelyn Fox Keller (1983) reveals that the methodology of Nobel Prize winner Barbara McClintock was to converse with and become a part of the organism she was studying rather than imposing an answer or trying to dominate her subject—a female as opposed to a male methodology.

I did both, though unreflectively. I interrogated my material and I listened to it. While I was in the field, I was more confident of the data produced by the more active and interventionist methods. However, I also let the material come to me, particularly in the neighborhood. This was a methodology that grew as much from my socialization as a Middle Eastern woman as it did from my training for participant observation.

The two styles produced different kinds of insights. The "male" methodology led to abstractions, generalizations about ethnicity, class, and state. The confidence that I had in the possibility of finding "laws," constructing macro-level theory, and predicting social outcomes on the basis of fieldwork were part of my academic training. As a result, I was then willing to make kinds of statements that I now would be more reluctant to propose. I forecast the collapse of the Lebanese political system long before it occurred, although then I assumed that a class-based social revolution would take place. Again, before the war, I argued that there would be an increased politicization of religion as the ruling elite tried to bolster the basis of its control over the population (Joseph 1975). With a kind of confidence and ease, I later wrote a lengthy piece on the theoretical relationships between kinship, class, ethnicity, the state, and the world system (Joseph 1978b, c). These insights, it now seems, came out of an academic, "male" anthropology.

At the time, this approach probably dominated my notion of science. As a result, I did not, for example, pay as close attention to systematically assessing my observations on the emotional content of the politicization of religion. Had I felt more legitimate about these observations, it might have been possible to foresee psychological aspects of the rise of religious fundamentalism in the region.

What I did pay attention to, however, were the complexities of social relationships. It was here that my training as a woman and the more "female" methodology enriched my research the most. While I was not conscious of merger as a method, I lived it perforce of my own persona. This aspect of my research lingered with me more deeply and problematically than any other. Its grip on me was personal and therefore a source of ongoing reflection. It is partly responsible for my shift to women's studies and for the beginning of a project on the nature of the self in the Middle East.

Women researchers may not gather different information from men if they are not atuned to or do not legitimate their different sensibilities. The question is not the superiority of one methodology over the other, but rather the different kinds of insights each produces. The problem is that many of us have been taught to value the one over the other. As I come increasingly to see the connection between the professional and the personal, I see those methodologies as enriching each other.


### Subject/Object; Professional and Personal Journey


Research has led me into a journey of self-reflection. I thought of myself as going to Lebanon because I was interested in a theoretical project on plural societies. I did not realize that I had embarked on a personal journey as well.

Scholars who research their countries of origin have perhaps the opportunity to combine the personal and professional in a way that others may not. My journey may have been made possible by the fact that I had left and returned to Lebanon, giving me a chance to become a person of two worlds.

This insider/outsider status brought with it another—that of subject/object. As I moved toward the study of women in the Middle East, I found that my personal experience became increasingly relevant to my research. My responses to events and situations became data for me to reflect upon along with observations of the behavior of other Middle Eastern women. The relationship to my self as subject/object brought an immediacy to my reading of the research of others. I could check their reports against my personal experience. The differences, as well as similarities, became points of departure for further inquiry. There is a constant engagement in this particularistic and privileged relationship to research.

I find myself now wondering how it is that people do research on questions or people far afield from their selves. Even though I was unaware of it at the time, my guess is that something more personal than an intellectual interest in pluralism took me back to Lebanon.

Abstractly, I have for years asserted that we are always studying ourselves. I think I did not know how true that was for me. My understanding of this search deepens as I find myself inching toward questions closer to the construction of the self. This is perhaps the most luxurious aspect of my present work. It utterly matters to me, as I am embedded in it.

It is probably not accidental that I initially researched the politicization of religion. I was making peace with my having left behind my own deeply religious upbringing, and searching for a social domain in which secular choices and identities could be sustained.

Similarly, it is probably not accidental that, as I became more interested in the women's movement in the U.S. and grew into an understanding of my own issues as a woman, I was drawn into researching women in the Middle East. Perhaps researching one's country of origin begins—or ends—in part in a search for the self.

# 3

# At Home in the Field

SORAYA ALTORKI

T his chapter focuses on the particular issues I faced in conducting fieldwork among members of my own status group in my own society in Jiddah, Saudi Arabia. It shows that despite certain immediate advantages, such as intimate knowledge of the vernacular, the ability to quickly "set up shop" in the field, and familiarity with the people and environment, a number of problems also had to be confronted and resolved. These included the requirement of abiding by norms expected of me as a native; overcoming the reluctance of informants to provide me with direct answers to my questions concerning religious practices, intra-family conflicts, and the like; and resocializing myself into my own culture, from which I had been separated for a number of years due to residence and education abroad.

More importantly, I argue here that as a Saudi Arabian and as a woman, I was able to gain access to an important domain of urban society: the area of domestic relations. While most of the literature on women in traditional Arab society in general and Saudi Arabian society in particular is based on misinformation, hearsay, and ahistorical interpretations, my investigation has shown Saudi Arabian women to be far from the passive and oppressed group that has been suggested by conventional discussions. I also argue that the female indigenous anthropologist studying her own society can play a major role in providing a more balanced analysis of the role of women in Arab politics and society.

49

## Going to the Field

My decision to conduct my first field research in the Arab world was motivated by personal rather than academic reasons. The shattering defeat of the Arab world in 1967 occurred only five months after I had arrived in the United States to study for a Ph.D. in anthropology at the University of California, Berkeley. It left me, along with many Arabs, stunned, totally confused, and robbed of my sense of national dignity. In the wake of these compelling and agonized feelings came a period of deeper questioning. Conferring with fellow students on the Berkeley campus, I came to the conclusion that attempts to remedy the situation must begin with a thorough and scientific understanding of the conditions of contemporary Arab society. So I set my mind upon conducting field research in the Arab world.

Although studying one's own society was not so novel in anthropological circles during the 1960s, the predominant trend was the study of "others." Thus, it was with animation that I explained to my dissertation committee members at Berkeley why I did not really want to go to Mexico or conduct my inquiry in the U.S. Instead, I insisted, I wanted to study folk religion in rural Egypt.

Arriving in Egypt with my dissertation prospectus in hand, I set myself the task of getting permission and clearance to do my research. Feeling quite at home in Egypt, I anticipated few problems, for after all I had been raised in Egypt from middle school through college and could bank on that experience to inch my way through the bureaucracy. My naive assumptions were sobered by new realities that had resulted from the devastating defeat of 1967. Nasser's Egypt had begun to close in on itself in the effort at reconstruction. This meant tighter controls on foreigners in the country and on their mobility between cities. Being an Arab made little difference in this specific instance. Non-Egyptian Arabs living in Egypt were also confined to their cities of residence, and traveling within Egypt did not include wandering into villages located off the main roads. My intention to find an appropriate village to live in for the period of fieldwork was therefore out of the question. It was also impossible to work in the city, since the research permit and clearance in any case did not seem to be forthcoming. This, of course, had nothing to do with my being Arab or a woman, but instead was due to formal changes in Egyptian society and the pervasive negative attitude toward social science research. Six months had now elapsed since my arrival in Cairo and, as there was still no indication that I would get the permit, I decided that I must locate another site for fieldwork. Thus, it was with great determination that I sent out my new proposal to my professors in Berkeley. This time, I was really going "home."

## At Home in the Field

Having been socialized many years in Egypt and identifying with its people, I had regarded it, on one level, to be my home. On another level, however, I had been brought up in a Saudi Arabian family committed in great measure to that country's cultural heritage and the observance of its cultural norms, even while selectively observing certain Egyptian values and practices. Throughout my college days, I had been reminded that I could not do what my Egyptian girl-friends could do, because "our" traditions were different and for "us" such behavior was unacceptable.

Besides, it was not only the constraining elements of Saudi Arabian culture that molded my growing-up experiences in Egypt, but also the rich rewards that I reaped from kinship support and shared cultural knowledge. These provided for me the security of a closure that was not attainable in Egypt. Thus, Saudi Arabia was home for me on a more fundamental level.

Arriving in Jiddah, my native city, I knew I wanted to study urban life. Although the entire northern portion of the Arabian Peninsula was virtually unknown to social scientists, yet early travelers and even scholars avoided its study in favor of the nomad and the camel. Barring Hurgrouje and Burton, almost nothing was known about urban life. In retrospect, I believe that my choice to focus on urban society was partly a reaction to the stereotypical view of Saudi Arabia as a society of nomads and oil wells.

There were also social constraints to my choice. I knew that, as an unmarried woman, I could neither travel alone in the country nor wander around with the nomads. Living alone, anywhere in the country, was out of the question. Thus, for many considerations, an urban-based study seemed most appropriate, and the city of Jiddah the most convenient.

The realities of being an unmarried woman in many ways dictated my field of research, although it did not determine my choice of research topic within that field (Altorki 1986). This essentially meant that I could work with women and that I had limited access to men. Within these bounds, my choice was absolutely free.

I was encouraged to study elite families because such studies are rare in anthropology. The history of anthropological fieldwork has been a study of commoners, the poor, and the marginal. Anthropologists, whether working in their own society or in another, have traditionally studied people whose status is below their own (see Nader 1969). An inquiry into elites was important on another score. The study of the influential and powerful is essential to our understanding of how current power distribution in society is conceived and maintained. It also guides us in locating the potential for transformation and change. Constituting the peak of the social pyramid, the elite make the decisions that affect all other social classes. There is no doubt that sources of stability can reside with other classes, but the latter cannot be comprehended in isolation or independently of those who wield economic and political power in the social system.

## Insider/Outsider

Being literally at home in Jiddah, I was spared having to worry about the problems of settling in that most anthropologists face when entering the field. Furthermore, I needed no research permit (or if I did, I never bothered to find out) and no letters of guarantee. Neither was I required to make commitments to local authorities and research institutes concerning the conduct of my work and the use and distribution of my data.

The people I studied saw me as one of themselves. Some of them had ties of kinship and friendship to my family. Others knew my family members by name. This state of affairs provided me with significant advantages. Others, working in their own society, have observed similar benefits in knowing the culture and consequently being able to select their research agenda in consonance with what is most expedient for the research task, and what is most feasible within the limits of what will be allowed by the subjects under investigation (see Stephenson and Greer 1981:126).

However, some facets of my life concerned my informants. Why, for example, was I not a married woman with children, like all my peers? And why was I still living abroad, rather than residing in Jiddah, awaiting marriage? My unmarried status at the age of twenty-two made me somewhat of an anomaly. More distressing to the older women among whom I worked was the conclusion that I was more interested in following my studies than in settling down to married life. Although the role of an educated woman had come to be accepted by the community at large and the elite in particular, the problem was in the priorities this role took over what was perceived to be the more important aspect of gender role, namely the status that marriage and motherhood bring. According to both men and women, it is these dimensions of womanhood that are primary. In fact, given the segregation of Saudi Arabian women from men, and their isolation from public life, marriage and motherhood become a woman's avenues to maturity, security, and greater prestige. Being a member of the society, I anticipated this and was well prepared to deal with its consequences.

Although women come of age with marriage, and prestige for them is attained by motherhood, my status within the community had to rest on other things: it relied greatly on my education. Lacking husband and child, I predicated my adulthood on education and depended on the community's acceptance of it as a legitimate goal for women to attain. Men and women alike respected this, although never failing to remind me of the fundamentals of my role as a woman. As one older woman put it to me: "Education is good, but women are weak. No matter how much money they have, no matter their education, they cannot manage without men. May Allah save your father and your brother. But you have to start your own family." That statement accurately reflects the dependence of women on men, a dependence that also correlates with their segregation in Saudi Arabian society. But my role as a Saudi Arabian woman, educated abroad, permitted me more flexibility and autonomy. For one thing, my interaction with men who were not my relatives was tolerated.

My long absence abroad was an additional factor leading to more mobility. While abroad, I had been immersed in a different way of life, and hence women and men alike did not expect me to conform totally to the cultural norms governing the relationship of men and women in Saudi Arabian society. My absence had a complex effect on my reentry into my own community. On the one hand, it allowed more maneuverability in my role as an unmarried woman, and, on the other hand, it made conformity especially expedient in strengthening my ties to my informants.

Repeatedly, men and women expressed their surprise and approval when my behavior showed conformity to Saudi Arabian culture. They were, for example, delighted that my many years in Egypt had not changed my accent to Egyptian. Whenever I showed observance of norms that young people my age had begun to modify, members of the older generation were astonished and particularly delighted. Those of the younger generation, however, saw such conformity as awkward and continued to remind me that times had changed: "Nobody is observing such things these days."

For example, norms of deference to older siblings necessitate that they be addressed in specific terms. To an older brother and kinsmen his age the term is *sidi*, which means "my master." My use of these terms of address was welcomed by all, barring girls of my age who by then were seeking to substitute as equivalent for the term *sidi* those of *akhuya* (my brother) and the sobriquet *abu flan* (father of). In doing this, I took my cues from young men who had obtained their college education abroad, sometimes through graduate school, and who continued to use traditional terms of reference in addressing older female siblings and other kinswomen in their age group.

It was in the same spirit that I observed some norms of modesty, particularly those related to veiling. Such practices were changing at the time of my fieldwork, so that the families I studied showed the whole spectrum of veiling practices, from those who had considerably modified its use to leave the face bare, to those who still observed the traditional practice of covering the face as well. While visiting the homes of the latter, I made sure to conform and to cover my face carefully. This gesture of respect did not go unnoticed: women and men alike commented that my many years abroad had not made me behave like a "foreigner."

The years abroad had been spent as a student, and now I had come back as a researcher with the intention of recording a way of life that had not previously been studied. Everyone understood that role. Female education was not a novelty. Girls were sent to *faqihas* (informal traditional schools) as far back as older informants could remember; and formal girls' schools were opened by the government in 1960. By the time I went to the field, the first women's university had already opened in Jiddah. College education was thoroughly acceptable for women; indeed, it had become greatly valued.

Thus, I had no problem in defining part of my role to the subjects of my research. I wanted to study social life, family organization, rituals, beliefs, and customs, and to document how these have changed for the younger people in the study. In another way, my role was more ascribed. My return to Jiddah meant taking my place in a family and getting involved in the various ramifications of family life. It also meant belonging to a class with the task of conforming to the behavior of that class. I was aware that I could in fact not conform to that behavior, but I had little choice with regard to involvement in family life.

The ascribed aspects of my role, i.e., gender, age, and kinship, were more fundamental in people's perception of me, which may be unavoidable in doing research among one's own people. My education was important in allowing me to explore areas of social life (e.g., more access to the world of men) that other women could not undertake. Despite my research objective, known and accepted to all the families, I remained primarily a Saudi Arabian woman. As such, I was known to some as the daughter or a sister of a friend, while to others as a member of a lineage they knew from other mutual friends. These considerations were always present in my interaction with others. While criteria centering on the individual are not without relevance in structuring relations, the world of these elite families was in the first instance structured by consanguineous and marital ties, and in the second place by friendship and business networks.

Within this world an individual—whether man or woman—is deeply embedded in the 'aila (family). One's status is, to a considerable degree, ascribed by the status of the 'aila. Individual achievement is an avenue to mobility, but clearly it is the achievement of men and not of women that is associated with family prestige. Recent changes in the wider society have introduced more emphasis on individuality and an increase of distance from the 'aila. This is evidenced in neolocal residence patterns, more individual involvement in marriage choice, relative reduction of parental authority, independent career choices for men, and less observance of traditional obligations to kinsmen (Altorki 1986).

On the whole, I experienced no problems in establishing rapport— that quality in the relationship between the ethnographer and the host community that the introductions to ethnographic monographs rarely fail to mention, but which probably involves the most enigmatic aspect of our methodological trademark: participant observation. I spoke the language, and the trademark itself had no special meaning for me, although, as I will explain, it had very special implications in my case.

In short, I found practical advantages in my particular field situation: unencumbered by bureaucratic impediments, comfortably set up in my family's home, fluent in the vernacular, and personally known in some of the households I was to study, I could begin my research under very auspicious circumstances—or so it seemed until I realized the implications of being an indigenous anthropologist. I discovered that almost every one of the advantages had its negative side.

In a very real sense, my fieldwork experience was a process of resocialization into my own society. Although I was raised in a Saudi Arabian family, my long years of residence abroad had established considerable distance between me and my society. The advantages were that much of the culture was not so familiar that it could easily escape my notice. This problem in the collection of data has been observed by other ethnographers working under similar conditions (cf. Spradley and McCurdy 1972; Ablon 1977; Stephenson and Greer 1981), but it is one that can be overcome by rigorous training. The researcher can counteract familiarity by close observation, meticulous recording of ethnographic scenes, and detailed probing to uncover the "taken-for-granted" world he or she may share with members of the community being studied.

Living at home meant that I had to assume the role expected of a family member in my position within the household group. The ordinary field situation reversed itself in my case. I became what may best be described as an observant participant. My primary duty was to participate. To observe became an incidental privilege.

My status did not afford me immunity from observing all the taboos and attending to all the obligations my culture prescribed for me—an immunity usually granted to foreign anthropologists. I had to accept severe restrictions on my movements and on my interaction with other people. For example, I had no freedom to move in public on my own, and challenging any norms of conduct would have jeopardized my relationships with the families I had decided to study. Had I not conformed, I would have risked ostracism and termination of my research. Persistently, if slowly, I achieved a precarious balance of roles that allowed me mobility and freedom to do my research as well as to be accepted and taken seriously. I became a conscious witness to my own resocialization as an Arab woman in my society and thus learned and comprehended many aspects of this role in the best possible manner.

This, perhaps, is one of the hidden advantages of being an insider. For example, veiling norms can be observed and described by an outsider, and one can also learn about the meaning of veiling by soliciting relevant information from informants. Yet the participant charged with the task of abiding by the norms experiences the constraints, to be sure, but also the rewards of these norms on a more basic level. In that sense, my resocialization generated data on an experiential level different from that to which an outsider could bear witness. This point has also been observed as a merit of indigenous research elsewhere. Aguilar, for example, summarizing the pros and cons of this kind of research, mentions that its advocates insist "that the covert culture of the insider has the heuristic value of lending psychological reality (or cultural reality) to ethnographic analyses" (1981:16).

My status affected my research in another way. Restricted possibilities for movement outside the house and pervasive segregation of men and women in public confined the research predominantly to the world of women. These realities affected the choice of topic for investigation. I could not study market or political relations, for example. Neither could I investigate any other subject in which men, rather than women, are the dominant actors. Family organization seemed the most accessible for a female researcher, and elites became my focus. Within that, my emphasis was on how ideology and practice affect and are influenced by one another. But, as noted elsewhere, elites are the least accessible to inquiry, especially through the technique of prolonged participant observation. The families I elected to study formed closed groups, and although the observation of and participation in their daily lives was possible for me as a member of the group, even I could gain their confidence only through patient approaches along the lines of friendship.

Although generous hospitality is highly valued behavior, there remain degrees of formality that the families must always maintain vis-à-vis the whole community. Only with considerable caution can a nonmember see their lives as they live them, as opposed to how they want the rest of the community to perceive them. For example, it takes a long time, coupled with intensive interaction, before people allow a friend to move within their home free of the façade of formality exhibited to outsiders. Indeed, it took between six and eight months before I could develop the friendships that made close observation of their daily lives possible to the degree that my presence was more or less ignored.

Being an insider has even more serious consequences for research. Information may be withheld when it relates to behavior that must be concealed from public knowledge. If one is outside the system, one's awareness of goings-on may not be problematical. But as a participant, the researcher constitutes a threat of exposure and judgment. Lewis explains this situation very well:

> There is a growing fear that the information collected by an outsider, someone not constrained by group values and interests, will expose the group to outside manipulation and control. . . . The insider, on the other hand, is accountable; s/he must remain in the community and take responsibility for her/his actions. Thus, s/he is forced through self-interest to exercise discretion (1973:588).

This was one of the hardest areas to overcome in doing research among one's own people. For example, family solidarity and cohesion are greatly valued. Verbally, men and women endorse the ideal of love and support between siblings; respect and obedience in filial relations; and honoring family duties of financial support to the needy and maintenance of elderly parents. In practice, the older generations approximated many of these ideals (Altorki 1986).

But family conflict does occur, and younger generation members have begun to modify family obligations in general. Differences over inheritance constitute the most serious threat to family solidarity—a threat that mounts as the stakes become higher and people's wealth increases. The ideal remains that such differences must be kept out of the public eye and should be reconciled between family members without recourse to the courts. So important is this family ideal that information about conflict, especially that considered to be serious, was at first not revealed to me. I learned about such conflicts indirectly from domestic servants working in these homes who, by coincidence, happened to be related to women working in my family's household. On other occasions, I obtained relevant information from women with whom I had established such strong ties of friendship that we had come to be considered "sisters." This family idiom symbolized our enclosure in the same kinship group and, by implication, showed our interest in protecting that group and shielding it from public criticism.

On one point, my learning about family conflicts was fortuitous. Is it conceivable that I would have returned from the field with the belief that the ideal of family solidarity was the reality? By being an insider, and from my own kinship network, I "experienced" the fact that reality was different and that disagreement can escalate to conflicts between family members. The problem, however, was in collecting data about conflict from the other families to uncover patterns in its expression and management. What, for example, were the patterns for the expression of intra-family conflict? How was it managed, and what are the patterns for its resolution?

In this respect, my status as an insider prevented people from divulging such information for fear of having it exposed to the wider community. Obviously, disseminating information about intra-familial conflict to the community also implies that the disseminator, i.e., the indigenous anthropologist, has judged it negatively and is now taking an active role in censoring the behavior it bespeaks. While the question of exposure to the public can be bridged by trust and confidence in the researcher, the threat of judgment is harder to overcome. Being a participating family member implies, of course, subscribing to the cultural norms and values of the group and to the sanctions that follow a breach of valued behavior.

These considerations are different for a foreign anthropologist. As an outsider investigating family organization and inter-familial conflict, she or he must gain the confidence of the people and be trusted not to expose family differences to the community. But outsider status does not imply shared cultural knowledge, and thus protects the outsider from applying the same moral judgments. The non-indigenous researcher is outside the system, and for this very reason people may not conceal family differences to the same degree as they would from a member of their own group. In collecting relevant data, the indigenous researcher is twice bound and must be able to overcome barriers to confidence and to potential value judgment.

Other social scientists have made similar observations. Aguilar, for example, highlights the constraints indigenous status may place on access to data (1981:21), although, as he points out, other anthropologists claim the opposite (1981:18). However, the Saudi Arabian case indicates that while confidence can be established, a morally neutral judgment is harder to demonstrate. An effective strategy is to be drawn into the same closure that allows sharing of such delicate information. In my case, the idiom of kinship and the ties of close friendships provided such a closure.

My general familiarity with these families had another irksome draw-back. My informants presumed that I knew my own culture, and for a long time they either misinterpreted my questions as implying an unbe-coming skepticism or failed to appreciate that I truly did not know what I had asked them to explain. This was especially true for knowledge of religious beliefs and rituals, which for me was a difficult area to explore. Such knowledge is essential to an adult Muslim, and any queries about it reveal a lapse in religious duties. Fed up with my questions, an older woman put it to me this way: "Are you not ashamed that you do not know how to pray at your age? What then did they teach you abroad?"

This revealed to me the cultural givens of the community and the cultural repertoire indispensable to membership in it. The best research strategy to circumvent this role was to openly admit my ignorance and to blame it all on my long absence abroad. Women and men patiently ex-plained matters to me in a desire to resocialize me as a Muslim Arab woman. In fact, it was especially pleasing to the older women, often illiterate, to instruct me despite my higher formal education.

These considerations have been well described by Stephenson and Greer. They note that while familiarity with the culture under study can be a bonus, prior knowledge of the people studied provides no guaranteed advantage. The expectations people may have of the investigator could make it more difficult for her or him to break out of fixed patterns and thus serve to restrict the work at hand (1981:129). The role that the community attributes to the researcher may inhibit other relationships and bias the researcher's thoughts. Moreover, the role ascribed by kinship to the indigenous anthropologist may forcefully draw that person into factionalism within the community and thereby limit the work that can be accomplished. Sometimes, such problems can be circumvented by conscious strategy. As Stephenson and Greer observe, "the researcher can mitigate the effects of already established roles by emphasizing some over others" (1981:127). Arguing beyond this, the Saudi Arabian material, as I will show, suggests that flexibility can be achieved by capitalizing on the ambiguity that periods of social change can bring to the rigid definition of roles (see Papanek 1964).

In any case, being a woman who had been educated abroad through graduate level definitely had some negative effects on my research. It made the women, particularly those of the older generation, cautious in discussing their beliefs and practices with me. Repeatedly, they evaded my questions and remained quiet, and they even gave me views different from those they actually held. This was especially true in areas where change and reformulation of the traditional culture had taken place.

For example, a major area of change was in the religious domain. The present Saudi dynasty based its conquest and unification of the northern part of the Peninsula on religious reform rooted in the Wahhabi interpretation of Islam. Upon conquering the Hijaz and forming the Kingdom of Saudi Arabia (1932), the regime took it upon itself to disseminate Wahhabi Islam and to forbid any practices that diverged from it. Members of the older generation among the families I studied came to learn that many of their religious practices, such as visits to the shrines and tombs of saints, were deemed sinful and blasphemous. Different interpretations of religious rituals were now taught in school books and broadcast in the mass media.

As might be expected, assimilation of the new interpretations has neither been uniform nor complete. Thus, when I interviewed older women about the stoning of the *shaytan* (devil)—a basic ritual in the pilgrimage—many of them were evasive. When they did explain the ritual to me, they said that the act is, in fact, symbolic: "The *shaytan* does not actually reside in that pillar, and the stoning is symbolic of man's triumph over evil." This was the official interpretation of the ritual as disseminated on radio, television, and in school books. The same woman who gave me the above interpretation on a different occasion counseled a contemporary of hers who was on her way to the pilgrimage to "collect the small sharp pebbles for the stoning because they hurt the most."

Behind the behavior of these women was the disturbing apprehension that, by virtue of my education, I would judge them as ignorant and belonging to another era. Such fears have their roots in the changes that the society is undergoing, where members of the older generation find some of their beliefs and practices, especially religious ideas, criticized or redefined.

Being a member of the research community in the strictest sense of the term led to a fairly egalitarian relationship with the families I studied. Thus, the data I collected in the field came from an egalitarian model of researcher-informant. Age, gender, and kinship were the only critical variables that structured my relations in the field. In all other respects, norms of strict reciprocity guided and informed our interaction. This extended from exchange of visits to the exchange of gifts that underlie the women's network in Jiddah society. I entered these exchanges as an equal partner. As a member of the community, my role in them was structured by the circle of kinswomen and affines of which I am a part.

Anthropologists often describe the asymmetry in their relationship to the people they study. Such asymmetry is bound to affect the data we collect in the field and the "facts" that we present in our ethnographies (cf. Rabinow 1977; Crapanzano 1980; Dwyer 1982). Recently, we have become conscious of the dynamics of the field situation and of the invisible clues that structure our interactions with others. Eickelman, for one, has indicated the relevance of people's perceptions of the ethnographer to what they tell him, and the distorting effect this may have on the theories we develop on how the social system works (1981:90). A critical component of this perception is the power symmetry or asymmetry between the two parties in the field situation.

In studying families like my own, I minimized the power disparities between us, thereby reducing the effect of this variable on the data. Moreover, I was not really troubled by considerations of equity in my researcher role. Anthropologists tend to agonize over reciprocity with the people they study. In a sense, anthropological research is an invasion of other people's lives, an objectification of others for the "transcendental" purpose of understanding how societies work and what informs and guides behavior. In the process of doing this, the anthropologist must face considerations of equity and of doing something to improve the conditions of those under study, or at least to help redress the imbalance inherent in the relationship between researcher and informant. Opinions here have varied from those who consider the imbalance to be permanent, immune to efforts to eliminate it altogether—except perhaps for those working in their own society (Rabinow 1977:78)—to those who believe that some parity may indeed be possible (Wax 1952; Golde 1970b; Ablon 1977).

The specificity of my research made such considerations irrelevant. In the first place, I was completely involved in a network of reciprocal exchange of services, visits, and gifts. The elite status and powerful position of these families precluded considerations of using them to advance the career aims of this anthropologist. However, the invasion of "their" lives, the description of the disparities between the ideal and the real in their social worlds, and the exposure of their innermost experiences could potentially generate a sense of guilt and a feeling of betrayal, were it not for the saving effect of distance inherent in my role as researcher.

There is no doubt that the ethnographer working with people other than her or his own may have similar dilemmas in divulging information told in the confidence of friendship and intimacy. But the dilemma takes on greater dimensions when the research community is composed of one's own childhood friends, family groups, and associates. Anthropolo-

gists who have worked among their own people have made similar observations. Nakhleh who worked in his native village of Rameh, Palestine,
observes that for the outsider the people studied are at best friends with
whom he may identify and become very close. But for the indigenous
researcher, they are his kinsmen, co-villagers, and compatriots. As such,
he shares their aspirations and their problems (1979:345). However, it is
important to recognize that identification with the people studied is not
a necessary precondition for scientific research and inquiry. Nor is it
uniform for all those who work in their own society (see Messerschmidt
1981:8). Similarly, non-indigenous social scientists may, and do in fact,
identify with the people they study and become ideologically committed
to their problems and aspirations.

Describing and analyzing the culture of one's own community is also
affected by the realities of one's group membership. Colson observed that
such considerations may inhibit an ethnographer working in his or her
society from the possibility of expressing opposite views, more so than
those ethnographers who have the immunity of being outsiders
(1982:255). While all ethnographers have to deal with questions of confidentiality and exposure of data, for those who return to live with the
people they study—and even more so for those who are participating
members—these considerations have more drastic consequences. It is not
whether a book will be read or not, assigned or banned from use. It is a
question of potential and severe ostracism for the ethnographer. Stephenson and Greer suggest that confidentiality of data is especially problematical for the indigenous researcher because it is known from experience
what will happen to informants if such information is traced back to
them (1981:128). More importantly perhaps is the researcher's concern
for the misuse of published information by governments and power elites
against the people studied. As Nakhleh observes, this is undoubtedly a
matter of greater concern to the indigenous researcher (1979:399).

## The Position of Women in Arab Society
### Ethnographic Reality and an Insider's View

How, if at all, did the opportunities and constraints encountered during fieldwork affect my understanding of women in Jiddah society? Did
the participants' status reveal a novel perspective in the understanding of
power distribution along gender lines in Saudi Arabia? These are the
questions I want to address in this section. I shall do so by looking at

my data in the context of what is known about women elsewhere in the Arab world.

At the time of my research, that is, before the recent deluge of publications dealing with women's studies, the generally accepted anthropological view of the position of women in Arab society differed little from their image in Western folk knowledge. Both ethnographic and lay opinion attributed an oppressed, servile status to the Arab woman, who was seen as deprived of rights. The institution of polygyny; the preferential, if not exclusive, right to divorce held by men; and the seclusion of women sufficed to convince outside observers of their extremely underprivileged position.

Yet, as anybody familiar with the literature will readily admit, this concept did not derive from observation, but rather from a series of flaws in the study of Arab culture. First, literary interpretations of Quranic verses and Islamic philosophical and theological literature have sometimes taken out of context statements relating to the personal status of women in Islam. More often, these interpretations equated ideological imagery with cultural reality. Second, many generalizations about male-female relationships that might have been true for the public arena in Arab societies were uncritically extended to the private, domestic arena as well. Third, most empirical work that has informed the traditional view was restricted to the more accessible formal sociopolitical organizations, which were quickly cast into a theoretical mold developed through ethnographic research in other regions in the world.

These mistakes were compounded by a lack of research done by women, who, precisely because of the pervasive segregation of the sexes in many Arab societies, alone could study the domestic culture of male-female relationships. Recent studies that have analyzed these relationships in different parts of the Arab world have radically challenged the traditional view of such societies (cf. Cunnison 1966; Aswad 1967; Mohsen 1967; Dwyer 1978; Farrag 1971; Altorki 1973, 1977; Nelson 1973b, 1974; Eickelman 1984).

One of the fallacies inherent in the accepted theory of Arab social organization concerns the alleged passive role of women in marriage arrangements. However, as van Baal rightly asserts, "the object-role of the women in the marriage trade monopolizes the argument to the extent of ignoring the possibility that this role, instead of being a matter of passive submission to the order of the males, could be the outcome of some form of female preference" (1975:71).

As far as Saudi Arabia is concerned, the key to a more accurate understanding of the role of women is an analysis of the way in which they influence decisions that affect the basic organizational structure of their society. Because that structure is defined by family connections, marriage is a critical process through which women exercise power, because they have traditionally controlled decisive information relating to marriage arrangements and thus have managed to manipulate these arrangements. Without the participation of women in marriage negotiations, men could not obtain sufficient information to create major unions, alliances they ideally would like to have. To the extent that marriages are the chief means by which a community reproduces itself, women enjoy a major part of the responsibility of arranging this reproduction. Thus, the idea of the unquestioned supremacy of men and the complete subservience of women in Saudi Arabian society is reduced to myth (Altorki 1977, 1986).

A sociological myth is a paradigm rendered obsolete by a different model that has greater empirical validity. I suggest that when an ethnographer's access to information is severely curtailed, then paradigms must of necessity be constructed on the basis of hearsay, appearance, and unverifiable inferences. In the case of the study of domestic relations in Arab society, such paradigms are the consequence of the limited access of male ethnographers to relevant data. I believe that under these conditions, only female researchers can possibly have easy access to the data needed. More specifically, I would argue that female indigenous researchers will have a particular advantage in this respect, although I am prepared to admit the possibility that a foreign female anthropologist might, under the most favorable fieldwork conditions, also gain such access in the long run. But this would be at the expense of spending much time in the effort.

In order to appreciate the crucial importance of an insider's view for an understanding of the reality of women's power in urban Saudi Arabian society, one must know that in Jiddah, in spite of its appearance as a modern, perhaps "Americanized" city, all social classes are still primarily structured by kinship and secondarily by friendship ties that extend a person's network of social interaction beyond family connections. For women, these networks have traditionally delimited the total realm of their universe of interaction. Today, in spite of an increased mobility outside their homes, women's social and psychological welfare still depends on the satisfactory maintenance and management of their networks, although the nature of these networks has changed.

Marriage creates a special bond within one or between two extended families. If a marriage occurs between members of the same extended family, as, for example, in the case of cousin marriage, this affinal link strengthens the already existing consanguineous bonds. If the marriage is with a person from outside this group, it then establishes a new alliance between two extended families without prior consanguineous ties. Principally, marriage within the extended family reinforces existing lines of reciprocal support and common interests. Marriage to a member of another family extends such lines beyond the network provided by the consanguineous family.

The family constitutes a person's reservoir of economic security, political influence, social support, and psychological succor. In Saudi Arabian society, family and friendship links combine functions, exclusively for women and in large measure for men, that in Western countries are divided between distinct reference groups outside a person's family. These links entail an elaborate system of reciprocal relationships involving rights and duties. Many of these relationships are activated in casual contexts of informal visiting and sporadic exchanges of favors. They are ritually expressed and reinforced on special occasions, such as birth, naming ceremonies, marriage, divorce, sickness, and death. In the case of life crisis events, participation of network members is mandatory. A person's failure to participate at such junctures without an acceptable excuse implies a rejection of her or his role in the network. It may severely disturb a family link and possibly terminate a friendship if a subsequent attempt at reconciliation through a formal apology fails (see Koch et al. 1977).

It is on these occasions and during casual visits that the role of women—as brokers of vital information affecting the continuation of established relations and the creation of new networks—enters the realm of exercising power over the decisions of men. Women, much more so than men, control the creation of new links of affinity within and between families.

The situation is paradoxical: the very segregation of the sexes that prevents women from gaining access to information and authority in the wider society creates the conditions for their far-reaching control over a man's destiny insofar as it is linked to his marriage. This control is reduced, but is still by no means negligible, in cases of intra-family marriage, which often follows from mutual expectations long held by the fathers of the prospective couple. Even in this case, norms of social distance between potential marriage partners limit a man's knowledge about a prospective bride: while planning marriage to a woman from another family, men are completely dependent on the information that women alone can establish and choose to divulge. Despite the subtlety and informality characterizing the politics of women in arranging marriages, their exclusive control of relevant information indeed enables them to determine the decisions that are nominally the prerogative of men.

## Discussion and Conclusion

This above description of my field study and findings indicates that my inquiry may be seen as the most indigenous sort of ethnography possible. Undertaking this kind of research has specific consequences for the researcher's role in the field. One may assume that his or her own role will be primarily structured by gender and kinship and only secondarily by the variables by which the researcher elects to define her- or himself to the community. My education and research interests opened wider vistas into the world of men despite my gender role, and made my interaction with non-kinsmen possible and acceptable. Thus, I interviewed and observed men of all generations in these families. But while I had to be more careful with men my age, I had relatively unencumbered access to men of the older generation. With respect to the latter, the age differential between us put them in a status similar to that of my parents, and I often addressed them as "uncle," a device indicating that the possibility of marriage between us was prohibited. Men from elite families who were closer to me in age were, of course, potential marriage partners. As a result, I had to observe more social distance from them and strictly follow modesty norms in conversation, gesture, and attire. A breach of these norms would have compromised my reputation as an unmarried woman and thus would have reflected negatively on the standing of my own family in the community.

The severity of sanctions for violation of such norms is a consequence of both the importance of marriage bonds in structuring social and economic ties between families and the role parents play in the creation and maintenance of these official bonds. Modesty norms, in their extreme form of veiling, ensure the separation of women from men. They reduce individual initiative in marriage unions that may arise from freer access of the sexes to one another.

Thus, while I could interview and observe men, my research drew its data more heavily from women than from men. This, I believe, is an inevitable outcome of working in a society where sex segregation is mandatory. My being a member of the community with the task of abiding by the norms placed more constraints on me than it would have on a foreign female ethnographer, who would have better opportunities to work with men. But both of us would have a substantial advantage over a male ethnographer insofar as access to gender-related knowledge is concerned. Working under the same conditions, male researchers would have no access to the world of women. Their research would be entirely limited to the society of men. It is therefore accurate to conclude that in sex-segregated societies, the role of a female researcher is less limited than that of her male counterpart when the subject under study includes women as the major participants. For contexts involving social relations of both men and women, the way will be less open to the male than to the female investigator, who will be able more comprehensively to study these relations than a male will. This of course does not imply that the one perspective is a more complete view of society than the other. Both are partial views in a multidimensional perspective of social reality.

My field experience also suggests that education and periodic absence from the society could, in fact, be avenues toward role flexibility and allow more mobility, with less conformity to norms governing female behavior in a sex-segregated society. These avenues of role flexibility were possible due to the changes taking place in Saudi Arabian society, together with the conditions of flux and transition attendant upon those changes. While customary patterns of behavior are changing, new patterns have not yet been fully established. The transitional period is best characterized by ambiguity rather than by fixed patterns (Altorki 1986). This ambiguity makes for role flexibility, a phenomenon that in the Saudi Arabian case has allowed some freedom from ascribed roles (cf. Papanek 1964).

However, it is not always possible to escape ascriptive roles, even for someone like myself who had been long absent and educated outside her own society. Factors of change did not, at the time of my fieldwork, affect a redefinition of gender roles in Saudi Arabian society. Thus, elements of continuity in the traditional culture made a compromise necessary. Consequently, as I have detailed above, conformity to traditional expectations of my gender role was sometimes a more effective strategy in my fieldwork. While it is true that, as a participant member, one's conformity is often inescapable, the upshot of this conformity, when volunteered, was better rapport and stronger ties with the subjects of my research. In the process of my own resocialization, my role as researcher oscillated between taking advantage of the few ambiguities that change had brought to gender roles, on the one hand, and, on the other, conforming to those components that persisted in the face of change.

There were other advantages to being indigenous. I was able to study the elites as an equal and to participate in egalitarian relations of reciprocal exchanges with the families I studied. Precious few studies exist of elites in anthropology and fewer still that are predicated on the researcher's egalitarian relations with informants. More often Westerners have conducted studies of Third World elites, especially in preindustrial societies. This theme has been cogently argued by Lewis, who maintains that the relationship between the anthropologist and his informants is af-

fected by membership in the dominant European group, whereas the insider has the advantage of familiarity with the workings of the informants
without the baggage of European provenance (1973:582, 588).

Despite difficulties in the study of elites, it must be pointed out that
at no point have I found that the methods developed in social anthropology were inadequate for an ethnological study of the position of women
in my own society. But as I have tried to demonstrate, the Western theoretical frameworks used to interpret the relationship between men and
women in Arab society misrepresent social reality. Such conceptual problems could perhaps be most readily recognized and solved by an indigenous anthropologist. To understand the role of the "invisible" women in
the domestic politics of Saudi Arabian society required that the data be
gathered by one who had a place in their midst.

While this chapter documents advantages and insights an indigenous
researcher may bring to the study of her society, I also acknowledge the
relevance of the perspective of the outsider. The Saudi Arabian case may
present extreme difficulties for non-indigenous anthropologists, even if
they are women. But if problems of access to information are overcome,
social scientists irrespective of origin can contribute valid insights that
can correct misconceptions derived from inadequate knowledge. In this
way both the insider and the outsider may contribute to the development
of anthropology as a truly universal science of culture.

# 4

# Fieldwork in My Egyptian Homeland

## Toward the Demise of Anthropology's Distinctive-Other Hegemonic Tradition

SOHEIR MORSY

Affected by anti-imperialist struggles and changing global relations, the evolution of critical anthropological thought has challenged traditional disciplinary claims of objectivity and ethical neutrality. As Third World and radical critiques of anthropology exposed the discipline as a Western-dominated "child of imperialism", anthropologists began considering not only the history of the "people without history", but the history of anthropology itself (cf. Asad 1973; Copans 1975; Huizer & Mannheim 1979; Leacock 1982; Wolf 1982). Calls for "reinventing anthropology" (Hymes 1974) followed critical assessments of the assumption of "objectivity in anthropology" (Maquet 1964). Within a sociology of knowledge framework, feminist anthropological discourse exposed the androcentric bias of the discipline, along with its paradigmatic implications, and charted a course "toward an anthropology of women" (Reiter 1975). Similarly, many Third World anthropologists rallied around the slogan of "decolonizing anthropology" (Stavenhagen 1971) and some went so far as to suggest the concept of "indigenous anthropology"(Fahim 1982a).

Beyond the ideological functions of anthropology as a discipline, recent anthropological debates have also raised questions about how the social identities of differentiated groups of anthropologists (e.g., female, Third World, Western) have affected research formulation, data collection and analysis. Contrary to conventional anthropological wisdom, it has been argued that an adequate definition of an anthropological study

69

should not only dictate its object, but also the social identity of its subject, the anthropologist. Theoretical progress rests not on the denial of anthropologists' multidimensional identities and ideologies, but on comparison of our different socially mediated constructions of reality. Recent theoretical developments related to the study of women's roles in society provide lucid corroboration of this contention.

For the Arab world, critiques of orientalism have exposed the political character of social inquiry (cf. Abdel Malik 1963; Said 1978). Moreover, the research and publications of some Arab women, including anthropologists, now pose serious challenges to this long-standing orientation of Western intellectual history with its characteristic tendency to dehumanize Arab women (cf. Abu Zahra 1970, 1982; Joseph 1975; Mernissi 1975; Altorki 1986).

This chapter contributes to anthropological discourse on the sociology of knowledge through the presentation of an Arab female's recollection of her first fieldwork experience among peasants of her Egyptian homeland. While I reject the idea of a monolithic "indigenous" anthropological orientation on epistemological grounds, I recognize the significance of documenting the field experiences of Arab women researchers. These are important contributions toward expediting anthropology's reluctant recognition of its knowledge as socially constituted truth rather than "scientifically established facts" (see Morsy 1983). To this day, the traditions of anthropology's colonial past continue to haunt us and are clearly reflected in some contemporary practices. An academic community controlled by Western intellectual elites continues to practice a form of scientific colonialism that maintains the "distinctive other" tradition. Accordingly, outsiders are judged to be better qualified to undertake the study of dominated societies, and males are assumed to be more objective in their analysis of female social behavior. Thus, selective recognition of the observer's social identity and its relation to theoretical formulation is practiced under the guise of scientific methodology. By contrast, this account of the fieldwork experience of an indigenous female anthropologist departs from anthropology's traditional focus on alien "others." It derives from a politically motivated interest in *our* Arab society, including its relations to others.

## Graduate Study: Why Anthropology

Travel to the U.S. from my home city Alexandria, Egypt, three weeks after celebrating my fifteenth birthday has in retrospect proved to be a most significant event in my life. Living in the "melting pot" crystallized two very important dimensions of my social identity. My interactions with African and Black American students who admired Nasser (as an architect of African unity and a defiant anticolonialist) activated my awareness of my African identity, which had been effectively suppressed by my British schooling (in Egypt). But although my African heritage took on special significance (particularly in relation to the civil rights movement in the southern part of the United States where I studied), it was my Arab identity that proved to be of greater import, gaining unprecedented significance with the outbreak of the 1967 June War between Israel and the Arabs. Watching television coverage of the sufferings of Arab civilians and the humiliating defeat of the Arab armies was a most agonizing experience.

As my feelings of sadness, helplessness, and humiliation subsided, I went through a period of unrelenting soul-searching that led me to very serious questioning of why and how such a historical catastrophe had befallen my people. Answers to questions that I asked myself and shared with others proved far from satisfactory. Hence my resolve to turn to "science."

My readings in search of explanations of my homeland's underdevelopment and answers as to how it can be transformed, prompted me to focus on the lives of the poor, exploited, and powerless. Among the powerless, the status of women took on special significance as I contemplated an Arab feminist's description of *us* as "sitting ducks" and easy targets for oppressors from within as well as from without. In short, my attention turned toward ordinary people, away from the heroes of our distant Arab past and from contemporary politicians who had led the Arab nation to the brink of cultural annihilation.

Concern with "ordinary" people and the subordination of women led me to anthropology, a field that I later came to recognize as generally the study of the powerless par excellence. I read Margaret Mead's fascinating accounts of cross-cultural variation in sex roles and examined classical works of anthropologists or prototypes thereof who had worked among the very people whose ways of life concerned me. Three years after the outbreak of the 1967 war, I applied for admission to an anthropology program of graduate study.

## Anthropological Training:
### Reconciling Personal Motivation and Academic Socialization

Contrary to my inflated expectations of anthropological academic training, I realized that academic anthropology was a very restrictive framework for the design of emancipatory social life. Very early in the course of graduate training, I realized that anthropology's traditional/ methodological orientations would not lead me in the direction of my original motivation. In light of this, I could not comprehend my classmates' interest in the discipline's subject matter and fieldwork tradition simply as an intellectual exercise. Furthermore, I was horrified by reports of anthropologists' involvement in intelligence gathering activities (see Boas 1973).

In addition to "discovering" parts of anthropology's colonial past, and its neocolonial present (see Frank 1975), I was confronted with the discipline's dichotomies of objective/subjective evaluations. I learned that the anthropologist "must behave *as if* he has no judgment, *as if* his experiences were inconsequential, *as if* the contradiction between his origins and his vocation did not exist . . . Moreover, he will imagine that he has no politics, and he will consider that a virtue" (Diamond 1974:94).

My readings of the Middle Eastern anthropological literature provided me with insights into the workings of local forms of social organization, but shed very little light on their national, regional, and global dimensions or on the complexities of social transformation (see Asad and Owen 1983). Assuming that indigenous researchers are more likely to present comprehensive accounts of the region, I examined the works of some Arab anthropologists. I soon realized that the Arab world's dependency extends to the intellectual realm.

As my training in anthropology progressed, I confronted the contradiction between my motivations for studying it and the discipline's paradigmatic implications. My interactions with some Third World and female graduate students, as well as my readings of radical anthropologists' critical evaluations of the field, helped me reconcile my political motivations with the requirements of academic socialization. Through such interactions and readings, I learned of the contradictions within the discipline itself (see Asad 1973).

I rationalized my continuing commitment to anthropology by defining anthropological knowledge as a means, not a goal. Rejecting the "distinctive other" tradition, I reasoned that unlike Western researchers, my study of "my people" would be to *our* benefit. Furthermore, I convinced myself that anthropological knowledge, as a form of power, has the potential for use not only as a means of exploitation, but also as an instrument of liberation, the critical factor being the political framework within which it is applied. But over the years, as my political conscious- ness developed, I realized the difficulty of attaining the condition that would unleash the potentially liberating force of "anthropological" knowledge.

I now recognize that while academic training does not offer us strate- gies for liberating "our people," it empowers us to articulate and defend their interests, *if* we so choose. This note of conditionality is intended to suggest the variety of political persuasions among anthropologists, be they non-indigenous or indigenous. But no matter who we are, it is worth considering that, in using anthropological knowledge as support for un- popular political positions in defense of "our (powerless) people," we should be prepared to confront charges of unprofessionalism and various labels of personality aberration, not to mention accusations of extremism.

### Gender, Power, and Illness: Formulation of a Research Focus

Just as my social identity and prior experiences influenced my choice of anthropological training, the formulation of my dissertation's research focus was similarly affected. Beyond the original motivation for pursuing anthropological graduate training, and certain requirements of academic socialization, the choice of the gender and health systems as focuses of research relate to both my personal and academic backgrounds. My iden- tity as an Arab female and my undergraduate training in bacteriology undoubtedly prompted my interest in the cross-cultural study of gender and my choice of medical anthropology as a primary area of graduate training.

As a child, I did not experience the type of severe discrimination imposed on females reported by other Egyptian women and recently brought to the attention of Westerners through the writings of Nawal El- Saadawi (1979, 1983). Indeed, my sensitivity to gender differentiation did not develop until my arrival in the United States as a teenager. Questions and assertions about the oppression of women in the "Muslim East" sen- sitized me to female subjugation. Stereotypical characterizations of Arab women put me on the defensive and forced me to research the subject in order to present coherent arguments in defense of my cohorts. Consider- ation of various dimensions of Arab women's social roles led me to serious thinking that eventually transformed me from an apologist confronting

Western devaluation of Arab women to an anthropologist focusing on a variety of theoretical issues concerning us. My preliminary concern with women's issues developed into an interest in cross-cultural variation of gender systems during the earlier part of my graduate education.

During the first year of graduate study, my initial acquaintance with a few female graduate students developed into a friendship based on the shared interest in women's studies as well as certain dimensions of the rejectionist political outlook that had developed on U.S. campuses during the 1960s. By the end of the first year in graduate school, we had established our Anthropology Women's Collective. The ideas discussed there reflected the emerging ideology of the women's movement in the United States and its impact on anthropology. As a result of feminists' efforts in the field, women had been reintroduced into the anthropological theoretical arena as rational choice makers, adept at manipulating their social environment in their own best interest in spite of normative constraints to the contrary (see Davis 1983).

This interpretation coincided with my own inclination, based in part on early age socialization among strong-willed, powerful women. I had grown up in Egypt recognizing the control exercised by my paternal grandmother, a powerful matron and the "boss" of a household of seven sons, numerous grandchildren, and several domestic employees. My own mother was no less powerful in our nuclear family, deciding on all details of our life ranging from choice of schools to control and management of family property. During discussion sessions in the Collective, I recalled that while the adult women of my family projected a public image of submission to the "word of the man of the house," they were in fact the real power behind the scene. Such recollections facilitated the adoption of current anthropological feminist orientations that differentiated between the appearance of subservience and the reality of influence and power in the public and private domains respectively (cf. Friedl 1967; Rosaldo and Lamphere 1974). Although I recognized that not all Arab women are necessarily as powerful as my female relatives, I thought that they are nevertheless good manipulators who get their way through devious means, including resorting to illness.

While no doubt affected by my undergraduate training and subsequent selection of medical anthropology as a major area of specialization, my selective focus on the health system in relation to gender differentiation was also prompted by certain theoretical considerations. I reasoned that examination of illness would be particularly relevant to my anticipated study of culturally prescribed role behavior, including that related to gender differentiation. Since definitions of illness are intimately related to deviations from such behavior, I expected that careful study of such illness-related deviations would contribute to understanding role expectations themselves (see Stein 1976). In short, I defined the dialectical relationship between illness and health as a probe of certain dimensions of social life, notably male-female power relations. But theoretical rationalization aside, my concern with illness was probably also prompted by a long-held belief that resort to illness is an effective strategy of manipulation, particularly among women (see Morsy 1978). I considered illness as a "weapon" that women use to overcome constraints related to what I believed to be only overt relative powerlessness.

### Preparing for Fieldwork

Aware of the importance of fieldwork as an anthropological rite of passage, I began preparation for this dramatic ritual well ahead of time. About a year before I started fieldwork, I traveled in the Arab world with the aim of selecting a community where I could examine the relation between gender and the health system. Affected by anthropology's "distinctive-other" tradition, I reasoned that working among non-Egyptian Arabs would be more appropriate. But as I visited some rural areas it became evident that the people who I considered as subjects were no more "otherly" than the Egyptian peasants among whom I eventually decided to work. Moreover, travel in my own country rekindled the original motivation that drew me to anthropology.

Although my initial entry into anthropology had coincided with the discipline's crisis of conscience, and the increasing admission that the distinctive-other tradition is fundamentally a political rather than a methodological issue, I was still confronted with the assertion that going to Egypt for fieldwork is inappropriate for an Egyptian. I defensively explained that I had never lived in an Egyptian village before and that my social background is very different from that of peasants. I now recognize this defensive posture as an illustration of how anthropological academic socialization promotes ideological conformity and internalization of the Cartesian separation between observer and observed.

In addition to maintaining loyalty to anthropological traditions by deciding to work in a rural community, I began searching for a small-scale setting that would lend itself to a holistic study. In spite of my problem orientation and preparedness to utilize the techniques of statistical sampling, as well as other forms of rigorous methodology, I set out to locate a village that could be studied in its totality. Given the high population

density of Egyptian Nile Delta villages, the village of Fatiha (a pseudo-
nym), which I eventually selected, seemed to be a reasonable size, since
its population had not reached more than 3,200. But village size was not
the only attraction. In addition to general economic, political, and social
characteristics that typify Egyptian villages, my chosen site had resident
traditional healers and access to public biomedical health care facilities as
well as physicians.

## Doing Fieldwork:
### The Anthropologist as a Female, Upper-Class Compatriot

I embarked on my trip to the field with much anticipation and great
confidence. I knew that as a woman in my society I would have privileged access to female spheres of activity. Conscious of my linguistic
skills, ease in getting along with people, and ability to detect the subtleties of my female compatriots' behavior, I expected my study to contribute to the enrichment of the impoverished literature on gender in the
Arab world. But aware of my indigenous status, and anthropology's prejudicial attitude towards the emic assessment of insiders, I was determined
to carry out my research in accordance with the highest standards of
rigorous methodology. Beyond preparation of a dissertation that would
certify me as a bona fide anthropologist, I wanted to produce a high
quality medical anthropological study. I reasoned that such a study, undertaken by an insider and a feminist, would undermine the discipline's
distinctive-other methodological standard as well as orientalist descriptions of Arab women's powerlessness and passivity. Ironically, striving
toward this goal prompted an increasing commitment to current Western
anthropological standards of fieldwork methodology and scholarship.
Once in Egypt, my family's connections, which had proved useful in
the selection of a research site, continued to facilitate my work. A psy-
chologist friend kindly offered her expertise. Intermediaries led me to a
local physician who became a valued collaborator during the course of
fieldwork, and necessary security clearances were expedited through my
father's friends in high places. Although delighted by the tremendous
help prompted by my insider status, on occasion I found it necessary to
firmly reject certain offers of assistance that conflicted with my research
priorities and objectives. An extreme example of such "undesirable" help
was a police officer's suggestion that I reside in the provincial town and

visit the village "whenever I wanted," escorted by one of his men. I politely declined and explained the residence requirements of my research (see Davis 1983:11). To those who eagerly offered their assistance to make me comfortable, this explanation no doubt must have seemed strange.

Although my husband and children did not live with me in the village, their photographs, letters, and later occasional visits always proved helpful in allowing me to project the locally valued image of a mother and the wife of a university professor. My husband's presence in the village on the first day of my residence there proved invaluable in defining certain significant dimensions of my social status to the people of Fatiha. Luckily, we had arrived in the village on the day of the annual celebration of the *mulid* (saint's day). Together we were introduced to a very large number of villagers. We were assured of my safety among the people of the village. Men and women generously committed their care, help, and support. The widow whom I had carefully chosen as a landlady assured us I would be "in her eyes," that is, well protected.

In time, villagers' curiosity about how my husband could "do without me" for the extended period of my residence in the village developed into an attitude of sympathy for me. It was understood that work demands forced me to be away from my family for so long. Although I no doubt represented an extreme case, the villagers understood my situation in light of their acquaintance with other urban women who are required to be away from their husbands because of the demands of their "bread earning." They pointed to similarities between my case and that of the female physicians and the female dentist in the nearby provincial town.

While my knowledge of Arabic, perceived kindness, humbleness, and simplicity facilitated my acceptance by many villagers, my rapport-building skills proved less effective among some others during the early days of my fieldwork. To a few men and women, my prolonged stay in the U.S. was grounds for suspicion of the real purpose of my interest in their village and the details of their lives (see Fahim 1977). I had arrived in Fatiha less than a year after the 1973 October War between Egypt and Israel, when many Egyptians had still not been made to forget (through the mass media), the role of the U.S. in supporting the Zionist state. Unfortunately, I became the target of the anger of some of the villagers. For example, during a household census-related interview with an old woman, her fury was unleashed on me when I asked her about the composition of her family. I was unaware of the fact that one of her sons had been reported missing, possibly dead or imprisoned by the Zionists. She screamed at me and told me to leave her alone, ending our conversation thus: "Go ask your Americans, where did my son go?"

However, aside from a few suspicions of my "real" intentions and the "true" function of my typewriter and tape recorder, my role was generally interpreted as that of a documenter of a way of life subject to rapid change. In reaction to my stated concern with Egyptian peasants, many villagers were clearly pleased that I considered their way of life, including their traditional medical beliefs and practices, important enough to be worthy of serious study. Older women in particular took pride in their knowledge of health-related practices and were demonstratively pleased with me for recognizing the worth of traditional wisdom.

As my research got under way, the female dimension of my identity encouraged women's willingness to express their thoughts and beliefs relatively freely. Not only did women develop warm relations with me and seek my advice regarding child care and health in particular, they also readily engaged in conversations dealing with general national and even international issues, including the recent 1973 war. The range of topics we covered during our numerous discussions belied universalistic theoretical generalizations that depict women as particularistic and private-sphere oriented (see Ortner 1974). In fact, some of the older women knew more about the history of the village and its relation to national politics than most of the younger village males. Some of the more detailed comparisons of rural social relations before and after the 1952 revolution came from these elder village women.

But, as expected, not all women exhibited the same degree of confidence in their beliefs or the willingness to share them with an outsider such as me. During my early interviews, some women clearly felt uncomfortable. Their sense of inadequacy was amplified by their male kin who would sometimes laugh when I questioned the women of their households, noting that the women "do not know." But as I insisted on the usefulness of female opinions, men started to take a less active role when I interviewed the women in their presence. In fact, they eventually tended to welcome me on arrival at their homes and then leave me with the women for long visits.

Given my critical posture toward male anthropologists who, for the better part of the history of the discipline, have provided us with male-biased information, I was well aware of the necessity of correcting for my expected propensity to women. But beyond managing to collect data, which on processing would yield a more balanced account of male-female relations, my fieldwork experience in some ways curtailed my very critical evaluation of male ethnographers' accounts. While my identity as a female facilitated access to women and encouraged them to freely express their beliefs (in spite of attempts on the part of some men to control the process of elicitation), my publicized support of women's rights *did not* prompt women to deny their belief in the "natural" condition of male dominance. The story completion tests that I administered to village children showed that the ideology of male dominance is upheld by female villagers from a very early age onward. Consequently, I began to consider the possibility that reports of male dominance by male ethnographers are not necessarily misrepresentations of social reality prompted by the researchers' gender identity. I reasoned that the shortcoming of their traditional reporting procedures is not that they misrepresent dominant ideologies, but that they assume their unfaltering effectiveness in guiding women's and men's *actual* behavior.

My relatively free access to women did not necessarily ensure distortion-free female-related information. In cases where I was introduced to women through the men of their families, initial conversations with the women were definitely constrained by the presence of their male kin. But although subsequent conversations with women alone yielded less guarded responses, it became evident that the difference was not simply a function of the presence of a male. As illustration, I recall the case of a woman who in the presence of her daughter, a college student, assured me that in their family women, including herself, do not work in the fields. During subsequent encounters with her, and after I had become a friend, she admitted that she contributed to her family's work in the fields. As I talked about the hardships faced by the peasants, and the work burdening women, she readily admitted her sufferings. Evidently, similar to men, women like to project the ideal image of female seclusion. Women's isolation in the sphere of reproduction remains a mark of status in Fatiha as in other parts of rural Egypt (Tucker 1983:330). In short, regardless of whether the source of information is male or female, there is no substitute for sensitivity to contradictions in respondents' statements and regular cross-checking of information.

Beyond the general advantage of access to female domains of activity afforded by my gender, specific aspects of this identity gained particular significance in certain situations. The threat of vulnerability experienced by other female anthropologists (see Golde 1970) was in my case controlled by my status as a married woman of upper class origin. I was never subjected to sexual advances during the course of my fieldwork in rural Egypt. Moreover, my purposeful adoption of the modest dress style of older village women, and repeated announcement of my underestimated age, spared me from the experience of being perceived as sexually threatening, as some female anthropologists have reported (see Golde 1970). Far from attempting to adopt a 'pseudo male role' (Bujra 1975, as cited in Gregory 1984:322), I flaunted my motherhood, thereby facilitating my access to some very important village ritual activities, notably those related to birth and the postpartum period. As the mother of three children, including a son, I was not likely to be considered envious of another woman giving birth, particularly if the infant should turn out to be male. In addition to the opportunity of attending a number of births, I had free access to mothers and infants during the postpartum period when they are considered particularly vulnerable to the power of the evil eye.

In spite of my awareness of the necessity of extending equal attention to the activities, concerns, and beliefs of both men and women in Fatiha, my interaction with these two groups was undoubtedly unequal and most definitely affected by my gender and class identity. For although I developed excellent confidential relationships with individual women and men, including my female field assistant and her male counterpart (both of whom facilitated my acquaintance with the people of the village), my interaction with women as a group differed *qualitatively* from my relationships with men. The gender barrier was clearest with regard to certain shared group activities from which I was excluded as a participant in view of my upper class identity. Whereas I freely participated with women in joke-filled conversations about sex, I was not involved in similar encounters with men. Sometimes I noticed that the lively conversation of a group of men sitting in front of the grocery store in a village alley would abruptly stop when I drew near (see Jenkins 1984:158). I later learned from some women (who heard it from their husbands) that the men had been exchanging sexual jokes which came to a halt upon my approach. In other cases, restricted access to male-shared group activities was self-imposed. Although I was invited to men's smoking gatherings, I chose not to attend, not only because I was a nonsmoker, but because I did not want villagers to think I was. However, the men who participated in such gatherings, knowing that I was interested in studying every facet of village life, had expected me to attend as an observer.

Nonetheless, while I have no doubt that another anthropologist—not necessarily a male—may have interacted with the men of Fatiha in ways that I have not, I generally did not encounter any serious impediments to wide-ranging observation and participation. In the Nile Delta Village of Fatiha, where sexual segregation is far less pronounced compared with other parts in Egypt (cf. Morsy 1978; Abu-Lughod 1985a; Hopkins 1985), I did not encounter the vast sacrosanct territories that some acquaintances had warned me of prior to my departure for the field.

As an educated woman of higher class origin than the villagers I interacted with, I had no difficulty whatsoever in discussing a variety of issues with male villagers. Many of the men saw me as something of a doctor-in-the-making, who could discuss a variety of topics without shame. I found no problem discussing highly personal matters with men, such as sexual intercourse and pregnancy, as well as a variety of health problems including sexual impotence. In setting the tone for the serious discussion of such matters, I pronounced the appropriate notation "no embarrassment in religion," a well-known statement based on the fact that sexual matters are discussed in the Quran.

Unlike the case of some other anthropologists who are reportedly considered by their hosts to be child-like, I was never cast in such a role. Village men as well as women did not expect someone of my background to share some of their beliefs or follow certain of their practices, but they did not necessarily assume that I was ignorant of such beliefs and practices. However, contrary to their assumptions, I in fact did not know a lot of what I eventually learned from them about different dimensions of their lives. Some villagers used to point out that the kind of questions that I raised indicated that I knew a lot about peasants. After long conversations, during which I would point to similarities between the lives of the villagers of Fatiha and those of the peasants in other parts of the world, some villagers would conclude that although I was aware of generalities about their life-style, I wanted to know exactly how they compare with other peasant communities. Still others would insist that I already knew what they were about to tell me, but that I wanted to hear it from them and to see the differences between men and women. It may be reasonably concluded that none of these evaluations of the nature of my work indicate that the villagers considered my questioning attitude to be child-like.

Thus, not unlike the "flexible position" occupied by the "foreign female field-worker" (Papanek 1964:161), my behavior in Fatiha, including my interactions with men, was subject to minimal restrictions. Neither female nor male villagers perceived me as "just a woman." To them I was above all an educated urbanite of higher social position than themselves. But unlike a complete stranger, I had a clearly recognized status in their system of social hierarchy. As such, they did not consider me subject to local gender role expectations.

The implications of my identity as an upper-class woman were well recognized by the villagers. They had been acquainted with other females of comparable status, including the female absentee landowning descendants of the village's former Turkish rulers, as well as agricultural specialists, teachers, and physicians (in whose presence male villagers undress and respond to questions about intimate details of their lives). Thus, my behavior as an urban professional was not alien to villagers' expectations.

My interest in their way of life and opposition to the political system that legitimized the exploitation of the peasantry formed the basis of a relationship based on trust that is seldom extended to outsiders.

The flexible position that I occupied in the course of my fieldwork in the village of Fatiha (as well as in other Egyptian villages I studied) proved far removed from the prediction that ". . . a woman field-worker from a non-Western background, e.g. another Muslim country, might encounter attitudes among informants and within herself which would make it *impossible* for her to achieve such flexibility" (Papanek 1964:161; emphasis added). The type of data that I, a "woman field-worker from a non-Western background" and from "a Muslim country," was able to collect, substantiates the fallacy of this statement. As an upper-class compatriot of the villagers of Fatiha, my conformity to certain local gender-role expectations was voluntary. Wearing traditional village attire and covering my head was in no way forced upon me by local expectations. In addition to being a matter of convenience, which allowed me to sit on the floor freely and protect my hair from dust and lice, this form of dress was also an expression of my genuine respect of village norms of conduct, a gesture that the villagers appreciated but did not expect.

The villagers' awareness of my national and class identities was of consequence not only with regard to their expectations of me, but also in relation to the information they presented to me. Conscious of my status as an educated urbanite, and assuming that I am not likely to believe claims of supernatural healing, some villagers denied knowledge of traditional medical practices, and some went so far as to condemn them as "nonsense of the peasants" or "nonsense of women." But when I brought up the possibility of psychological relief resulting from such practices, the same persons admitted their own experiences with the *rawhaniya* (spiritual healers) and even cited the Quran to substantiate their belief in the power of sorcerers. My later observations in the village showed that they not only believe in the "nonsense" of traditional medicine, but in fact acted upon these beliefs in the treatment of illnesses that afflicted them.

Fieldwork for me has not been accompanied by feelings of impotence or powerlessness (Golde 1970a:12). I never felt that I was "operating from a position of powerlessness" (Jordan 1981:188). The powerlessness that I stressfully recognized was widespread among Egyptian peasants, and particularly among females. Being a carrier of the dominant culture, I never felt that in the course of fieldwork I was learning "slowly, as does a child, the codes of the local culture" (Jordan 1981:188).

My own relative *powerfulness*, assumed by the villagers, was clearly demonstrated to them on several occasions during my residence in the village. The villagers were particularly impressed by the way I handled bureaucrats, including health care personnel who visited the village. While my demanding attitude towards these government employees (including a public health physician, whom I criticized for carelessness in giving local infants the oral polio vaccine) enhanced my social standing in the village even further, it also raised expectations of me as an urban patron. Through appropriate contacts I helped some villagers obtain urban employment, assisted a young village woman in gaining admission to college dormitory facilities in a distant province, and generally acted as an intermediary in facilitating access to services, particularly those related to health.

Aside from trying to reciprocate my hosts' generosity through offering one service or another, I also gave gifts. At the beginning, I gave only collective gifts. Using the village school, I distributed pencils, erasers, paper, and other school supplies. As I started to become involved in health-related activities, I took gifts of sugar, tea, fruit, and sweets to families of sick persons. In a few cases, I also helped schoolchildren with their homework. But no matter what help I could offer to the people of Fatiha, I always felt that I was the one who came out ahead. I had no illusion of ever reaching a state of balanced reciprocity in the course of the fieldwork transaction. Even the villagers' generous sharing of the intimate details of their lives did not prompt a similar degree of self-disclosure on my part. I established confidential relationships with only a minority of Fatiha's people. Exploitation does indeed seem to be "inherent in the art" (Hatfield 1973:26). For their part, the villagers were well aware that I would be the primary beneficiary of the information I collected in their village. They knew that I would use this information to become a *doctora*.

Confronting the reality of the relationship of unequal exchange in which I was engaged with "my people," I often wished I had gone to medical school instead of training as an anthropologist. As the latter I could not help alleviate the sufferings of the villagers, much less eradicate illness, poverty, and deprivation. I could only theorize about people's medical beliefs and practices, or so it seemed to me during the course of fieldwork when data had priority over politics, the initial driving force that had led me to anthropology. My sense of powerlessness was not in relation to the peasants among whom I lived, but in connection with the problems and injustices that plagued them and the academic methodological standards that haunted me.

As I adapted to village life and grew attached to its people, the once eagerly anticipated visits to my hometown became tension-ridden. I did not experience culture shock and depression in the field, as reported by other anthropologists, but rather when I left rural Egypt to visit my urban relatives. Sharing third-class train rides with peasants gave me the opportunity to observe their humiliating treatment at the hands of fellow Egyptians. Once in Alexandria or Cairo, the long hot showers and luxurious bedding, although enjoyable, also highlighted the gap that separates the people with whom I trace my social origins from those among whom I had chosen to live temporarily.

My visits to urban relatives always served as a reminder of the social markers and practices that differentiated me from the villagers of Fatiha: the type of food they ate, and which I shared during my stay in the village; the circumstances of their children's birth compared with the setting in which my female relatives and I had given birth; the burdening of their children with productive labor and the pampering of ours. Upper-class urbanites' evaluation of peasants being "more comfortable than us," having "limited needs" and "controlling Egypt's bounty," although infuriating, were nevertheless politically and anthropologically enlightening. Indeed, my repeat visits to the city during the first few months of fieldwork always confirmed my belief that the community of Fatiha could not be understood without situating it in a broader social context that includes Egypt's centers of political power. No amount of anthropological participant observation in the community could correct for the theoretical limitations of anthropology's atomistic models (see Jenkins 1984:162).

Contrary to descriptions of the anthropologist as an outsider who eventually becomes an insider, I never identified myself as the latter. Moreover, while many villagers grew to like and to accept my presence among them as a caring compatriot, like myself they recognized the limits of my incorporation in their midst. There were many social indicators that differentiated me from the villagers. In addition to material markers of differentiation, my very mission of research in Fatiha remained throughout my stay an important distinguishing element, as did my clearly recognized social class origin. I never pretended to be one of the villagers and the people of Fatiha never expected me to do so. As someone who wanted to see their lives improved, not only did I not want to be like them, I wanted them to change, to shed the yoke of oppression and exploitation. While they recognized my identification with their problems, they did not see me as one of them, but as one who cared for them.

In short, although I lived with the peasants of the Delta, ate their food, got bitten by the same insects, and waded through the muddy alleys of their village just like the rest of them, and although they accepted me as a caring fellow Egyptian, they nevertheless did not consider me to be one of them. To most of them such a consideration would have been nothing less than an insult, in spite of my assurances to the contrary.

Even the educated young people of Fatiha who, through the vehicle of social mobility could feel closer to me, expressed this in terms of them moving toward my social station rather than the reverse.

Although seldom noted by anthropologists, I have no doubt that my personality and the social skills I had acquired long before I started my anthropological training, facilitated the building of rapport and attendant sharing of information. But beyond researchers' multidimensional social identities and mastery of various skills, anthropological and otherwise, the type of information—to be processed into data—that we compile is also a function of the extent to which we are committed to very hard work in the field. No dimension of our identity as facilitator of data collection is a substitute for constant observation, participation, cross-checking, questioning and more questioning—in a word, perseverance. Thus while my gender helped me gain access to certain types of female-related activities, such access was but one element in the complex process of carrying out my first anthropological research project. My own resolve, the unceasing search for data, the constant awareness of getting a balanced account of social relations, along with anthropological skill, and certainly academic theoretical and methodological standards—all these factors and more have no doubt influenced the outcome of my research in the village of Fatiha.

### Rigorous Methodology: A Fieldwork Obsession

As I focused on the study of power relations in Fatiha, I never lost sight of the academic and professional power structure that affected me and would ultimately determine the validity of my theoretical and methodological claims. Over the course of graduate training, my original primary motivation of knowing and understanding "my people" had gradually been overshadowed by the immediate concern with "doing" anthropology and joining the ranks of the discipline's professionals. While the political motivation for acquisition of anthropological knowledge remained in my consciousness, academic requirements and standards dictated junctural priorities. Once in the field, the power of scholarship prompted the pressing need to collect hard data. Overwhelmed by the task at hand, I became aware more than ever before that any serious attempt to empower the peasants, and the women of Egypt, could not possibly be undertaken within the boundaries—theoretical, methodological, and political—of professional anthropology.

Throughout the period of my fieldwork, I was concerned with the fact that my passport to the world of professional anthropologists would be a dissertation that would be judged according to certain established professional canons. Although the chairperson and other members of the committee were supportive of my study and of my decision to work in my own country, I was aware of the fact that the intellectual product of my fieldwork would subject both my feminist and my insider rendering of social reality to the possibly less sympathetic scrutiny of the professional community at large. In spite of the revival and increasing legitimacy of women's studies around the time of my first fieldwork project, female anthropologists continued to complain of the resistance to the feminist research orientation within the anthropological professional community (see Bujra 1975:552–553).

Beyond anticipating such reactions to my own feminist orientation, I expected my insider identity to intensify them. For although an anthro-pologist's indigenous status may make her less of a "professional stranger" in her own society (Agar 1980), it may also make her less of a professional in the eyes of those who uphold the "distinctive other" standards of the professional community. Thus, in the earlier part of my fieldwork, my concern with understanding the lives of the people of Fatiha was severely compromised in favor of the goal of demonstrating technical expertise.

Although my research project in Fatiha involved a problem orienta-tion with a clearly predetermined focus on gender, power, and illness, this selectivity did not deter the influence of anthropological "holism" by which I had been affected. Abiding by the discipline's traditional wisdom of "write everything—you never know what might be important later," I proceeded to transform even the most trivial details of villagers' social life into data (see Jenkins 1984:155). The compulsive recording of infor-mation, trivial and otherwise, the obsession with counting and giving equal time to males and females, as well as impression management, had all reached extremes before I realized that the enthusiasm for data had developed into an obsession. It was a reflection of my attempt to correct for my emic inclination and to uphold professional etic standards. By representing information numerically, resorting to the assistance of biomedical professionals and using standardized biomedical research instruments, I was trying to transcend not only the anthropologist's "limits of naiveté" (Devons and Gluckman 1964), but also my "indige-nous" qualitative knowledge.

Aside from the high value that I attributed to quantitative and biomedical data, the very decision and concerted effort to collect it indi-cates that I did not simply want to understand villagers' definitions and management of illness. I wanted to translate their illness categories into objective, scientific data. While comparison of illness categories is no doubt a worthwhile effort in the cross-cultural study of health systems, it is the motivation for such an undertaking that is worth noting in view of the sociology of knowledge orientation of this chapter. I—an indigenous anthropologist—utilized the biomedical standards as a yardstick against which my people's definitions of illness were measured.

As I started to amass more and more hard data, I began to transcend the tension-ridden compulsion for rigorous methodology. The orientation that eventually came to guide my pursuit of knowledge among the people of Fatiha during the latter part of fieldwork involved strong identification with the object of study. I realized that my initial exaggerated commitment to rigorous methodology was nothing less than an attempt at objectifying others, setting myself apart from them, and reducing them to "things" being subjected to anthropological scrutiny. Exactly how I came to abandon this implicit conception of scientific methodology is not clear. However, I do believe that the kindness, generosity, and affection that the villagers showed toward me undermined my inclination toward objectivism. My reciprocal emotional attachment to the people of Fatiha stood in the way of this objectivism and, by extension, the extremes of rigorous methodology.

In my attempt to counter the stressful effects of rigorous methodology, I set aside time for leisurely visits that I undertook without mentally stored hidden agendas of questions to be slipped into conversations with unsuspecting hosts and hostesses. After such visits, I did not feel the need to run home and write up the data with any degree of urgency. The resulting social attachment proved to be not only emotionally comforting, but also an important means of understanding, which could then be translated into the desirable anthropological data. Unlike objectivism, which severs subject from object, the orientation that I adopted and that a feminist scholar has labeled "dynamic objectivity" (Keller 1983:20) did not deny the connection between myself as researcher and the villagers of Fatiha as objects of study. The bond of friendship that was forged between us enriched my understanding of individual and collective behavior in the research setting.

## Modifications of Theoretical Assumptions

At the time I started my fieldwork in Fatiha, I had been exposed to two major current theoretical positions. The first was the assumption of the universal subordination of women based on the alleged universal opposition between the public and private domains. The second theoretical orientation portrayed women as rational choosers and manipulators of their social environment, who wield a form of informal power that enables them to transgress structural constraints (see Rosaldo and Lamphere 1974). While I found the first argument rather weak in light of my knowledge of Middle Eastern society (cf. Nelson 1973a; Leacock 1974), I was thoroughly convinced of the second position. I believed that women, although not formally recognized as powerful, are nevertheless influential in the sense that they resort to various strategies of indirect control, including illness. But as my research in Fatiha proceeded, the anthropological differentiation between social structure and social organization extended to male-female power relations. The consideration of illness as a strategy of manipulation exercised by women was contradicted by developments that presented themselves and that I reluctantly came to accept.

During the earlier weeks of fieldwork, the idea of power-wielding women so dominated my thinking that I found many examples to support it. But I had failed to consider, during this early stage of my research, the adverse consequences of women's defiance and the specific conditions under which such adverse consequences could be avoided. While my observation of women's defiance and the study of illness illuminated the transgression of prescribed behavior, such transgressions in and of themselves did not clarify the structural bases that allow women to deviate from role prescriptions.

Although I had initially set out to prove the difference between women's apparent subservience and the reality of their power, my observation of power differentials *among* women and men prompted me to reconsider the utility of this orientation. The differentiation between appearance and reality helped me to understand how women adapt to an oppressive social structure. But it could not address my original concern with the basis of women's oppression. Methodological individualism with its focus on individual choices and actions proved of very limited explanatory usefulness. As an alternative, I began to consider the dialectical relationship between individual choices and societal constraints. It soon became clear that these constraints transcend village boundaries. Various manifestations of state control over the peasantry came into focus.

My research experiences in Fatiha convinced me of the limitation of focusing on the subject community in pursuing an understanding of the subjugation of women and the health system. I could not realistically claim to understand either male-female power relations or the health system without due consideration of the political power that the state exercises over the people of Fatiha. With this realization, I had finally begun to deal with the type of issues that had prompted my interest in anthropology in the first place but which had been overshadowed by the more immediate requirements of graduate training and the pursuit of professional accreditation. By the end of my fieldwork, the idea of separating the system of female oppression and the health system from Egypt's class structure and its integration into the global political economy became unthinkable. By then, my conception of "holism" had transcended the idea of thoroughness in data collection and involved a definition of the field as situated in a broader national as well as global context (see Koptiuch 1985).

## Conclusion

The foregoing exposé highlights subjective dimensions of the process of interaction between the anthropologist and "her people." Although the field experience I have described had different effects on my conception of identity and self, self-disclosure has been exercised only to the extent that it is epistemologically relevant. As a member of the "generation of Arab defeat" (Shukri 1985:129), I resorted to the social sciences in search of understanding my homeland for the purpose of changing it (see Bannoune 1985:358–359). While academic socialization proved ineffective in the pursuit of this end, the original motivation that prompted my anthropological training, along with my Egyptian Arab female and class identities, have no doubt influenced the research that I carried out in my own national setting. Nonetheless, the framework within which I worked was not fundamentally different from that associated with other anthropologists' rites of observation and elicitation.

While I cannot be easily accused of "mining Third World cultures" (quoted in Bannoune 1985:361), I did partake of the typical anthropological style of working among people less powerful than myself. The indigenous dimensions of my social identity noted above did not shield me from some of the general problems confronted by non-indigenous anthropologists (cf. Jones 1973; Bernard et al. 1984). Moreover, my choice of research topic and certain theoretical and methodological emphases of my study were compatible with general trends within the discipline. Even my critical posture toward anthropology's "distinctive-other" tradition and stereotypical characterizations of Arab women are not simply reflections of my "otherness," or an automatic defense of my Arab female cohorts. I share these orientations with some non-Arab researchers (cf. Fluehr-Lobban 1973; Nelson 1973a; Gran 1977). In fact, my rejection of the claim of complete objectivity derives from anthropology's own proclamation of the cultural conditioning of behavior and ideology.

The research focus in Fatiha, which was influenced by my own female Arab identity, was also in line with disciplinary trends. The acceptance of my topic as a legitimate focus of anthropological research is traceable to the revival within anthropology of interest in the study of the position of women in conjunction with the growth of the Euro-American women's movement. The obvious intensification of efforts to investigate the role of women in society is in turn related to the sociopolitical transformations taking place in Western industrial societies, the locus of anthropological professional power. In these societies, feminists have turned to anthropology to derive the empirical evidence that would support their politically motivated analysis. Under the influence of the trend of rectifying the androcentric bias of the discipline, the development of my theoretical perspective on gender differentiation was definitely affected by current theoretical assumptions.

As Arab female researchers, we no doubt have the opportunity to make important theoretical contributions toward the understanding of our own societies. But our direct experience in our homeland is only an opportunity for knowing, not knowledge itself (see Kaplan 1984:33). Research undertaken in our own societies may provide certain variant insights, and may involve advantages as well as disadvantages. Nevertheless, we cannot expect such locally performed investigations to yield distinctive indigenous conclusions. This is understandable in light of shared theoretical and methodological orientations among anthropologists of different national origins, the variation of such orientations within our national community of scholars, the intellectual dependency of the social sciences in the Third World, and the related "satellite" nature of local scientific output (cf. Goonatilake 1984; El-Kinz 1986; Morsy 1986b). Given that it is a particular social epistemology that limits the development of indigenous research priorities in the Arab world, any ambitions of developing such priorities require serious considerations of the necessary social changes.

# 5

# Gender, Class, and Origin

## Aspects of Role During Fieldwork in Arab Society

───────────────────────────── CAMILLIA FAWZI EL-SOLH

In response to the realization that absolute objectivity in the social sciences remains a largely unattainable goal, sociologists have increasingly begun to question the paradigm of the role of researcher as an objective instrument of data collection (see Roberts 1981). It is now recognized that the relationship between researcher and researched is influenced by many factors, some of which may well be beyond the control of both parties concerned. Either way, the type of relationship that researchers establish with those they study will almost inevitably have an impact on their access to relevant data. Far from viewing this fact as a "dangerous bias," there have been increasing calls among social scientists to recognize that the researcher's involvement with respondents "is the condition under which people come to know each other and to admit others into their lives" (Oakley 1981:58).

This chapter discusses aspects of my relationship with respondents during the study of an Egyptian peasant settlement community in Iraq (Fawzi El-Solh 1984). I argue here that far from being rigid, definitions of my role as an Arab female researcher were largely dictated by the situational context I happened to be in. I also argue that although the class barrier in Arab society may to a certain extent reduce the "commonalities of the female experience" (see Scheper-Hughes 1983b:112), this fact can be overridden by expectations based on the commonality of being part of the same cultural area and tradition.

## My "Self" as Part of the Arab World

My attempts to reexamine the many dimensions of my researcher role during fieldwork among Egyptian migrant peasants in Iraq has also led me to turn a renewed eye upon my "self": as an Egyptian who feels a deep commitment toward the Arab world; as a woman from a nontraditional social background coming to terms with some of the restrictive norms applicable to females in the area of my cultural origin; as a sociologist trained in a West German university who discovered how unquestioningly I had assimilated some models about my own culture.

Growing up in Egypt as the daughter of an Egyptian father and an Irish mother was in some ways a bicultural experience. I was fortunate in that my parents somehow imbued in me the flexibility of taking East and West in my stride and not feeling too lost between the two worlds. This experience, including my education in a German school in Cairo, proved to be important assets when, at the age of nineteen, I enrolled in a West German university to study for the equivalent of a Master of Science in economics and sociology. Much of what I encountered was unfamiliar, yet at the same time not too strange.

The freedom to spread my wings brought with it the thrill of discovery and self-discovery. Like many of my generation, I too did not remain unaffected by the burgeoning feminist movement sweeping America and seeping into Europe during the 1960s and early 1970s. Delving into feminist literature led me to turn a critical eye on the social conditions of women in my native Egypt as well as in other parts of the Arab world. But at the same time, I found myself becoming alienated by some aspects of the society in which I was receiving my higher education. Such alienation ended up reinforcing a sense of belonging to my part of the world, something that I had largely taken for granted during my childhood and early youth in Egypt.

But this identification was also indirectly encouraged by my field of study at the University of Cologne. Briefly, the preoccupation with the economic and sociopolitical implications of the European Common Market (EEC), which was the topic of many a lecture I attended, had quite an effect on me. I became intrigued by the possibilities of regional economic ties and more specifically by the benefits of an Arab Common Market (see Musry 1969) as a prerequisite to the lessening of inter-Arab strife. This interest was also affected by the novel (for me at least) experience of meeting students from other parts of the Arab world.

The ideas swirling in my head during my student days in Germany, regarding the implications of strengthening economic ties between the Arab countries, not surprisingly resurfaced during my period of employment in the United Nations Economic Commission for Western Asia in Beirut, Lebanon. Catching a glimpse of the resettlement scheme involving Egyptian peasant families during a trip to Iraq in 1976 excited my imagination and led to a prevailing interest in the impact of migration trends on socioeconomic ties within the Arab world. When I decided to apply for a Ph.D. course at the University of London, there was no doubt in my mind what the subject of my dissertation would be.

However, when I set out to study the Egyptian migrant peasants in Iraq, I was not particularly conscious of being an indigenous social researcher, beyond the fact that there were a number of advantages inherent in this status. My Egyptian origin implied in my mind a familiarity with Arab culture at large and a knowledge of the general aspects of my native society and its language. Furthermore, I not only believed that my Arab origin would facilitate my entry into the field; I also expected it to mean that I would require less time to carry out my study compared with a foreign field-worker with little or no direct knowledge of Arab society.

The wider implications of my gender role and indigenous status began to dawn on me very soon after I embarked on my study. I became aware that there were many more dimensions—advantageous as well as restrictive—to my researcher role in my own society than I had at first been conscious of.

### Introducing the Field

In 1975, a bilateral agreement was signed by the governments of Iraq and Egypt, decreeing that Egyptian peasant families would be resettled permanently in Iraq. The Iraqi government contracted to shoulder all resettlement expenses, including the provision of free housing and plots of land that these peasant families would be allowed to cultivate as individual holdings. One hundred settlers and their families were recruited by the Egyptian authorities from various provinces in Egypt, mainly, although not exclusively, from among landless tenants who were expected to have the agricultural experience necessary to become small landowners. They arrived in the spring of 1976 in the Khalsa Settlement, which the Iraqi authorities had built for them some thirty-six miles south of Baghdad.[1]

My interest in this new human settlement revolved around the type of community that had been developing. I set out to discover whether the geographical remoteness of the villages of origin, as well as the relatively alien socioeconomic environment—cultural similarities between

Egypt and Iraq notwithstanding—would have served to diminish the importance of these settler families' heterogeneous provincial origins to the point of encouraging the development of a cohesive community in Khalsa. Equally relevant to this focus was the study of the postmigratory changes that had or had not taken place with regard to specific peasant customs and traditions that were assumed to prevail in the contemporary Egyptian village (Fawzi El-Solh 1985). I was also interested in the type of relationships that had come to exist between these peasant families and their Iraqi hosts and neighbors.

### Politics and Bureaucracy: Impediments to Research

I arrived in Cairo at the beginning of the winter of 1978–1979 in order to collect information on the part played by the Egyptian authorities in recruiting and preparing the peasant families who had been resettled in Iraq. Although there were rumblings in the Egyptian press, reflecting the rising political tension between Egypt and the rest of the Arab world as a result of Sadat's Jerusalem trip in November 1977, I was confident that the importance of such a resettlement scheme for an overpopulated Egypt would encourage the officials concerned to cooperate with me.

As an Egyptian, I was naturally aware of the intricacies of dealing with the bureaucracy in my home country. Accordingly, I set about activating my contacts among relatives and friends in order to facilitate the process of making my way through the bureaucratic maze. Beyond this measure, I did not give much thought to my researcher role. I was convinced that the latter only required that I explain my interest in this type of resettlement scheme and its positive implications for regional economic cooperation within the Arab world.

Oblivious of the fact that any research undertaking involving a government agency requires an official sanction—I thought this only applied to foreigners—I set out to contact those officials who were said to have been directly involved with the migration project. No one thought of questioning whether I had secured the appropriate authorization until I made a request to view the relevant documents. I quickly found myself escorted to the security officials in charge, who just as quickly shattered my illusion that obtaining such a clearance was a mere formality. None of them expressed much interest in the topic of my research. Instead, they felt compelled to warn me that, given the political circumstances, it

would really be "inadvisable" to travel to Iraq. Since direct flights between Cairo and Baghdad were continuing uninterrupted (usually a reli-
able sign of the state of relations between governments in the Arab
world), I decided to ignore such remarks. But repeated visits to this security office failed to produce the necessary clearance and I left Cairo at the
beginning of February 1979 without having secured it. Trying my hand at
what Egyptians commonly refer to as *fahlawa* (which, roughly translated,
means to be carelessly daring; cf. Mayfield 1971) and bluffing my way to
these documents, did not get me anywhere.

A second trip to Cairo in January 1980 in order to supplement the
rather meager information I had managed to collect during my previous
trip was not much more fruitful. The Camp David agreement (concluded
in the autumn of 1979) had further isolated Egypt politically from the rest
of the Arab world. Direct flights between Egypt and Iraq had since been
suspended. The security office had no record of my previous application
to view the documents related to the resettlement of the Egyptian peasants in Iraq and I was advised of the need to reapply. More perturbing to
me were the thinly veiled warnings uttered by the security official in
charge, to the effect that it was "illegal" for Egyptians to travel to Iraq. I
wondered what had happened to all the Egyptians I had seen in the
streets of Baghdad the previous winter. But given the political tensions
between Egypt and Iraq at the time, I had no reason to disbelieve these
ominous utterings, specially since there were rumors circulating in Cairo
that a number of Iraqis had been deported. Unfortunately, I was at the
time quite unaware that an increasing number of temporary Egyptian
migrants of all skill categories were quietly making their way into Iraq via
a third country (mainly Jordan), a development to which the Egyptian
government was turning a blind eye.

### The Arab Female Researcher in Baghdad

Previous trips to Iraq had to some extent alerted me to certain realities connected with research endeavors in this country. Here too personal
contacts have to be activated in order to obtain the necessary security
clearance and research authorization. However, there is the added factor
that governmental circles generally do not view prolonged unsponsored
fieldwork as either necessary or desirable. Furthermore, although women
within the social periphery of Baghdad enjoy a relatively greater freedom
of mobility in comparison with other Iraqi urban centers, and although

the female participation rate in the labor force has risen tremendously over the past few decades, these facts have not necessarily been translated into a less formal relationship between the sexes. The many capable members of the Iraqi Federation of Women encourage the assumption that the gap between economic development and social change is not vast. But this is to some extent a fallacy. Although obviously decreasing, this gap is still very much in evidence even among the less traditional middle-class circles in Baghdadi society (cf. Joseph 1982; Rassam 1982). Such reality is particularly evident when compared with Cairene society, for example, regardless of the current Islamic fundamentalist wave that has been affecting segments of the urban middle classes in Egypt (see Mohsen 1985).

Cultural similarities between Iraq and Egypt, as well as the bond of a common language (notwithstanding the difference in dialects), precluded any feeling that I was a stranger in Baghdad. In fact, I almost unconsciously assumed my "Arab identity" by being sensitive to certain cultural expectations that I generally did not question in my native Egypt. For example, it would not have occurred to me to walk around alone after nightfall, not even in the commercial center of the capital, which continues to bustle with activity well into the night. Similarly, I was very conscious of the public places that were either barred to me as a woman (e.g., specific areas in the mosque, traditional coffee shops), or into which I could not easily venture without a male chaperone (e.g., certain restaurants).

But at the same time, I also perceived myself as an outsider in the sense of being non-Iraqi. Therefore I assumed I could afford to escape some of the restrictions applicable to Iraqi women in general. Specifically, although I was aware that it is for the most part difficult for an Iraqi woman to live unchaperoned, I believed that my role as an outsider would enable me to circumvent the type of protectiveness associated with this custom. I was also convinced that the relative freedom of mobility that this outsider role could be expected to accord me would be further enhanced by my marital status. In order to prove the latter and its concomitant respectability, I felt it opportune to have my husband accompany me to Baghdad and remain with me until I had secured the necessary research authorization.

Similar to other Arab countries, obtaining research permission in Baghdad necessitates beginning as near to the top of the bureaucratic ladder as possible, such nearness naturally being a function of the importance of the recommendations one has been able to secure. Once such authorization is granted, the researcher is sent to those lower echelon officials who are directly involved with the field or topic being studied.

However, the lower down this ladder we ventured, the more I found my-self relegated to the role of silent, tea-sipping wife while my husband did his best to explain my reasons for wishing to study the Egyptian peasant families in the Khalsa Settlement. Although being an Arab served to lessen the authorities' traditional suspicion of foreigners (non-Arabs in particular), this advantage was to some extent overridden by gender-role expectations which, I soon discovered, were less flexible than I had at first supposed. My official hosts did not share my self-perceived status as an outsider or a non-Iraqi, but tended instead to view me as an Arab member of their own society to whom, as a woman, certain customs were naturally applicable.

These expectations became particularly apparent during my attempts to secure accommodation inside the settlement. I had not given much thought to this issue during my first field trip to Iraq in February 1979, since I intended it to be a preliminary survey during which I was to decide on the focus of my study. But I had noted that a number of the houses, built for the administrative personnel in one part of the settle-ment, stood empty, and I had been assured by one of the officials that there would be little problem in renting one during the following winter.

Personal reasons as well as the outbreak of the Gulf War in Septem-ber 1980 forced me to postpone the second stage of my fieldwork in the Khalsa Settlement. Arriving in Baghdad during the winter of 1981–1982, my husband and I discovered that, not surprisingly, the war situation had invalidated the research authorization we had previously secured. This necessitated many rounds of visits to the relevant officials, during which we also broached the subject of my residence in the settlement. My hopes were quickly dashed, for the capital's chronic housing shortages had since my last visit spilled over into the area in which Khalsa is located. This meant that there was no accommodation available in the settlement. The possibility of lodging with one of the settler families did occur to me fleetingly, but was quickly discarded. Apart from the fact that the layout of the settler homes would not have afforded me the privacy I felt I needed to write up my field notes and keep track of the direction that my research was leading me in, there was also the fact that nearly all the households were letting out accommodation to temporary Egyptian mi-grants working outside Khalsa. But attempts to secure accommodation in the vicinity of the settlement, specifically in the nearby market town of Jisr al-Diyalah, which had the advantage of a regular bus service to Khalsa, met with conspicuous evasion on the part of the authorities.

Embarrassed that our persistent inquiries had ended up obliging some of the officials to offer me the hospitality of their own homes (which I wanted to avoid in order not to be identified with the authorities in the settler families' eyes), I reluctantly accepted the idea that I would have to remain in my hotel in Baghdad and find some way of commuting to the settlement. The inevitability of this solution finally dawned on me when I realized that, housing crisis apart, it was the fact that I was an Arab woman wanting to live without what was perceived to be an appropriate male chaperone that seemed to be the main problem. The authorities apparently had not understood at first that my husband did not intend to remain with me for the duration of my fieldwork in Khalsa. Once this was made explicit, my official hosts seemingly felt compelled to extend to me the protection that my status as an *ukht 'arabiyya* (Arab sister) warranted. As far as they were concerned, I was not an outsider to the extent that I believed I was. I was subtly made aware of this fact when one official, discussing my accommodation request over the telephone with a colleague, referred to me loud and clear as a *bunayya* (a young girl). By explicitly ignoring my marital status in the presence of my husband, he was apparently attempting very politely to convey to us the message that a higher official finally told us more bluntly—"We are not in the West"— and with this the matter was effectively closed.

A female researcher from a Western country might also have been refused permission to reside unchaperoned inside or in the vicinity of the settlement. However, I believe this would have been mainly because of security regulations applicable to most if not all non-Arab foreigners whatever their gender. I somehow doubt that a Western woman researcher attempting to secure accommodation would have met with the kind of disapproval that my husband and I were subtly made aware of.

## Problems and Solutions

My transportation problem was eventually solved with the authorities' gracious offer to have me picked up at my hotel every day at 6:00 A.M. (except Fridays) by the bus that transported government employees from the capital to the agricultural administrative center some ten minutes' drive from the settlement. The driver would pick me up again in Khalsa at around 2:00 P.M., unless I had been able to arrange a ride back to Baghdad before nightfall. I soon discovered that there was no point remaining in the settlement after sunset (around 6:00 P.M. in the winter). Because it became pitch-dark (a result of the blackout imposed by the war situation), one of the officials in the settlement felt obliged to accompany me on my visits to the settler families' homes, which was exactly the situation I was striving to avoid. Conscious that my fieldwork was to a large extent dependent on the authorities' good will, I did not ignore their hints that I should not be wandering in the settlement's alleyways after dark.

There were obvious disadvantages in being unable to live in the settlement. One was the limit this set on opportunities for participant observation as a means of supplementing data obtained through questionnaires. Another was the fact that the thirty-six-mile journey between the capital and the settlement took over two hours to negotiate because of traffic conditions during peak hours. However, the arrangement also had its advantages. To begin with, my arrival in Khalsa in a state-owned bus was an indication to the administrative personnel that I had secured authorization to carry out my research. After some attempts to accompany me on my visits to the Egyptian peasant households, these officials soon left me to my own devices. In my conversations with the settler families, I made a point of casually mentioning that my husband had insisted that I use this bus, not only because it was cheaper than renting a car but above all because it was safer, since I would not be alone in the company of a male stranger. This was one way of emphasizing my membership in the wider society of which these peasant families are a part. My explanation also made perfect sense, since everyone knew that using the public bus to get to and from the settlement necessitated numerous time-consuming changes. Another advantage of riding in this state-owned bus was the fact that the driver very soon became my barometer of the authorities' expectations about the duration of my study. I became conscious of this fact when, around two weeks after embarking on my fieldwork, he began to question me ever so persistently about how much longer I needed before I was finished.

The gender role that my official hosts expected me to conform to unexpectedly provided me with the solution to a problem with which I had been grappling ever since my first field trip to Cairo. The Egyptian peasantry's long-standing mistrust of outsiders encouraged me to stress my non-affiliation with the authorities. This seemed to me all the more crucial given the state of political relations between Egypt and Iraq at the time. I was worried that these settler families might think that the Egyptian government had sent me to report on them. Such considerations were reinforced by the fact that the National Research Centers in Cairo and Baghdad, both governmental agencies, had carried out a joint study in Khalsa during the first post-resettlement year.[2] Moreover, an Egyptian journalist had compiled a book about some of the settler families, and this had been published by a government agency in Iraq (Badri n.d.). There were therefore precedents which could well have encouraged the Egyptian peasant families in Khalsa to suspect that I was one more government representative who had come to collect information about them.

I had not yet decided how best to deal with what I perceived to be a delicate problem when, during my first field trip to Baghdad in February 1979, I noticed that it was almost taken for granted that I was Lebanese like my husband. I had unintentionally encouraged this impression by my habit of slipping into the Lebanese dialect when greeting one official or another. (It seemed nearer to the Iraqi dialect than my own native one, at least to my Egyptian ears.) My role of more or less silent, tea-sipping wife obviously prevented such an assumption from being put to the test. The impression that I was Lebanese appears also to have been reinforced by the fact that the letter of introduction issued by a high official, that also served as a clearance to carry out research in the Khalsa Settlement, simply referred to me as the wife of a Lebanese. Realizing this, I found myself impulsively explaining that I had in fact lived for some time in Cairo, hence my perceptibly Egyptian accent. None of the officials we met seemed particularly interested in my life history, beyond the fact that I was the wife of the man they had been requested to offer assistance to.

Encouraged, I decided to stick to this "national identity" during my fieldwork in the settlement. Accordingly, I introduced myself to the settlers as an Arab student from Lebanon who had come to write a dissertation about their customs and traditions for her English university professor in London. The peasant families' knowledge of the world outside their social horizon implied a familiarity with this role model. The explanation I proffered for my perceptibly Egyptian accent seemed equally acceptable. In fact, many were amused that I could "imitate" it so well.

At first, I tended to think I had perhaps attributed too much importance to the issue of my national origin and its possible negative impact on my research endeavors. But I gradually became convinced that having to live with the almost constant dread of being found out was well worth it. To begin with, it enabled me to assume the role of *ghareeba* (female stranger) in the settler families' eyes. Though being Lebanese and speaking Arabic meant that I was perceived to belong to the same part of the world as these peasant families, I was at the same time *ghareeba* enough to be permitted a host of questions the answers to which I could not be expected to know, however long I had supposedly lived in Egypt. I believe this served partly to distract attention from the class barrier dividing the peasant families' social world from my own. I was not a member of the social hierarchy in their home country and thus was not identified with upper-class Cairenes who, in the eyes of Egyptian villagers, are all too often indifferent as to how the rural poor fare. Being thought Lebanese also provided a common bond as outsiders in Iraq. In addition, it allowed me to discover what many of these families thought of the Iraqis among whom they had been resettled.

I tried to assuage my guilt by reminding myself that I held dual (Lebanese and Egyptian) citizenship and was thus, strictly speaking, not being dishonest. But I do not by any means wish to gloss over the ethical aspect of my action, since I believe that fieldwork ethics are a fundamental issue in the social sciences (see Barnes 1977; Dillman 1977). However, I also believe that many field-workers will at some point in their research find a measure of dishonesty unavoidable. In my view, the crucial question should be how much harm we thereby cause those we seek to study. I would like to think that, in my case, the harm was minimal. I paid a price through the almost constant dread of being found out during my field-work in Khalsa. My anxiety was compounded by emotional confusion when I discovered that the settler couple who had become my main informants came from a village only a few miles from that of my family in Lower Egypt, where my father is buried. I felt as if we were almost kin, a feeling made more poignant by their repeated claims of *wallahy, da akinnek wahda mennena* (by God, it is as if you were one of us). While this seemed to me the best indication that the social-class barrier between us had at least drifted to the background, it made the guilt I felt that much more difficult to bear.

### Entering the Field

Questions as to the best way of gaining access into the Khalsa Settlement were made more or less redundant during my first field trip in February 1979. As a matter of course, I was provided with an official car and the company of a research assistant from the Ministry under whose jurisdiction this resettlement project falls. My guide introduced me to the government officials who lived in the settlement and who were directly involved in its administration. To them I was one more visitor to be shown around this novel experiment of planned migration, albeit one who intended to make repeat visits.

Obtaining entry to the settlement during the winter of 1981–82 more or less followed the same pattern. To my surprise I found that two of the government officials I had met previously seemed to remember me, for they addressed me as Om Lina (the mother of Lina, which was the way I had introduced myself during my first visit to Khalsa). Again, I was first taken to the house of Abu Said, the Chairman of the Cooperative Society.[3] His official position, as well as the fact that he had to some extent assumed the role of informal leader in the eyes of most of the settler families, had led the authorities to particularly single out both him and his wife to introduce them to all visitors to the settlement. His wife, Om Said, also gave every indication of remembering me because, as she later explained, she had not realized that a *sitt zawat* (upper-class lady) like me also believed in prolonged lactation.[4]

The reiteration of our common bond as mothers somehow served to pave the way, for both Abu Said and his wife made a point of insisting that I use their home as the base from which I could set out to visit the other peasant families. Although I was touched by their hospitality, I was at first hesitant to be seen entering their home as often as they seemed to expect. I had gained the impression during my previous field trip to Khalsa that relationships between some of the households were marred by suspicion that, for the most part, appeared to be fed by their heterogeneous provincial origins in Egypt. Too much contact with one particular family could, so I feared, affect my relationship with the other households. Given my consciousness of the time pressure I was working under, I was perpetually worried that I would have very little chance of rectifying costly mistakes. But I very soon realized that this fear was largely unfounded. Although, by the time I was ready to embark on the second stage of my fieldwork, Abu Said's role as informal leader had become perceptibly eroded (partly as a result of the settler households' incipient individualism and their relative economic independence of one another), most of the Egyptian peasant families still held him and his wife in high esteem. A tall, elderly man, whose very reserve exuded dignity, Abu Said had left his mark by refusing, from the beginning, to be involved in any provincial factionalism. For her part, Om Said had earned the respect and gratitude of many settler wives by assisting them during the birth of their children without expecting any financial compensation. It was thus more or less taken for granted in the settlement that I too should defer to this settler couple.

Both of them very soon became my most valuable informants. Although illiterate, they were nevertheless extremely perceptive and from the start took it upon themselves to graciously but firmly point out to me which questions they felt to be ambiguous. They were not always right, as I managed to ascertain from other interviews, but their perceptions were generally astute and I came to value their opinion. The rapport I managed to establish with them was to some extent a function of the intangibles of our personalities: something "clicked" between us from the start.

But it was also based on our respective needs. They knew I relied on them for information and, given Abu Said's leadership role, they took such reliance for granted. At the same time, my regular visits to their home appear to have fulfilled their need for social recognition, which my intuitive attitude of according them the courtesy due to their status as my elders further emphasized. Like the majority of the peasant families in Khalsa, this settler couple perceived the advantage of migration in terms of social mobility out of the peasant stratum via the achievement of one or more sons in non-peasant occupations. To be able to claim a friendship with someone of my social background seemingly added to the fulfillment of their social aspirations.

### The Indigenous Female Urbanite and the Peasant

I was familiar with the Egyptian peasantry's way of life from childhood visits to my paternal family's village of origin, and from the peasant girls and women employed in both my own home and that of my relatives. Such knowledge was partly supplemented by Arabic novels, films, and television serials. Although not complete, this cognitive sharing nevertheless implied that there was no unbridgeable gap or dissonance between these Egyptian peasant families and myself. This fact was further underlined by my command of the Egyptian dialect. We shared a meaning system, an understanding of many tacit as well as explicit social situations that are an inherent part of our culture. My assumed role as a Lebanese enabled me to question those categories with which I, as an urbanite, was not sufficiently familiar without detracting from the cultural frame of reference we had in common.

In general contrast with the Egyptian village (see Zimmermann 1982), the settler families in Khalsa tended to guard their privacy, which meant that neighbors did not move freely in and out of each other's homes. This had the advantage that most of my interviews with the settler wives were relatively uninterrupted. Even if I met a settler wife chatting in the alleyway with other women, I would generally be led into her home away from the prying ears of her female neighbors.

It was apparent from the outset that although I had made a point of wearing what I believed were relatively ordinary unfashionable clothes, there existed a social class barrier between these Egyptian peasant women and myself. I therefore decided to initiate my interviews with them by introducing the universal themes of motherhood and child rearing into the conversation, bonds that we as women had in common regardless of the actual disparities in our respective ways of life. Furthermore, I attempted to enforce an informality between us by insisting that a settler wife continue with whatever she happened to be engaged in and by offering to lend a hand at one or the other chore. After some initial hesitation, most settler wives would concur, thus enabling me to avoid turning the interview into a formal question and answer session. However, not all of my offers of help appeared to be acceptable. At first I tended to attribute this to a fear of the evil eye (see Critchfield 1978). While this may to a certain extent have been the case, it appears that my social status also had an effect. The latter was taken to imply that there are specific chores that a *sitt zawat* such as myself could not possibly be used to (such as scouring the pots and pans with sand or hanging up the washing, for example). I realized that my offer of help could very easily be misunderstood as a patronizing attitude.

Therefore, whenever I met a settler wife who was particularly friendly and was inclined to prolong our conversation, I made a point of telling her about myself and my way of life. I knew she would very probably share such information not only with other members of the household, but also with her female neighbors living along the same alleyway. Such reciprocity would, so I hoped, add a social background to my researcher role by stressing the similarities rather than the differences in our respective ways of life, thus easing the settlement's suspicions of me as an outsider.

My gender and marital status afforded me the freedom of broaching subjects with the settler wives that a male researcher could not have and that an unmarried female researcher would have been expected to be too shy to talk about. Although intimate marital relations were never explicitly referred to, some of the settler wives who had made a point of inviting me to join them during their chats in the alleyway would in my presence freely joke about this subject. In fact they would often make innuendos which I admit I could not always follow. Since I was apparently the only *sitt zawat* of their acquaintance who did not consider it beneath her to be seen squatting with them in the dust of the alleyway, they were determined not to miss the chance of finding out as much as they could about me. They saw their opportunity when the conversation came around to the subject of circumcision. Many were openly puzzled by the fact that, similar to Iraq, female circumcision is not practiced in my "native" Lebanon, and proceeded to question me in detail about the particulars of my uncircumcised state. My obvious embarrassment at such intimate questions surprised and even confused them at first. I suspect it did not tally with the upper-class female stereotypes portrayed in

the Arabic films and serials, which they all avidly followed on their television screens.

By contrast, I at first found it difficult to introduce a similar informality into my contacts with the male settlers. I avoided seeking them out in
the settlement's two coffee shops, instinctively perceiving this traditionally male social space to be barred to me as a woman. My exclusion from
this male preserve was also emphasized by Abu Said, who once admonished me not to hang around in front of the coffee shop to talk to a
passerby. Attempts to interview the settlers in their fields were also firmly
discouraged by Abu Said. Implicit in his disapproval was a measure of
protectiveness, which he expressed by wondering aloud what my family
would think of my venturing into the fields on my own. However, apart
from fear of the evil eye, I also suspect that his hesitation was due to his
determination to avoid any probing into his own agricultural activities,
which could easily lead to unwelcome questions about his income.

Since the alleyway was perceived to be the social arena of women
and children, and men considered it shameful to be seen squatting there,
I had to seek the settlers out in their homes. At first, I could not help
feeling distinctly uncomfortable whenever I found myself either alone in
the company of a settler or the only female sitting with him and his male
visitors, who were generally from outside the settlement. The authorities'
protective attitude toward me as well as Abu Said's admonitions had
heightened my self-consciousness of what was and was not appropriate
behavior. In fact, I caught myself on a number of occasions demurely
tucking my legs out of sight under my seat.

My increased awareness of gender-role expectations in this cultural
setting also led me to avoid discussing subjects of a more intimate nature
with my male respondents. For example, it did not occur to me to find
out what they thought of the circumcision of their daughters. Nor did I
attempt to check if, similar to their wives, who found it inconceivable
that an uncircumcised girl could be fully trusted, they too would oppose a
son's marriage with an Iraqi girl.

However, I gradually realized that most if not all of my male respondents were oblivious to my discomfort or my instinctive compulsion to
erect a barrier of reserve between us. In the privacy of the settler's home,
it appeared that my gender role was of secondary importance compared
with the fact of my social class origin. It was expected that an educated
city woman, and a married one at that, would be used to sitting and
freely conversing with men. The settlers would accordingly attempt to
exhibit the kind of deference that they believed my social status warranted. Thus, I did not encounter any difficulty in broaching subjects

that, so I had learned from Abu Said, were generally considered to be male prerogatives: e.g., the cooperative society, reasons for growing specific crops, the type of fertilizer used, marketing problems, and so on. Such deference was also implicit in my male respondents' insistence in seating me in the front room where visitors were usually received. The formality of the occasion was underlined by the extended ritual of exchanging greetings and an avoidance of discussing the reason for my visit until I had been offered the appropriate refreshments.

But, however much I was treated as an honored guest in the male settler's home, outside this private sphere I was apparently expected to adhere to certain conventions applicable to me as a woman who, although she may have been a *ghareeba*, was nevertheless perceived as a member of the wider culture of which we were both a part. Thus, the same settler who conversed with me at length in his own home would, if he met me on the public road—i.e., outside the semi-privacy of the alleyway—confine our contact to a friendly but brief greeting, and hurry off. Abu Said was not the only one who considered it inappropriate of me to linger in a public place and engage someone in a lengthy conversation.

### Face-to-Face as Women

My female respondents were quite aware that my status as an educated *sitt zawat* afforded me certain liberties and a freedom of mobility that did not apply to their way of life. However, I gradually began to realize that Om Said and some of the settler wives with whom I was on particularly friendly terms would at times tend to ignore my social class origin. Although few had more than a hazy idea of what my "native Lebanon" was like, they nevertheless tended to judge me as someone to whom some of their own cultural expectations were applicable: Why did I only have one child and a daughter at that? Was I not worried that my husband could divorce me or take a second wife in order to have a son? After all, he was a Muslim, was he not?

Since few of the settler wives prayed or fasted regularly and even fewer considered it a priority to make the pilgrimage to Mecca (although this journey is cheaper from Iraq than it is from Egypt), I was not judged by my admitted neglect of these pillars of Islam. However, some of my female respondents felt it necessary to admonish me not to become like "them," i.e., Western women who, so it is said, all prefer to work like men rather than stay home to care for their families. Socialized from a young age to shoulder the responsibilities of household, child-rearing, raising fowl and other domestic animals, as well as working in the fields, these women perceived a higher social status to imply that they would never have to venture outside their homes in order to contribute to the family's earnings. Although they had contacts with working women (e.g., the primary school teachers, nurses, female agricultural technicians associated with the settlement), a role model also conveyed by the media, the majority of them were generally indifferent to images depicting women as indispensable participants in society's development efforts. Their postmigratory way of life attempted to reflect this ideal of female seclusion, since a settler wife generally never left the confines of her alleyway unless there was a compeling reason. Having to work outside the home in Khalsa was justified as an economic necessity, from which these peasant women expected to be absolved when they returned back to Egypt as the successful migrants who had done well during their stay in Iraq. They therefore found it difficult to comprehend why I did not sit back and enjoy my status as a *sitt zawat* and leave it to my husband to earn our livelihood.

My impression of being judged according to these peasant women's cultural expectations was deepened by a confrontation I once had with Om Said. I had remarked on the fact that, in contrast to boys, girls appeared to be circumcised at a relatively later age (usually around nine or ten years, but before the onset of menstruation). Om Said answered that it was necessary that a girl be "old enough not to forget the pain." Implicit in her explanation is the belief that this ritual with its pain would help check a sexuality that demands a measure of social control. Traditional Egyptian society believes that such control is necessary, since females are held to be incapable of curbing their sexual impulses by themselves (see El-Saadawi 1979). I found it hard to disguise my anger at the almost nonchalant way in which Om Said seemed to discuss what in my view must undoubtedly be a traumatic experience. It was impossible to be impartial about an issue that directly concerned me as an Egyptian woman, for I was aware that, but for my father's nontraditional mentality, I too could have been circumcised.

In retrospect, I realize that my anger had also been triggered by the desire to see the lives of these peasant women and their daughters improved not only economically, but also socially and politically. Rationally I was aware of the almost inevitable lag between economic development and social change. Hence, I was not unduly surprised to discover that, in contrast to sons, there were quite a few settler daughters of primary school age who were being kept home, in spite of the fact that primary education is compulsory for everyone living in Iraq. But I did not attempt to influence the settler parents, since I realized that they did not envision a role other than the traditional one of wife and mother for their daughters. I was convinced that whatever the future of these girls, it would hold more promise compared to the poverty that their parents had left behind in Egypt. But the custom of female circumcision was, to my mind, a very different matter. I could not shrug it off as an exotic ritual that only concerned me as an impartial researcher.[5]

However, Om Said was not in the least taken aback by my reaction. In fact, she put me on the defensive by insinuating that she viewed my uncircumcised state as distasteful and unclean. Moreover, she demanded to know, if a woman could stand the pain of childbirth, then why not put up with this "little pain" of circumcision, which would make her more attractive for her husband? While men, she confided, did not like a cold wife, they did prefer one who was not easily aroused, since this meant that they could always trust her.

I was at a loss to know how to counter these attitudes and I remember leaving Om Said's house in a state of confusion. I had always pitied my female compatriots who had had to endure the ritual of circumcision, even though I was aware that they were more fortunate compared with women in the Sudan, for example, where a more drastic form of this custom (infibulation) continues to be practiced (see Passmore Sanderson 1981). It had never occurred to me that such women might view my uncircumcised state with equal distaste. I began to see a previous remark by Om Said, to the effect that women who were sexually promiscuous had obviously not been "properly" circumcised, in a very different light.

## Models and Stereotypes

The separate questionnaires that I had set up for settlers and settler wives were a reflection of my belief that men and women in Arab peasant society generally inhabit different social worlds. By and large, I still subscribe to the view that since traditional urban as well as rural societies in the Arab world are to varying degrees sex-segregated, such separate questionnaires are generally unavoidable and will to some extent reflect sex- and gender-related knowledge. But fieldwork in Khalsa also taught me that implicit in the type of questions I had set up for the settler wife was the notion of the powerless peasant woman, a stereotype that I had more or less unquestioningly assimilated. Sociological as well as anthropological literature had to a large extent served to reinforce such a model in my mind.[6]

My fieldwork in Khalsa opened my eyes to the fact that many of these Egyptian peasant women were very subtly manipulating the circumstances of their way of life. Although the many postmigratory changes that have taken place in the settlement may not have perceptibly influenced traditional peasant notions of gender roles, I believe that there is some evidence to support the claim that these changes have left an impact on the relationship between spouses. The absence of the traditional female hierarchy based on age and status, to which the settler wife would have been subjugated back in her village of origin, has tended to reinforce her position in the nuclear family in Khalsa, since she may well be the only adult female in the household on whom the husband can rely. In addition, the settler parents' encouragement of their sons' educational achievement as a means of mobility out of the peasant stratum, has increased the wife's importance as an economic asset. Her labor contribution outside the household can make all the difference to the family's aim of income maximization. Much obviously depends on a settler wife's personality. But it appears that many of these peasant women in Khalsa have carved out a role by which they are able to assert themselves unobtrusively, however much they may adhere to the custom of publicly deferring to their menfolk.

I am unable to judge the actual extent to which a settler wife's postmigratory way of life has come to differ from her circumstances back in her village of origin in Egypt. However, recent studies that attest to the significance of the Egyptian peasant woman's entrepreneurial spirit (cf. Van Spijk 1982a, b; Sukkary-Stolba 1985) lead me to conclude that the stereotype of the powerless peasant woman is experiencing a well-deserved erosion.

### Outstaying my Welcome

After about the sixth week of my fieldwork, I began to be aware of a change in the attitude of some of the settler families toward my presence in the settlement. A greeting that had always been accompanied by the invitation to step in for some refreshment, gradually became a greeting only. More conspicuous was the fact that, whereas before one or the other settler family would always call off the guard dog if they saw me approach their alleyway, some of them would now pretend not to see me. Even the group of children who used to wait nearly every morning for my arrival, upon which they would burst into a chant of *al-sitt Om Lina gatt* (the lady the mother of Lina has arrived), ceased to make a regular appearance. Om Said finally admitted that some settler families, including those whom I had revisited in order to supplement some of my data, seemed to feel that I should by now have collected enough information about the settlement.

Whatever the explanation for this change, I tend to believe that it was also encouraged by the fact that I was seen entering the office of the local district administrator who had requested to see me. Since, in the settler families' eyes, this official is synonymous with the law, it is quite possible that they had become worried I could be reporting about them. Although everyone seemed to be aware of my contacts with two of the Iraqi administrative personnel living in the settlement (who had become my informants of sorts), the latter were generally well liked and were not viewed as "the authority" in the way that the district administrator was. I had hastened to Om Said's house to explain my visit to this official's office. To my consternation, she already seemed to know where I had been. Although she very patiently listened to my assurances that I had not discussed the peasant households' affairs with the district administrator, I nevertheless feared that the damage was already done. Very soon after this incident I began to notice the perceptible withdrawal of some of the settler families.

Not wanting to submit the apparent fragility of my friendships and relationships in the settlement to any further test, I decided to heed the hint that I had obviously outstayed my welcome. Bureaucracy had once again intervened to dictate the scope of my research endeavors.

### Conclusion

Being indigenous as well as female has a number of obvious implications for the Arab woman researcher's access to knowledge in her own society. Perceptions of gender role are not only dependent on the actual degree of sex segregation, but will, in correlation with a number of other factors, also vary according to specific situational contexts (see Clark 1983).

In my case, the Egyptian authorities appeared to be less concerned with my status as a woman researcher than with the fact that the focus of my study touched upon political sensitivities, from which I as an Egyptian was not immune. By contrast, to some of the officials I encountered in Iraq, my gender role and the behavioral norms this implied for a woman of Arab descent appeared to be the more crucial factors, overriding both social class and educational status.

My heightened consciousness of these cultural clues led me to be somewhat reserved during my contacts with the Egyptian peasant men in the Khalsa Settlement. But here too I found that the definition of my role varied according to its situational context. Thus, inside the home, it was my social and educational background that tended to dictate the boundaries of my relationship with the male settlers. In public, both my gender role and Arab origin implied that I heed at least some of the behavioral norms applicable to women in this social setting.

The self-limitation that I subjected myself to during my contacts with the male settlers was to some extent due to my hesitation to stretch the flexibility of my role to the limits of what would have been culturally permissible. In retrospect, I realize that this hesitation was not only influenced by my perpetual worry of not having sufficient time to rectify any offense I may inadvertently have caused. It was also affected by notions of male/female interactions in a traditional rural setting, which I had consciously or unconsciously assimilated as part of my socialization in the wider culture.

With regard to the settler wives, I never entertained the illusion that the friendliness and warmth that some of them exhibited toward me implied a complete dismantling of the class barrier between us. This barrier was always there, explicit in the very fact that I was not a peasant woman and was unlikely to assume this native role. Thus, I never really transcended my transitional status as temporary guest. Nonetheless, there were instances when my Arab origin and religious affiliation tended to override my social class status. Though I had seized the initiative of stressing the experiences that we had in common in our roles as wives and mothers, some of the settler wives perceived the implications of these similarities in a wider context than I was inclined to. Their judgment of my uncircumcised state is a case in point.

Although perceptions of my gender role as an Arab woman restricted my freedom of mobility in specific situations, I also believe that there are a number of positive aspects to this status. One obvious advantage of being a member of the wider culture lies in the time required to carry out research. Even when, as in my case, the field-worker may not be completely familiar with the cognitive world of the research community, the very fact that he or she will be able to operate on the basis of "minimal cues" (Agar 1980) is to my mind an indisputable asset. This will not only facilitate communication with the research community. In addition, the indigenous researcher can dispense with the services of interpreters, whose personal bias must be taken into account in the collection and analysis of data (see Owusu 1978).

While I do not negate the possible dangers emanating from a prior familiarity with the field (see Stephenson and Greer 1981), I would also point out that the foreign field-worker is not necessarily immune from the pitfalls of bias and omission (see Hsu 1973). Whatever the advantages that a field-worker may enjoy through his or her role and status in the research community, good data is ultimately dependent on training and ability.

I would generally concur with the view that there are numerous topics that a male researcher could discuss with peasant women, e.g., the type of work they carry out on the land, their marketing activities, which household chores they are responsible for, etc. (see Gregory 1984). However, I believe that it is not only the type of topic that is at issue here. In the Khalsa Settlement, for example, it is doubtful if I could have interviewed the settler wives in the privacy of their homes without the presence of male kin had I been a man, Arab or otherwise. Few male settlers would permit their wives to talk freely with male strangers, unless this were specifically requested by the authorities. Even then, a husband would have ensured that he was present during the interview. Furthermore, although many of the settler wives had quite astute opinions about a variety of subjects, few of them would have been inclined to express these views freely in the presence of a male stranger. Data gathered during this type of cross-gender research in societies where sex segregation is a fact of life will tend to contain a bias that may well be unavoidable.

Moreover, whatever the degree of rapport that a male ethnographer could achieve with female respondents in a research setting such as Khalsa, the fact remains that not only will he be unable to gather data touching upon the intimate sphere of their lives. Equally important is the fact that cultural perceptions of his sex role and social status preclude his acceptance as an honorary female in the social world of women, assuming that a male field-worker would accept such a categorization (see Scheper-Hughes 1983b:114). By contrast, the female field-worker in a sex-segregated society will, on the basis of her status, be able to maneuver in the men's social world, however much the actual flexibility of her role may be dependent on the degree to which the sexes are socially separated (see Pettigrew 1981). Although here too the possibility of biased data must be taken into account, I would claim that the female researcher can in such a situation cross-check her data more easily by taking advantage of her access to both the male and the female social spheres.

There is an additional aspect pertaining to indigenous researchers in the Arab world irrespective of their gender roles, namely their subjugation to the restrictions imposed by those in authority (see Fahim 1982a). National bureaucracies will not only tend to dictate the type of research undertaken, but can also decree what may and may not be published (see Colson 1982). Furthermore, as in my case, the intricacies of Arab regional politics may well have an impact on the Arab researcher's freedom of mobility.

Being indigenous in the Arab world also demands, in my view, a sense of commitment. This does not necessarily contradict the objectivity demanded by the social science discipline. Given the development needs in the Arab world, I believe that my role as a social scientist does not imply an impartiality. These needs demand a committed involvement in attempts to improve the quality of life of those whose fate has hitherto largely been ignored. The social scientist need not apologize for this type of ideological commitment. I do not mean to imply that foreign researchers are not necessarily interested in action-oriented research or are not committed to those they study. Rather, as Fahim (1977) and Nakhleh (1979) have also indicated, Arab researchers cannot easily escape the political responsibility associated with their research findings and publications.

## Notes

1. It was planned that Khalsa would be the first of many such settlements. Officials in both countries envisioned the eventual permanent resettlement of 50,000 Egyptian peasant families in Iraq. The Camp David Agreement led to the political isolation of Egypt in the Arab world and to the shelving of this officially sponsored resettlement scheme. A further settlement village intended for Egyptian peasants was instead populated by Moroccan peasant families.

This official sponsorship is a separate issue from the influx of temporary Egyptian migrants who have made their way into Iraq, a wave that began to gather momentum during the mid-1970s and reached a peak by the early 1980s with Iraq's need for replacement manpower because of the Gulf War. This peak has since ebbed because of the recession that has hit Iraq and many of the other oil producers in this region (see Birks 1983).

2. To my knowledge, this study has never been published (see Fahim 1982b).

3. The uniqueness of this resettlement scheme—there is only one Khalsa in Iraq, indeed in this part of the Arab world—undermines efforts at anonymity. I have therefore not attempted to give pseudonyms to my main informants.

4. This was in reference to an incident during my first fieldtrip to Khalsa. I had on one occasion stayed until dusk in the settlement, by which time a wet patch had spread on

the front of my dress. This was an obvious signal that it was high time to return to Baghdad to breast-feed my fourteen-month-old daughter. Om Said, who had witnessed my predica-ment, openly expressed her surprise, since she had been convinced that only poor women who could not afford the cost of milk preparations would tend to prolong lactation. Bottle feeding was at the time of my study a relatively widespread practice in Khalsa, especially among settler wives who used modern contraceptives. But even those who believed that lactation was an effective means of birth control supplemented this with bottle feeding when they were busy on the land or in the market.

5.  I do not subscribe to the Western feminist view that tends to focus on the issue of genital mutilation often to the exclusion of all the other socioeconomic and political ills that affect the lives of many women in Egypt. But, unfortunately, this particular Western feminist view has provoked a reaction among some Egyptian feminists who tend to deny that female circumcision is still relatively widespread among traditional urban and rural circles in Egypt (see Rugh 1985).

6.  Rogers (1975) presents an interesting overview and analysis of the implicit and explicit assumptions in the anthropological literature concerning women's subordinate role in peasant societies.

# 6

## Studying Your Own

### The Complexities of a Shared Culture

SETENEY SHAMI

$T$ here has been much discussion among anthropologists about the advantages and disadvantages of doing fieldwork in one's own society. All too often, the insider/outsider question is posed too simplistically as a dichotomy between subjectivity and objectivity. Underlying this point of view is the basic assumption that, as an insider, the indigenous anthropologist duplicates completely the culture of his or her informants. When this assumption is examined more closely, the real complexity of the issue becomes clear. Both anthropologists and their informants are more than bearers of certain ideas and values. They are social persons with a certain position vis-à-vis one another within a common social structure. The question then is not whether the indigenous anthropologist can be objective or not. Like any other social scientist, she or he has to first examine her or his own values and ideas critically. Rather, the question is how the relative social position of the indigenous anthropologist affects the methodology of research. Class, gender and ethnicity have definite implications for access to and rapport with the research community, as well as for the substance of data collected.

In comparing my two major fieldwork experiences, both in my "own" culture and yet quite dissimilar, I would like to explore some facets of this issue. This discussion focuses on the fieldwork aspect of the anthropological endeavour, on the collection of data and its interpretation in field notes. Another important issue is of course the theoretical examination of data. In this I believe that the insider/outsider distinction is canceled, the determining factor being the intellectual rigor with which the subject is explored. I do not believe that an insider somehow has an intuitive ability to theorize about his society better than an outsider. However, both have to depend on good data in order to theorize well, and it is the process of data collection that will be discussed in the following.

## Coming Home to the Field

For my doctoral thesis I spent twenty-one months (1979–1980) doing fieldwork among the Circassians, an ethnic minority group in Jordan. The Circassians had immigrated into the Ottoman Empire from the Caucasus in the 1860s, driven out by the southward expansion of Czarist Russia during this period (see Berkok 1958). At present they form sizable communities in Turkey, Syria, Jordan, and Palestine.

My own great-grandparents had been among the 1.1 million Circassians who set off on overcrowded ships and arrived at the even more overcrowded ports of Istanbul, where disease and famine were wreaking havoc. Harried Ottoman officials sent convoy after convoy to various parts of the Empire, where the immigrants established agricultural communities (cf. Eren 1966; Karpat 1972). Thus it was that my paternal grandfather was born in Galilee, Palestine, and my maternal grandfather in Kayseri, Turkey. My father left Palestine in 1948, part of the Palestinian exodus after the creation of Israel. He met my mother in Damascus, they were married in Istanbul, and settled in Amman, Jordan.

This story was very much part of my childhood. My parents had a great deal of ethnic pride. My maternal grandfather had spent twenty years writing the history of the Russo-Caucasian wars, and Circassian daggers and swords adorned our walls. Yet socially we were very much on the fringes of the Circassian community. We had no relatives in Jordan and spoke Arabic, Turkish, and English at home, thus rarely hearing the Circassian language spoken. So much so that as I was growing up, I entertained vague doubts about whether there were really a people called Circassians, or if they were something my parents had made up to complicate my life.

Thus, when I decided to study the Circassian community in Jordan, to what extent was I doing fieldwork in my "own" culture? At the age of twenty-three, how much of my own world view was molded by my Circassian background and how much by my three years of graduate school at Berkeley? Some years later, when I started my fieldwork in a squatter area of Amman and found myself entering the bounded universe of the women, watching them deal with the pressures imposed upon them by their gender, class, and kin, to what extent was I participating in a familiar culture? Was the common factor of being female enough to enable me to understand, and to make me part of what I was observing?

## The Middle Eastern Woman

It was, perhaps predictably, at Berkeley that I first came into contact with "women" as an academic topic, as a unit of analysis. For the most part, this was triggered by the questions that I came up against in the U.S. There were questions about the veil, arranged marriages, Islam, and patriarchal fathers. Truly, being a Middle Eastern woman seemed to weigh me down with a lot of cultural baggage. I could not answer many of the questions. For me, veiling had never been a consideration and I had always expected to go to college. My friends and I were certainly aware of arranged marriages and the cultural preference for boys, but we were not all aware that we were supposed to marry our parallel cousins—a revelation that, as an undergraduate in my first anthropology course at the American University of Beirut, I shared with my Arab friends in the dormitories. At Berkeley, people often said that I seemed very "Westernized." Was I somehow less Middle Eastern because I did not wear a veil? For the first time, I began to read critically the works on Middle Eastern and Muslim women.

From the community studies on the Middle East, I found it extraordinarily difficult to emerge with a picture of the Middle Eastern woman— she seemed a shadowy, vague creature, always on the edge of life. Mostly she was only mentioned as an object rather than as an actor in society. She appeared in conflict cases as a victim of an honor crime, or a divorced woman, or she was the "sexually threatening wife," or the "self-sacrificing mother," as illustrated in proverbs and folk tales (see Sweet 1974). Or the discussion would be phrased in terms of more or less "Westernization" (e.g., Patai 1955, 1967; Hamady 1960; Berger 1962; Churchill 1967). More satisfying were the studies that analyzed the effects of various factors—economic, political, ideological—on the position of women (see Aswad 1967; Mohsen 1967; Sweet 1967; Antoun 1968; Abu Zahra 1970). These studies also threw into doubt the orientalist image of the Islamic woman, which generalized about the status of Muslim women on the basis of interpretations of Islamic prescriptions and doctrine. This image blurred the distinctions between the variety of statuses occupied by

Middle Eastern women. Many anthropologists, generally nonspecialists in Islam, tended to incorporate these ideas uncritically. Thus, the image of the marginal position and personality of the Middle Eastern woman continued to persist in the literature and, even more so, in the popular mind.

As an insider, I knew that many of these images were false. The same applied to many other aspects of Arab society and culture that I read about. Yet I also realized that my experience was limited to my own sector of society and that I knew little about the realities of different social groups and classes. Whereas it was not difficult to see what was wrong, biased, or misrepresented in the anthropological literature, it was less easy to come up with an alternative view and approach.

When the time drew near to having to choose a research topic for my dissertation, this fact was brought home to me in full force. My family and relatives who had been supportive of my academic ambitions expected that I would naturally research a Circassian topic. I was not so sure. I had often been reluctant to be identified with Circassians as an identity that set me apart from my friends and the majority of society. Besides, its culture seemed boringly familiar as compared to many that I read about in the courses I attended. Yet intellectually the topic of ethnicity, in particular its politics, did appeal to me. It was also a topic of some importance in the study of Middle Eastern societies. The turning point came as I attempted to write a paper on this topic for a course. Many of my assertions rang false to me. I discovered that I simply was not sure what the dynamics of Circassian ethnic politics were. Thus, when I chose to do my first field study on the Circassians, my choice was not so much guided by how much I knew, but rather by how much I felt that I did not know about "my own."

### The Circassians in Jordan: Beginning

The Circassian community, numbering about 25,000, is clustered in the Jordanian capital, Amman, and six surrounding towns. They had been settled in these locations during several migration waves in 1876, 1880, 1885, and 1901. While the Ottomans considered this area *miri* (state) lands, in fact it was the summer watering grounds of the surrounding Bedouin tribes (see Hacker 1960). This led to armed clashes over pasturage and water rights until the turn of the present century. With the founding of the Hashemite regime in 1921, and the establishment of Amman as the new capital, the Circassians found themselves at the center of the new state and the opportunities it afforded. Gradually, they moved away from farming and became urban landlords, civil servants and army officers (cf. Abidi 1965; Aruri 1972). By the 1950s, class and status differences had become apparent within the Circassian community. As the old neighborhoods broke up and the surrounding villages became incorporated into the capital, communication within the community decreased and ethnic cohesiveness became harder to maintain. Ethnic organizations and clubs were founded to fill in the vacuum. Thus, when I came to do my fieldwork, the Circassian community was a heterogeneous one, reflecting all the divisions in Jordanian society, as well as the divisions based upon traditional status considerations.

I did not want to study only one subcommunity or subgroup. Rather, I was interested in questions of ethnicity and national integration, and in understanding factors that affect ethnic cohesiveness in the context of the national polity. This meant understanding the internal structure of the community in all its complexity, as well as its articulation in the wider society. I especially wanted to be able to analyze fluctuations in ethnic cohesiveness over time. My research objectives combined with the geographically scattered nature of the Circassian community meant that I could not just walk into the community. I had to seek out informants and work within their networks in order to construct and define the boundaries of the Circassian community, as well as to discover how and where it intersected with the rest of Jordanian society.

It seemed natural to start by interviewing my parents' Circassian acquaintances, most of whom were middle- or upper-middle-class urbanites. Many of them were regarded as leaders of the Circassians, and I believed that interviewing them would get me off to an excellent start. I looked through the research proposal I had written in Berkeley to remind myself of the crucial issues, bought a notebook, labeled it "Fieldwork Notebook No. 1," and went visiting.

Those first interviews left me feeling very inadequate. I knew that I wanted to hear about ethnic identification, patronage, leadership, and conflict resolution, but I did not know how to phrase the questions in meaningful terms. All too often, as my informant looked at me helpfully, expectantly, my mind would go blank. The fact that I had easy access to the people, which seemed to be such an advantage at first, in fact meant that I had obtained access before I had formulated the right questions. I had as yet no idea of the real structure and dynamics of the community. So, by default, these first interviews turned into sketchy accounts of the history, customs, and general "superior" qualities of Circassians, as fondly imagined by the informant. When I asked about interethnic conflict, I always heard the same old stories about a few clashes at the turn of the century, and rosy pictures of the present—or at best, "Well, that's politics and we won't go into that." Many of these people were politicians or high-level civil servants, and years of habit had made them instinctively cautious about what they said and revealed.

Another "type" that I came into contact with during this initial phase was the "expert," who would be introduced to me with the words: "So and so knows everything about the Circassians." Generally, these were people who, for a variety of reasons, had withdrawn from active participation in the community, had read the few available books, and tended to build original but dubious theories. They tried to tell me what I should be studying, as opposed to what I wanted to study. One who had drawn up a complicated classification of the branches of Circassianology kept wistfully asking: "Won't you change your mind and study our national costume?"

Later, I realized that these interviews had in fact yielded much interesting data. For instance, the fact that visiting those leaders did not bring me into contact with the rest of the community was in itself significant. In their large quiet houses we would sit sipping tea, and there were never any visitors dropping in as I later saw in other Circassian households. They never volunteered to introduce me to others, although they would mention names of people that I should meet. When people later complained about the growing social gap between leaders and the community, it began to make sense. As for the "experts," they had an important function in the community. Cut off from their roots, starting to lose their cultural distinctiveness, Circassians were vitally interested in proving to themselves the ancient origin and importance of their language, history, and "race." These concerns had never been important to me, and at first I did not appreciate the urgency with which they discussed them. Having heard many of the stories before, I was neither interested nor stimulated. I was laying too much emphasis on getting what I wanted to hear and dismissing what they were telling me as somehow not being data, because it was not new.

Things began to change the day I received an invitation from two young women, students at the University in Amman, who had heard about my research on the Circassians. They lived in a small town to the north of the capital, where the local branch of the Circassian Charity Association was organizing a party to commemorate its twentieth anniversary. Since this was an important occasion, they suggested that I attend.

Overcoming my diffidence, and telling myself that sooner or later I would have to venture from the relative comfort of one-to-one interviews, I went to the party. It was in full swing when I arrived and it looked as though the whole town was there. The men on one side of the room, women on the other, teenagers hanging around together on the edges, and kids literally sprinkled everywhere. For the first time I was among "real people" and the dynamics of interaction were absorbing. I mentally began composing field notes. The young women who had invited me introduced me to some of the women and thus I met Lina, who became one of my best informants, my closest friend, and the moving force in my fieldwork.

This young woman with the quiet voice, herself exceptionally observant, would constantly ask me questions: What did I think of this? Did I notice that? (Often I had not.) What was I doing about x, y and z? Most importantly, Lina grasped immediately that I did not want to be taken from one Circassian "expert" to another, but wanted to meet and talk to people in their normal day-to-day setting. Within a few days, she had taken me to meet an elderly couple ("They are real Circassians"); a young couple with three children and a mother-in-law ("A typical family— notice how they respect the mother-in-law"); and a middle-aged couple with two daughters ("A modern family—they do not mix with Circassians"). Next she introduced me to some people who were involved in activities of the Circassian Charity Association and who invited me to attend their meetings. After that one thing led to another and I could write in my field notes that "my fieldwork is under way."

### A Circassian Household

I became a frequent visitor in Lina's home and through it was introduced to Circassian family life. It took me a week to move from the small formal sitting room, with its statutory velvet sofa, four armchairs and three coffee tables, to the rest of the house. The large kitchen was the main gathering place of the family. Lina had three sisters and two brothers. Their father was an invalid and rarely about. Their mother was an energetic woman who described with nostalgia her childhood on the farm. She helped me, with a great deal of amusement, in my efforts to improve my Circassian vocabulary. In a quiet way, Lina's mother ran the household by rules that she enforced unobtrusively, but firmly. The house was always very neat and orderly. Chores were divided up among the women, and the boys helped with the shopping and the heavy work. The different personalities of the members of the household had been worked out and were reflected in the division of the chores. Tasks did not duplicate one another and the work was divided up evenly. When Lina started spending a fair amount of time accompanying me on my round of visits, she quietly rearranged her schedule without negotiating with the rest of the family, but in such a way so as not to disturb the structure that had been set up. Although, compared to mine, this was a large family where there were always relatives and neighbors about, there was also a great deal of privacy. In terms of structural space, bedrooms were crowded and rooms had multiple functions. But people had different interests and pursued them individually.

After some time, I noticed that I was hardly writing anything down in my notebook about my visits to Lina's house, other than specific things she had said or stories recounted. I was not describing their interaction among themselves or with me. This interaction was structured by Circassian values of formality and avoidance within the family and kinship group. Although the traditionally high degree of formality had relaxed a great deal in the Jordanian context, contemporary Circassian households continued to exhibit aspects of these characteristics. Particularly persistent was the attitude that emotions were made to be suppressed. There was also the attitude of non-confrontation in conflict situations. One pretended that conflicts did not occur and that they would disappear if sufficiently ignored. This usually worked. I began to see that this aspect of Circassian culture was very much a part of myself. I had never before realized how much my own family reflected Circassian attitudes toward interpersonal interaction.

Lina was also my greatest proof of the inadequacy of the literature on Middle Eastern women. Her activities and personality stood in sharp contrast to the standard images. She was a graduate school teacher, intelligent, well read, and extremely interested in understanding differing viewpoints on any matter. Her soft voice and quiet demeanor at first gave the impression that she was shy until one realized that, in fact, she was very self-possessed. She had a quick sense of humor that could be vented equally on herself or any of her friends, who differed in age and sex and came from different ethnic groups. Lina had been the first woman in her town to be elected to the local committee of the Circassian Association, thus paving the way for those who followed. She became a valuable source in my research, as well as a useful indicator when it came to measuring community cohesiveness and communication. I would often be astonished at how quickly she managed to hear about some event or decision that I had witnessed at a meeting of the "elders." She had a lively interest in politics and often had the "inside story" of some event or another on the local or national scene. At first her comments would be riddled with tantalizing statements such as: "Well, you know what that clan is like," or "The women of that village are obviously different."

Whereupon I would exclaim that I did not know. By the end of my fieldwork, Lina told me with a half-exasperated smile: "You made me think so much about Circassians—things I had never bothered with before."

### In the Public Sphere

Going by what I had read in the literature on the Middle East, and given my research focus, I started my fieldwork with the assumption that most of my contacts would be with men as the prime actors in the political public sphere. I expected to interview women only in order to assess the impact of this public decision making on their lives and to see what informal power, or influence, they may wield. I certainly did not expect to obtain my entrée into the community through a woman, or to see how often men and women got together to discuss, plan and often disagree on matters of ethnic policy. Neither did I expect to find such a large number of formal women's groups. This is not to claim that inequalities did not exist. They did, but men's and women's spheres of activities often intersected, a fact that was of immense help to me during my fieldwork.

Within the Circassian community, the largest public arena for the overlapping of activities was in the various ethnic organizations. There were two sports clubs, the Circassian Association and its branches, and a newly founded Tribal Council. The people involved in these organizations represented all sectors of the community and held many differing viewpoints on the shape of things to come. Women, both married and unmarried, were involved to various degrees in a majority of these organizations. In effect, ethnic organizations brought the community closer together, while at the same time creating an arena for the expression of factions and tensions, including tensions along male/female lines.

My presence at the meetings, even in all-male committees, was not viewed as too much of an aberration, since there was already a precedent of women serving on these committees. Another facilitating factor was the cultural attitude of Circassians toward unmarried women. The latter had a great deal of freedom of action in Circassian society. There would be a mixing of the sexes at the large dancing parties held during wedding celebrations. Furthermore, girls were free to receive male visitors in their homes, and the parents would not intrude on such occasions, as long as the strict etiquette of speech and behavior was maintained. Thus, relative permissiveness was the custom as long as a woman was unmarried. After marriage, however, women were expected to restrict their activities and not venture too often outside the household. While Circassian girls were widening the arena of their autonomy, Circassian women had, at the time of my fieldwork, begun to challenge their social position. They too were forming committees and, much to the chagrin of the men, they were achieving excellent results, not the least of which was the establishment of a primary school of Circassian children, which taught the Circassian language and history, in addition to the regular curriculum set by the government.

Soon a large part of my fieldwork consisted of attending various committee meetings. There a number of topics would be discussed, ranging from routine business to the planning of events, to matters of ethnic concern. Since these meetings were held weekly and there were also many subcommittees, I ended up going to a meeting a day and often having to choose between alternatives. At first, when a committee member would invite me to attend one of these meetings, and take it upon himself to introduce me to those present, the assumption was that I was coming for one time only and that I had specific questions to be answered. I would then explain that I wanted to join them regularly, to see what kind of issues were important to the community, as well as the manner of discussion and decision making. I would also give my "little ethics speech," emphasizing that if there was anything they did not wish me to write down, they had only to say so. At this, I would be given a little speech in return, welcoming me, praising my "ethnic patriotism," which had led me to undertake this valuable research, and emphasizing the democratic way in which decisions were reached.

They would then generally proceed to ignore me and get on with the business at hand. This was especially true of large meetings such as those of the Tribal Council, where up to forty men would gather monthly to discuss community disputes and interethnic conflicts. These meetings were held at a different town or village each time, so that they could reach the whole community. While my presence had no effect on the formal proceedings, my arrival at the meeting would have some impact. I would usually try to be taken to the meeting by some members of the council. But, since the location varied all the time and the meetings were open to all, there were always a few people who did not know me and would therefore be surprised by my presence. There would be some whispering as someone took it upon himself to explain who I was, who my father was, and what I was doing, whereupon I would receive a smile and a nod of recognition. My arrival would also cause a little confusion as to where I should sit. Generally, the chairs were arranged lining the walls, sometimes two or three rows deep. As a woman, I was worthy of respect and should be sitting with the most important people, i.e., at the head of the room, facing the main entrance. As a relatively unimportant guest (I had no high-ranking job or standing in the community), I should be seated toward the sides and to the back. As a young Circassian, if I were following tradition and proper manners, I should be standing, preferably by the door. At one meeting, the problem was solved by one of the more outspoken members who, tired of different people motioning me to different chairs, said: "Until the end of her research, we will treat Seteney as a man." This effectively banished me toward the back of the room, where I sat and wrote my notes freely. It was an excellent arrangement from my point of view.

## A Niche in the Community

Gradually, I grew into an appendage at all kinds of events and my attendance was taken for granted. I was also distributing a questionnaire, gathering statistics from government departments, collecting oral histories, and going back to the politicians, now armed with penetrating questions. By the midpoint of my fieldwork, I had created a niche in the community as a researcher, and most people I met would already have heard of me. Even the Circassian police-woman, whom I met when paying a parking fine, looked up after writing my name on the receipt and asked if I was the one doing research.

At this stage, I also started taking photographs and found this increased my popularity, especially when I gave slide shows for those I had photographed. The camera also increased my access to all-male domains. One day, someone mentioned that his son was getting engaged and that the delegation of kinsmen was going to go and ask for the girl's hand in marriage. When I began asking questions about the procedure, he told me I was welcome to join them if it helped my research, adding as an afterthought that it would also be wonderful if I photographed the ensuing wedding celebrations. I only wish that I could have photographed the look of surprise on the faces of the bride's kinsmen when they saw a woman, armed with a camera, accompanying the bridegroom's delegation. After a brief attempt to hustle me into the inner room where the women were, and loud protests and whispered explanations from "my" delegation, they took it in their stride and I was able to observe the ritual at first hand.

As I became a familiar figure in the community, reactions to my presence began to undergo a change. This was particularly apparent when

I was with small groups of people who were very involved in community activities and organizations. Previously, they had accepted me as an observer. Now, however, they began to ask me about my findings and conclusions. Significantly, most of their questions centered around language and history. This sent me running back to my neglected "experts" for more detailed interviews, focusing this time on their personal biographies and how they had become interested in studying their ethnic heritage.

Furthermore, at some of the committee meetings people started to ask me for my opinion and evaluation of their activities. The members of one newly elected and energetic group were interested in upgrading their activities, as well as extending their power vis-à-vis other committees in the same organization. Knowing that I attended all meetings, they made an attempt to pump me for information. Seeing that I was not receptive, they dropped the attempt—they had other sources of information. However, they were still genuinely interested in hearing my opinion of their plans. Surprising even myself, I would find that I had no opinions. I listened, noted differing viewpoints and wrote them down, but without developing my own reaction to what was being said. These were not issues that affected me personally—the running of the school, the form wedding celebrations should take, the problem of alcoholism, etc. They interested me only as data. My own sense of identity was not involved in these issues as was theirs. Thus, I listened to their discussions quite neutrally.

The logical outcome of my presence at these meetings was that finally I came to be seen as a possible recruit. Predictably, this happened mainly among my own age group, with young men and women who were interested in organizing social and cultural activities. They would try and involve as many people as possible and I was an easy target, since I was always around. Lina chuckled when I told her, and gave me further food for thought: "Just wait until you come back after finishing your thesis. You won't be able to get away that easily."

## Fieldwork in the Wadi

My second major fieldwork experience involved a totally different community. The Wadi is a squatter slum area in the heart of Amman, comprising about 300 households. It lies on the slopes and bottom of a narrow valley adjacent to one of the large Palestinian refugee camps in Amman. With a few exceptions, the Wadi is inhabited by Palestinian households which, for a variety of reasons, were unable or unwilling to live in refugee camps. The area was first settled after 1948, but more than half the families moved in after 1967. The quality of buildings in the settlement is fairly poor, with the majority of houses composed of one or two rooms with concrete floors and walls and a zinc roof. A courtyard with a small toilet and kitchen and a grapevine in one corner complete the picture.[1]

My interest in studying the Wadi arose out of the fact that it had been one of five squatter urban areas designated for an upgrading project by the World Bank and implemented by the municipality of Amman. The Wadi, however, had not been upgraded due to a planned road which, if constructed, would cut through it and displace a number of its inhabitants. However, it had been part of the thorough survey carried out in 1980, focusing on the physical infrastructure of the area. In addition, a survey of child health had been carried out. I was therefore interested in comparing the changes that had taken place over the five years since the surveys were carried out, and also in comparing changes in the Wadi with those in areas that had been subject to upgrading. The main emphasis of the fieldwork would be on child health as affected by family, household, and community environment. This naturally also meant an understanding of the history of the settlement in this area as well as an understanding of its social structure.

Delays in funding meant that I had to start working in the Wadi, while at the same time carrying a heavy teaching load at Yarmouk University, Irbid (some ninety kilometers away from Amman). This did not provide the best context for fieldwork and necessitated the help of a full-time assistant in order to be able to carry out the fieldwork at all. We gradually established a routine whereby we would go to the Wadi for two or three consecutive days, while the rest of the week my assistant would work on the field-notes, to be reviewed later by me. We picked an initial sample of eighteen families from the 1980 survey, selecting for different household structures and for variations in terms of income and geographical location. But our selection was flexible and open to change for, as we went along, we naturally included other families who were part of the networks of those we visited.

### The Beginning

As opposed to the Circassian fieldwork, here was a bounded community, spatially and economically delimited. Although it soon became clear that being squatters per se was not necessarily the definitive feature of the community, yet—to me—coming down the steep stairs from the main road and descending into the jumble of concrete and tin houses below, there was a definite sense of coming into a self-contained world where any outsider was immediately discernible. There was a definite sense of being an intruder in a way that did not exist even in the adjacent areas.

Another immediate sensation was that this was a world composed mainly of women and children. Although, as we were to discover, young men gathered in the evenings at favorite spots in the alleys, at no time were men—fathers and husbands—much in evidence. Instead, they were to be found on the main street, in the coffee houses, or sitting in front of shops with their friends. To some extent, the whole of the Wadi is an extension of the private sphere of the home. The households themselves merge as their members, in particular the children, flow from one house into the other and overflow into the street. Whereas children are usually carefully dressed before going out into the main street, within the Wadi they run around half-dressed and barefoot. Infants crawl unhindered in and out of their courtyards in alleys where no vehicles can enter.

Socially, the Wadi is a stable community with a small amount of in- and outmigration. The residents have some sense of identity as co-squatters in this area, especially at times of insecurity, as when a land-owner threatens legal action, or when the threat of "the road" coming through is resurrected in the press. However, the most important networks and groups are kinship-based ones, which extend into adjacent neighborhoods, into the refugee camps, and beyond. Within the community, every two or three households form units among which reciprocity is most intensive. Women visit freely and constantly between these households, and the children eat, sleep, and play comfortably in whichever home they happen to be at a given moment. A tree or a rocky unbuilt area provides a gathering place for all the women of the adjacent households.

It was difficult to know how to begin fieldwork in the Wadi. The best way would have been to go with someone who had friends or relatives in the community, but I was unable to locate such a person. I did not feel like just going and knocking on a door. Nor did I want to go with the municipality officials who had worked in the area, since I did not want to be identified with any governmental institution. Thus, when a woman who was carrying out a short one-day survey in the area as part of her doctoral thesis offered to take me along, it seemed to me the best way of meeting people in this community.

Among the houses we visited that day was Um Abed's home. I felt very drawn to this woman, a large, self-confident person full of ideas on the upbringing of children, the behavior of neighbors, and other issues.

Another, in my view, attractive feature of Um Abed's household were her daughters. While the mother was being interviewed, I sat with Khawla, an eighteen-year-old who had just finished high school and was recovering from a badly burned leg. I was most impressed by her manner and interest in what I wanted to do, and thought she might be able to take me to relatives and neighbors who had small children. Here, I was unconsciously proceeding on a Circassian assumption that the unmarried daughter would be more free to help me than her mother. I knew that the families in the Wadi generally restricted the comings and goings of their daughters. But, when I heard that Khawla's blind older sister was attending university, I believed that this particular family accorded its daughters some freedom of movement. I was wrong, for I found out that the norms concerning what was acceptable behavior were imposed differently upon the different members of the same household. Furthermore, Khawla had a definite role in the household as the only daughter not attending school. On subsequent visits, I was never able to sit with her for any length of time since, once her leg had healed, she became a whirlwind of activity. Khawla was her mother's right hand and was gradually taking over the running of the household. Thus, it was Um Abed herself who was free to take me around the community.

On my next visit to Um Abed's house, I took my mother with me. During this visit, I explained to Um Abed that I was a teacher at Yarmouk University and what the purpose of my research was. All the families in the Wadi had a relative or acquaintance studying at the university and knew that people there did "research." Thus, though they had a rather vague idea of what research entails and were constantly surprised at how long it took us to finish it, such activity was not totally unfamiliar to them. The university affiliation also successfully established that I did not report to a governmental authority. Indeed, "university research" apparently did not hold any connotation of practical application for the people of the Wadi.

My mother and I also answered a great number of questions about ourselves. In a society where family is an all-important institution in structuring social relationships, it stands to reason that the people of the Wadi wished to place me within the context of a family. In the Circassian research, this presented no difficulty, since people knew my family, or at least knew of them through other Circassians. The situation differed in the Wadi, where my family was not known. As my mother and Um Abed talked about various things and compared mothers-in-law, a feeling of warmth and an air of "so you're not so different from us after all" was definitely established. Apart from helping to place me within a context, my mother's visit also established my respectability. It implied that my family knew of my activities. On my third visit to this household, I went through the same explanations for the benefit of Abu Abed, who welcomed me into the family and expressed his readiness to help me in any way. I had finally established my entrée into the community.

## A Wadi Household

Sitting in Um Abed's house, the contrast with my previous experience in Circassian households struck me immediately. Here nothing was familiar, everything was new. Um Abed's house was larger than average. Her husband had worked in a construction company for fifteen years. Although there had been lean periods when the construction industry was at an ebb and the company had withheld salaries for weeks on end, a period during which the household ate less well, Abu Abed was nonetheless among the luckier inhabitants of the Wadi in that he had a steady income.

When I first met the family, the house was composed of three rooms: the parents slept in one, the four boys in the other and the five daughters in the third. There was a partially roofed courtyard providing space for multiple purposes: cooking, washing, visiting. During exam periods, the six children who were attending school would be sprawled all over the yard, studying under their mother's strict eye. Two tiny rooms, which had belonged to Um Abed's parents-in-law before their death, now served as a kitchen and storage room. This is where the family also had their weekly baths. A separate toilet was at the far corner of the courtyard. The roof of the house was the private domain of the eldest son—who at the time was doing his compulsory military service—where he entertained his young male friends, who would hurriedly cross the courtyard and climb up the steep stairs along the side of the house.

Two of the daughters had been born blind. One was at a special school for blind children. The other, Feryal, was encouraged by her parents to continue her university education. Um Abed explained that this was necessary, since it was doubtful that Feryal would ever marry and so needed a means to support herself. The family therefore had to make the necessary sacrifices and suffer the expense of her schooling. Feryal had a small cubbyhole in which she studied, as well as a cassette recorder and a braille typewriter. The family had also paid to have a telephone connected so that Feryal could call her friends to arrange for lessons or for being picked up and taken to and from the university. Feryal was often out when we visited Um Abed's home, and was constantly making plans for more outings. She realized that she was privileged in the amount of free-dom she had. "Sometimes," she once explained, "I go too far and go out too much—but I've gotten used to it and can't stop."

On the other hand, Khawla, who wanted to attend university so much, was not allowed to do so since it was too expensive. In anger, she had refused to have her high school diploma framed and hung along with the others on the wall. She often made bitter jokes about having become a "professional" housekeeper and about the fact that she was only taking a short cut to marriage without the detour of a university education. Khawla's role in the household was typical for most girls in the Wadi. As daughters in a large family, young girls are gradually charged with a vari-ety of tasks and responsibilities. The process starts at a very young age with preschool children of both sexes being sent to run errands, borrow money from relatives, or come in to hold a younger sibling and give it its bottle. Children may also perform these services for neighbors and rela-tives living close by.

Once the child enters school, her or his tasks are somewhat de-creased. The exception is the elder girl who, from around the age of eight onward, will start to take on more household responsibilities and share in the care of younger siblings. By adolescence, the chores and errands that the young girl has been carrying out since her childhood will be trans-formed into active responsibility for specific household tasks (e.g. baking bread, preparing certain meals, and above all the daily chore of washing clothes). The mother may gradually hand these tasks over to her daugh-ter, but will tend to retain control, such as over the cooking of the main meal which requires her "special touch."

A very close relationship generally develops between mother and daughter. They begin to share authority over the younger children, and the elder daughter will tend to supervise their comings and goings, medi-ate in their quarrels, and so on. This is not to imply that major decisions will be in the elder daughter's hands. However, they may not be in the mother's hands either, but rather be considered the father's domain. The fact that the daughter reflects and shares the mother's role in the house-hold may be observed in the joking rivalry that tends to develop between them over the husband/father's attention and affection. It is interesting to note that even when several girls are out of school, or are of an age to run the household, only one, usually the eldest daughter, assumes this role. The others will tend to help out only by running errands and doing chores sporadically. Thus, they may have a significantly larger degree of leisure and freedom of movement in leaving the house and visiting rela-tives and girlfriends.

This relationship between mother and daughter is never completely cut off after the girl's marriage, so long as she continues to live nearby.

Especially later on in life, when her own daughter has taken over the running of the household, she will stop by her elderly mother's house and tend to her needs because "her daughters-in-law do not take care of her properly." At the same time, she will complain that in spite of all she does for her mother, the latter prefers the children of her sons and of her ungrateful daughters-in-law over her grandchildren through her daughters.

It is thus not difficult to understand that women often express the wish to bear daughters, saying that "a daughter remains for her family." Some women hope that their first-born will be a girl because a daughter is "a support for her mother." This stands in clear opposition to the husbands' attitude, namely that a girl is a continuous source of worry, even after she marries, whereas a son is no burden at all.

The situation in the Wadi households stood in contrast to what I had observed in Circassian homes. One such contrast was the overwhelming and continuing awareness of housework. Um Abed, relaxed and confident as she was, never felt compelled to sit with her visitor if she was cooking or supervising some task, while the older girls would be almost constantly scurrying back and forth. The tea, coffee, and fruit, although offered with complete sincerity and genuine hospitality, always left me with a sensation of having been prepared in a great hurry and in the midst of interrupting other chores. Although Um Abed's household may have carried this to extremes, this preoccupation with housework was typical in the Wadi households.

It was through observing the work in Um Abed's household, and specifically Khawla's role in it, that the importance of the daughter to her mother became obvious, to the extent that although there was a clear preference for boys, no woman would want to have male children only. As one woman with no daughters put it: "A girl stays loving to her mother, as for those (pointing to her four boys), they will all leave and pay me no attention. They will become like other men." Obviously, whereas a mother does not feel that she has any real authority over her sons, she believes that she has a hold over her daughter who is an important source of support.

## The Women of the Wadi

In the Wadi my female assistant and I found ourselves encapsulated in the women's world. This was partly due to the nature of our research.

However, it was also the only way to gain entry into this community where, in contrast with the Circassians, there was a definite women's world. When we did meet the men—husbands, fathers, sons—interesting conversations would follow which we would try to steer toward such issues as the history of the Wadi, and community problems and actions, in the belief that these were topics concerning which men would be more artic- ulate than women. However, such conversations would generally take place only if immediate family members were present. If there were other relatives or guests, then the men would sit apart and confine themselves to exchanging the briefest of greetings with us.

At the outset of my fieldwork in the Wadi, I had feared that the obvious fact that we differed from the women would prove to be too much of a barrier for friendships to develop. Would we be rejected because of the way we looked, dressed, and behaved? It turned out, however, that there existed categories in the Wadi into which we fit and which served to explain us.

Although they constituted an exception, there were nonetheless un- married women of our age who worked and therefore had a certain degree of freedom of movement. Muna, who was to become our friend, was one such woman of around thirty years of age who was supporting her two younger brothers through college by her job as a secretary in a well-paying institution. Originally from Gaza, her father had encouraged her to do well in school. In her last year of high school, her mother became ill with cancer. Since the father was in Saudi Arabia, Muna had to take over the running of the household and take on the care of her mother. This af- fected her school grades. Although her father had wanted her to go to the university, her exam average was insufficient. Instead, she went to a secre- tarial training center. Graduating at the top of her class, she had had a hard time finding a job since, as a refugee from Gaza, she was not a Jordanian citizen. She was eventually successful and had been working in the same place for nine years.

Living with her brothers, one married with four children and two in college, Muna occupied a rather peculiar position in the community. As she herself put it: "They do not approve of me, but they still like me." While this can to some extent be attributed to her personality, her stand- ing in the community went beyond this. Thus, it is Muna who is asked to inspect and give her opinion on the apartment that a bridegroom in the community is to provide for his bride. When Muna's younger sister quar- reled with her mother-in-law and came home in anger, it was understood that she was coming home to Muna and not to her brothers. In the period of negotiations that followed to effect a reconciliation between mother- and daughter-in-law, it was Muna who played the key role. This pointed to the fact that it was Muna who was perceived to be the head of the household, composed of herself and the two brothers she was supporting. Her other married brother, with whom she shared the house, was only in charge of his wife and children. But Muna nevertheless kept herself at some distance from the community and was often critical and caustic in her comments. She considered herself a rebel, not merely because she worked outside the house. She herself put more emphasis on the fact that she had refused to marry her first cousin.

Thus, we two fit into one category, namely that of working unmarried women. We also fit into another category, that of being *madani* (townsfolk) as opposed to *fallahi* (peasants). Even though most of the people thus categorizing us had been born in Amman or in other cities, especially after the emigration from their villages in Palestine, they still regarded themselves as *fallahi*. When asked to describe the difference between the two categories, interestingly enough place of origin was never referred to spontaneously. Rather the differences were seen in terms of dress, makeup, and dialect. When asked whether place of birth was not the crucial factor, some agreed, but many disagreed, saying that this would make them all *madani*, which was not true. A *madani* woman was one who wore short skirts and not the Palestinian embroidered dress (this fact applied to all the young girls in the Wadi); a *madani* woman wore makeup (which we did not, but many of them did); and finally a *madani* woman spoke differently, with a city dialect (which we did, as did some of the Wadi women, but only outside—never within the home). Being *madani* was thus such a fluid concept that we could fit somewhere within its sphere. Still, every now and then, if we used a word or said something that identified us as *madani*, someone might ask us in surprise: "Are you *madani* then?" And another woman would answer her: "Of course they are, can't you tell?" Alternatively, when mentioning an aspect of our family life or ideas on marriage and customs that brought us closer together, there would be the pleased comment: "So, you are *fallahi* after all."

The real factors that made me an outsider were class and ethnicity. In my opinion, the former variable was more determinant than the latter. In terms of ethnicity, many women were not sure who the Circassians were and I did not elaborate on the issue. The subject was mostly brought up because of my Circassian first name. However, the conversation rarely led to a discussion of origin, but rather to questions of marriage customs and Circassian food. The fact that my father was from Tiberias in Palestine also helped bridge the ethnicity gap. In addition, however, each village and region in Palestine is perceived to have its own "customs." Thus, when they asked me about "your customs of marriage," for example, they were not referring to anything more foreign than the equally strange customs of their next-door neighbor of forty years who originally came from a different region in Palestine. Their neighbors were also seen as speaking different "languages," and examples were constantly being given about differences in dialect. Coming from a complex social order in Palestine, the women of the Wadi were not at all unidimensional in their perception of social groups.

Although the class factor is not to be minimized, there were other factors that brought us together. The best proof of this was that class differences did not prevent the development of friendships and warm relationships between us and the women of the Wadi. In some ways, being outsiders meant that we were not an integral part of the complex networks wrought by the women and were thus not identified with any one family or group. As one young woman who was going through a difficult period of negotiating her status with her husband's family put it: "I really wait for your visits and miss you more than I miss my sisters. I can tell you all sorts of things, and I know you understand and that it will not cause me trouble to tell you these things, the way it does if I talk to someone else."

## In Retrospect

It may at first seem that doing research in one's childhood environment and speaking familiar languages is the very antithesis of what fieldwork is "supposed" to be. However, adding the role of researcher to one's preexisting role-set means contact with groups, ideas and events that would otherwise never have been experienced. Thus, an already well-known fact in anthropology is confirmed: that cultures, beyond the simplest small-scale societies, are not homogeneous. The indigenous anthropologist does not come into the field with all the knowledge and experiences generated by the various and complex structures of society. The two fieldwork experiences I have described raised quite different methodological and theoretical questions. The nature and objectives of the research determined which aspects of my identity were relevant in the establishment of rapport and thus what kind of data was made available to me.

Fieldwork among the Circassians posed a number of difficulties for the traditional anthropological method of participant observation. Since I did not want to limit my study to one group within the community, this meant that I had to secure access to all sectors of Circassian society, which cut across many classes and residential areas. This necessarily required a great deal of freedom of movement as I moved at all hours from wealthy neighborhoods to small houses, to villages, to farms, to offices, to clubs and associations. The Circassian community did not represent one specific life-style or one set of behavior. This made it imperative that I not be restricted to the women's world in the community. Circassian cultural attitudes of relative permissiveness toward unmarried women were undoubtedly a facilitating factor. In addition, the fact that I lived with my parents established my respectability, while at the same time giving me the required mobility. The latter would certainly have been restricted if I had lived with another Circassian family, an action that, incidentally, would have been very hard to explain.

In the Circassian research, I felt that all avenues were open to me. Common ethnicity overrode class and gender differences. Being the daughter and granddaughter of people whom my informants knew or could remember, would immediately establish the atmosphere of trust which is essential for good rapport. In addition, the fact of my being Circassian established in my informants' eyes enough motivation on my part to be involved in such a research project. While other anthropologists may often have to justify their interest, mine was automatically put down to "ethnic patriotism." This allowed me access to information, opinions, and emotions that I have no doubt would have been denied to a non-Circassian. On the other hand, it also laid a heavy responsibility upon me. To a community that was undergoing a great deal of change and anxiety about its ethnic identity, my research seemed to confirm its "specialness" and the reality of its cultural distinctiveness. Often my informants would thank me for my efforts, irrespective of whether they expected to see any results from the fieldwork. There was a certain insistence that I be present at every meeting, every wedding, and every gathering. My presence somehow became proof of the "Circassianness" of the event.

This impelled me to observe a strict neutrality vis-à-vis the various groups and factions in the community. I could not spend too much time with or be recruited into the activities of one particular organization or club at the expense of others. This was not difficult, since there was a definite limit to my identification with these types of activities. Although they interested me as data, they did not engage my sense of identity. Yet, sitting in Lina's house, there would be no strain or feeling of distance. I have no doubt that if my research topic had entailed a close examination of family dynamics, this would have required a great deal more conscious effort on my part to question and note behavior and nuances that were too familiar to me.

As opposed to the Circassian research, my participation in the life of the Wadi was very much structured by the variables of class and gender. Since the actual topic of research concerned child health and the domain of women, I naturally did not attempt to break out of this sphere. However, access to the men of the community was still important for certain kinds of data. I only sought such access via the women, that is, by becoming an accepted member in the family. I did not try to enter the men's world on their own terms, as I had in the Circassian research. This was essential for maintaining my credibility in the eyes of the community, since the Wadi was much more sex-segregated than the Circassian community.

Another important factor was that the Wadi was a much more spatially defined community. Thus, the mores imposed on women were imposed upon me as well, as soon as I entered the community. This fact limited my access to data on certain kinds of community action and decision making. Although I could hear about such events from the men in the families that I visited, I could not observe them first hand or meet and talk to all those involved. As for the class difference, while it helped explain my research activity as a necessary part of my job, as well as my mobility in and out of the Wadi, it nevertheless created a gap that had to be negotiated and overcome mostly by my personal behavior and attitude. As one woman put it: "When we first heard that you were a university professor, we were worried about what you would think of us and the way we live. But you have been so simple and natural that now I think you can go into any house in the Wadi and be welcome." It is clear to me that the evaluation of my behavior as "natural" was due to my conducting research within the boundaries defined for the women in the Wadi community.

Comparing these two experiences brings into focus the oversimplification of considering both communities as my "own" in the same way. In both cases there were ideas, values, and patterns that I recognized immediately. In no sense, however, was my fieldwork a confirmation of things that I already knew. And if, after my first research, I felt that I now "knew" Jordanian society, then the second research once again threw this knowledge into doubt. The contrast between Circassian households with their understated discipline and the Wadi households with their bustle and life; the different roles and relationships between mothers and daughters, men and women; Lina and Muna—both firmly part of their community, and yet stepping out of the roles prescribed for them. All these contrasts show up the difficulties involved in generalizing about "Middle Eastern society" and "Middle Eastern women."

## Notes

1.  According to a 1980 survey of the area, the average size of a household was 6.58, with a density of 3.54 persons per room. The average income of the household was JD 90/month possibly earned by two members of the household. Work was mostly in small-scale workshops, the construction industry and low-level government employment (see Urban Development Department, 1980: Summary Tables of Comprehensive Social-Physical Survey, Amman). Services such as water, electricity, and sewage were only extended gradually into the community after 1969, and the area is still largely dependent upon services such as schools and clinics provided by UNRWA to the camp. The main environmental problem is the wide ditch that cuts through the settlement, carrying waste water, sewage, and rain water, and causing floods in the winter.

My research on the Circassians was supported in part by a grant from the National Science Foundation (grant no. 7912265) and a grant from the Wenner-Gren Foundation for Anthropological Research, Inc. The dissertation was entitled "Ethnicity and Leadership: The Circassians in Jordan" (unpublished Ph.D. dissertation, University of California, Berkeley, 1982).

My research on the Wadi was made possible by a grant from the International Development and Research Center in Canada. The anthropological study was one component of the "Amman Follow-Up Health and Population Assessment" project, co-directed by Dr. Leila Bisharat and Dr. Seteney Shami, and conducted under the auspices of the Urban Development Department, Municipality of Amman. A special acknowledgement is due to Ms. Lucine Taminian, graduate student at the Institute of Archaeology and Anthropology, Yarmouk University, and research assistant on the anthropology study.

# 7

# Fieldwork of a Dutiful Daughter

LILA ABU-LUGHOD

I n the summer of 1985 I returned to the Bedouin community in the Egyptian Western Desert in which I had spent nearly two years doing fieldwork. Five years had passed since I had left to go home (to the U.S.) to write my dissertation. I was excited about visiting the people with whom I had not only lived for the period of fieldwork, but in a strange way even more intensely in the following years as I thought and wrote about them. I wanted to know what had happened to them but I also wanted to make them real again. My memories had become increasingly limited to those incidents I had incorporated into my writings and those aspects of their lives I had analyzed. In the process of abstracting from my field notes and putting together a picture of their lives through reflection on my experiences with them, I feared I had made of them something mythical.[1]

Seeing them again was exhilarating but also jarring. I had forgotten much that I had come to take for granted when I lived among them, especially concerning the nature of my relationship with them. Although a great deal happened during my short visit, to highlight the issues about field research that I want to explore in this chapter I will recount two aspects of the experience that I found emotionally difficult.

I was welcomed back with tremendous warmth tempered with formality that included the special treatment accorded all guests. This treat-

139

ment was reminiscent of what I had often observed when family members, like sisters and daughters who had married out of the community, returned home for visits. I thought that some of the formality might have been in recognition of my achievements: I had received my degree and obtained a job as a professor. I had brought a nicely bound copy of my dissertation as a gift, figuring that even if people could not read it, they would know I had written a book that was a tribute to them. But people expressed little interest in the dissertation, felt deeply sorry for me when I described the life I was leading, and were concerned with only one thing: Was I married and had I had any children? I had fully anticipated being asked about these matters, but was surprised by the way that hardly a moment after greeting me, women would begin questioning me. Even the men asked each other under their breath. This reaction confirmed what I already suspected and had, during my fieldwork, encouraged and at times resented, namely, that they saw me primarily as a female. It was hard not to feel inadequate as women excitedly told me of the young women in the camp who, in my absence, had married and had one or two children, and generously shared with me various magical cures for barrenness.

The visit was personally trying in another way. I sensed a greater emphasis on piety and Muslim identity, which may have been an artifact of the timing of my visit; it was right before the Great Feast ('id), always a period of heightened religious activity and sentiment. It might also have applied only to the families to whom I was the closest, families from which several members had in recent years gone on the pilgrimage to Mecca. Or perhaps I had just forgotten what it was like to live in the Middle East. In any case, unlike in the past, I felt that the fact that I never prayed was conspicuous. Even more problematic were my host's disquisitions on the subject of religion. On several occasions he lectured me on the glories of the Quran, the importance of living where one was surrounded by Muslims, and the dangers of living with the infidels (if you live with them you become like them). He assured me of God's grace toward those who return to the faith. Asking me questions about my life in the U.S. inevitably led to suggestions that I should move to Egypt. These were not unfamiliar themes. He had often spoken to me of such matters in the past, but this time his tone was more urgent, and my discomfort and sense of hypocrisy more acute. The problem was that I had presented myself and was perceived as the daughter of an Arab and a Muslim. Yet, I was also the daughter of an American, had been born and raised in the U.S., was in numerous ways culturally more American than Arab, and I was not religious.

Both factors, that I was a woman and that I was of Arab descent, had consequences for the sort of research I could do and the types of relationships I could establish in the field. Furthermore, these two aspects of my identity combined to place me in the position of what I will call a dutiful daughter. And being a dutiful daughter doing fieldwork led to a privileged view of one crucial issue in Arab society, the meaning of modesty for women. Thus, with the contributors to this volume I share the experience of being a woman studying in a sex-segregated society. Unlike most of them, I was in the peculiar situation of being neither completely a cultural insider, nor a total outsider. As an Arab-American, I was in an ambiguous position that, as I will show, had both advantages and awkward disadvantages.

### Initial Contact

The terms of my relationship with the families with whom I had lived had been set during my fieldwork in 1978–1980, so I will describe that experience before exploring the consequences of these terms. I had arrived in Cairo at the beginning of October 1978 and had ensconced myself in an unpretentious pension frequented by generations of Arabists, Egyptologists, and scholars of modest means. In the many years since I had last stayed there as a young girl traveling with my family, nothing much had changed. This meant, of course, that the lumpy beds, the plumbing, and the gentle hotel personnel bore the inevitable marks of old age. Outside, however, the city seemed to be in the throes of change. The progressive dilapidation of old buildings had in some cases led to their collapse, and in other parts of the city, construction of massive new luxury hotels was under way.

I familiarized myself with the city, more crowded and noisy than ever, and awaited my father's arrival. Here the reader might pause. I suspect few, if any, fathers of anthropologists accompany them to the field to make their initial contacts. But my father had insisted that he had some business in Egypt and might just as well plan his trip to coincide with mine. I had accepted his offer only reluctantly, glad to have the company, but also a bit embarrassed by the idea. I did, after all, like to consider myself an adult.

Only after living with the Bedouins for a long time did I begin to comprehend some of what had underlain my father's quiet but firm insistence. As an Arab, although by no means a Bedouin, he knew his own culture and society well enough to know that a young unmarried woman traveling alone on uncertain business was an anomaly. She would be suspect and would have a hard time persuading people of her respectability. I knew of the negative image of Western women, an image fed by rumor, films, and insensitivity to local standards of morality and ways of communicating. But I had assumed I would be able to overcome people's suspicions, first by playing up the Arab half of my identity and not identifying with Westerners, and second by behaving properly. I was confident of my sensitivity to cultural expectations because of my background. Not only had I lived in Egypt for four years as a child, but more significantly, I had also spent many summers with relatives in Jordan. Being part of that household carried with it expectations about conformity to the codes of conduct appropriate to Arab girls. My many cousins had also provided models. I felt I had internalized much that would help me find my way with the Bedouins and not offend them.

What I had not considered was that respectability was reckoned not just in terms of behavior in interpersonal interactions, but in the relationship to the larger social world. I had failed to anticipate that people such as the Bedouins, for whom belonging to tribe and family are paramount and the education of girls novel, would assume that a woman alone must have so alienated her family, especially her male kin, that they no longer cared about her. Worse still, they might suspect that she had done something so immoral that her family had ostracized her. Any girl valued by her family would not be left unprotected, to travel alone at the mercy of anyone who wished to take advantage of her. This applied especially to an unmarried girl whose virginity and reputation were critical to a good match. By accompanying me, my father probably hoped to lay all such suspicions to rest.

So after making contacts in Cairo, we set off for Alexandria. There we spoke with social researchers conducting a study of the Mariut Extension, the site of a land reclamation and resettlement scheme in the Western Desert. The director of field research generously offered us accommodation, and a promise to introduce us to his Bedouin contact. When we drove out to this town and met this man, my father explained that his daughter, who had been raised in the United States, wished to improve her Arabic and to learn about their society, and would need to find a good family with whom to live. After some deliberation, the man guided us to a hamlet consisting of scattered houses and tents. We were greeted by a number of men. My father went with them into one of the houses while I, along with a couple of the female researchers from the Mariut Project, were invited by the women into a nearby tent. We did not stay long, piling into the van over the protests of our hosts who wished to slaughter a sheep for us, as they would for any honored guest. The Haj, head of the community, was not there. Instead my father had spoken with his brothers, and had left him a letter explaining the situation and placing me under his protection. When I returned the next day, the Haj welcomed me and said that he would be happy to have me live with them.

## The Partial Insider

This introduction to the community profoundly affected my position and the nature of the work I could do. First, it identified me, despite my initially poor linguistic skills and apparent foreign mannerism and dress, as a Muslim and an Arab. My Muslim credentials were shaky, since I did not pray, and they knew that my mother was an American. But most assumed that I shared with them a fundamental identity as a Muslim, and my father's speech was no doubt so sprinkled with religious phrases that they believed in his piety. This rubbed off on me. Many times during my stay, I was confronted with the critical importance of these traits to their acceptance of me. As always, the old women and the young children bluntly stated what most adults were too polite to say. The hostility they felt toward Europeans (*nasara* or Christians) came out in violent objections the children had to my listening to English radio broadcasts; an old woman's horror at the thought of drinking out of a teacup a European woman visitor had just used; and comments made about an American friend who came out to visit me (whom they liked very much) that she was good "for someone of her religion."[2]

It was also clear that I came from a good family and good stock, so they could accept me as a member of their household without compromising their social standing. They often mentioned my father's beautiful Arabic and the fact that he was not an Egyptian but "from Jordan," as he had been introduced. These Bedouins believe that all non-Egyptian Arabs are Bedouins, speaking a decent dialect and living as they themselves do. So they considered my father a fellow tribesman and a person with noble roots (*asl*), a characteristic linked to morality that they deny to settled Egyptians.[3]

This raises an important point regarding the issues under consideration in this volume. While the limitations of access and acceptance of the total outsider are obvious, the limitations of being an insider have only recently begun to be seriously examined.[4] It must be remembered that the insider, for example the Arab studying an Arab group, will identify and be identified with a particular class and way of life, not to mention nationality and ethnic group. As long as anthropologists do not "study up" as Laura Nader (1969) advocates, or study their own class (as did Altorki 1982, 1986), they will be distinguished from those they study by greater wealth, education, and standard of living in a way that leads their informants to liken them to other relationships with social superiors or members of the dominant groups in the country. Foreigners, except in colonial situations, might be less easy to place socially because they would not fit into a ready-made social status.

Had I been an Egyptian (non-Bedouin), I would certainly have faced a set of problems my non-Egyptian identity allowed me to avoid. The Awlad Ali Bedouins are a somewhat suspect minority within the Egyptian state who resent the increasing imposition of state authority and restrictions on their activities. They distinguish themselves clearly from settled "Egyptians" or "people of the Nile Valley" (hal wadi n-nil), urban and rural, in linguistic, sartorial, cultural, and moral terms. Although always polite to Egyptian researchers and others, the Bedouins I knew were ambivalent about these people and guarded in their relations with them. In part this was because Egyptians were associated with the government. Partly it may have been because Egyptians had attitudes of superiority based on their greater education and "modernity." But it was also because of the antipathy Bedouins feel toward these people whom they perceive as less moral and less pious, qualities they attribute to an inferior bloodline.

Blood, in the sense of genealogy, is the basis of Awlad Ali identity. No matter where or how they live, those who can link themselves genealogically to any of the tribes of the Western Desert are 'arab, as opposed to Egyptians. The use of the term Arab to distinguish themselves from their Egyptian neighbors implies the Bedouin claim to origins in the Arabian Peninsula and genealogical links to the pure Arab tribes who were the first followers of the Prophet Muhammad. It also suggests their affinity to all the Arabic-speaking Muslims of the Middle East and North Africa who, because of the commonality of origin, they assume to be just like themselves.

In contrast, some Bedouins characterized Egyptians as mixed-blooded or impure. Others attributed to the Egyptians Pharaonic origins, as the following story of their ancestry told to me by one Bedouin man suggested:

"When Moses escaped from Egypt, the Pharaoh and all of the real men, the warriors, set off after him. They left behind only the women, children and servants/slaves (khadama). These were the weak men who washed women's feet and cared for the children. When Moses crossed the Red Sea, the Pharaoh's men drowned chasing him. This left only the servants. They are the grandfathers (ancestors) of the Egyptians. That is why they are like that now. The men are women and the women are men. The man carries the children and does not take a seat until he sees that she has."

At the bottom of this concern with ancestry is the belief that people's nature and worth are closely tied to the worthiness of their stock. Nobility of origin is believed to confer moral qualities and character. By crediting Egyptians with no line to the past, or more insulting, a line to an inferior, pre-Islamic past of servitude, this man was making a statement about their present worthlessness. The ignominy of origin is a metaphor for present shortcomings. Bedouins value a constellation of qualities that could be captured by the phrase "the honor code." Although the content of this code cannot be explored here, a few of the Bedouins' criticisms of Egyptians are telling.[5] Men variously described Egyptians as lacking in moral excellence, honor, sincerity, honesty, and generosity, at the same time claiming these as Bedouin traits. They consider Egyptian men cowardly and fearful and Egyptian women lacking in modesty and propriety. The ease of social intercourse between Egyptian men and women and the perception that Egyptian women rule their men are special sources of the Bedouins' disdain and sense of moral superiority.

The Bedouins' attitudes toward actual Egyptian individuals they encounter are more complex than these abstract statements suggest. Many of the ideas the Bedouins have about Egyptians are based on hearsay and the imposition of their own interpretations on reported behavior. Few of those living in the desert have much opportunity to see Egyptians at home or to interact closely with them. But sometimes, as the following incident shows, their ideas are confirmed when they have such opportunities. During the holidays celebrating the Prophet's birthday, an Egyptian army officer, friend and business-partner of the Haj, decided to bring his family for a weekend visit to the Western Desert. Before going to a beach resort, the family spent a day and a night with us. The officer was a powerful man spoken of with a certain awe. These were city people who were accustomed to a certain standard of living. The Bedouins knew that. They went all out to treat them as honored guests. Their visit occasioned a great deal of commotion including the purchase and preparation of special foods, a massive cleanup, and the rearrangement of the household to vacate rooms for their comfortable accommodation.

Given what everyone knew about the laxness of sex segregation among the Egyptians, they were not surprised that the women and girls ate with the men and spent time as a group in the men's guest room. However, the evening's events were unexpected. After dinner, the man, his wife, their daughter, and his wife's sister all retired to their rooms, only to emerge in nightclothes and bathrobes. They then sat in the men's guest room chatting with their host and his brothers. This immodesty of dress sent waves of shock through the community. Next, people were scandalized when they realized that husband and wife intended to sleep in the same room. Although the Bedouin husbands and wives sleep together under normal circumstances, they would not do so when visiting; each would sleep with members of his or her own sex in the same room as the guests. The public admission of active sexuality implied by the couple's wish to sleep in the same room was considered the height of immodesty. Yet everyone was polite, the values of friendship and hospitality outweighing the deeply offended sense of propriety. Perhaps even more importantly, the Bedouins excused their guests' behavior because they recognized that the Egyptians were another sort of people whose lack of pedigree made it difficult (although not impossible) for them to behave with honor.

A second indication of the ambivalence Bedouins feel toward Egyptians is the way they treated young university women who worked on social research projects in Bedouin areas. Such young women would turn up periodically to fill out questionnaires on a variety of subjects. In the women's world, they were treated graciously, respected for their education and their clean elegance and embraced for their vulnerability as young women for whom the Bedouin women and children felt an empathic affection. Mixed with the fascination with their clothes and jewelry and their marital statuses was a confusion about the meaning of the more scandalous and improper aspects of their dress: their loose, uncovered hair, painted nails, eyeshadow, and lipstick.

As I came to understand how the Bedouins perceived the Egyptians, I was glad that they saw me as distinct, and grateful that my father's being a different sort of Arab had enabled me to be incorporated as a morally superior "tribal" Arab. It also cleared me of political suspicion, for if outsider anthropologists are often suspected of being CIA agents, indigenous anthropologists are suspected of being government agents. Since, wittingly or unwittingly, many Awlad Ali live outside the law, carrying unlicensed firearms, smuggling, avoiding conscription, and trying their own cases according to customary law, their relationship with the Egyptian government authorities is tense. An incident that occurred within the first month of my stay immediately reassured members of my community that I was not a government agent. I had gone, with the Haj and the Field Director of the Social Research Center project, to inform the district's Security Officer of my presence and my intent to study the Bedouins. A few days later, while I was away in Cairo, the Security Officer and his men came to the house. According to the Haj's wife, they questioned my new hosts about me and asked to search my suitcases. The Bedouins refused to let them, telling them my suitcases were locked (which they were not). My hosts were angry. I, like them, now appeared to be the victim of what they perceive as government harassment, which they always find an affront, and they felt protective.

Their acceptance of me as someone without the upper- or middle-class pretensions of Egyptian city people was made easier by my own behavior. Although the Bedouins disparage people of the Nile Valley, they do recognize that these people, especially from the urban areas, also entertain fears and prejudices about them. Many perceive the Bedouins as backward, dirty, uncouth, untrustworthy, and rough. Others more sympathetic to them merely wish to educate and assimilate them, seeing their way of life as an embarrassing anachronism in today's Arab world.

Perhaps it was because I did not share any of these views that people said of me that my "nose was not up in the sky." It may have been an advantage for me to be familiar with, but not from, any particular Arab society, so that I did not see them through the lens of common Middle Eastern assumptions about the place of Bedouins in society. I had always been intrigued with nomads and had been attracted by their image as free and noble. My assumptions about them were Western ones, positive and perhaps overly romantic. In fact, I had at first been disappointed to find that the Awlad Ali were sedentarized, living mostly in houses rather than tents, riding in Toyota trucks rather than on camels. But I later became convinced that the Bedouin social system and ideology represented the essence of the system found in other Arab societies.

I was actually surprised at the extent to which Bedouin attitudes toward kinship and family, and toward morality in particular, were familiar to me because of my background. A whole set of experiences I had had with my paternal relatives, my grandmother, aunts, uncles, and cousins, and even conflicts I had had with my father as I was growing up in America and wanting to be like other Americans, illuminated what I was seeing among Awlad Ali. At the same time, what Awlad Ali explained to me also helped me to interpret the fragments of that Arab part of my life that had not seemed to make sense because I had never experienced them as part of an ongoing social and cultural system. Insofar as I was an insider, someone who had lived at times in the Arab world (in Egypt, Jordan, and Lebanon), who was treated in certain contexts as a member of an Arab family network, and who identified with aspects of the culture and people, I had the indisputable advantage of encountering the familiar and having a head start in understanding the basics of what I saw (cf. Nakhleh 1979; Messerschmidt 1981; Fahim 1982a).

But I also faced the problem of only being partially culturally Arab. First, although Arabic was quite familiar to me and I could get along in it in Cairo or among Palestinians, even if I could not say much that I wanted to, the Bedouin dialect was totally unfamiliar and initially incomprehensible to me. I suspect someone whose mother tongue was Arabic would have picked up the Bedouins' Libyan dialect more quickly than I did, but I did not have the basic fluency in Arabic upon which to build. Men were the easiest to understand and when women spoke directly to me, I fared better than when I listened, uncomprehending for long months, to high-speed conversations among themselves. It was from the children and from the way people spoke to them that I picked up the basics of the Bedouin vocabulary.

Second, the presumption that I was an Arab and a Muslim led my hosts to expect me to be less ignorant than I was. This was most difficult in matters of religion, where confessing ignorance would have been tantamount to admitting religious failings that would have implicated my father's piety (that he had not made sure that I was properly educated in religious matters). The fear of revealing my ignorance hampered my investigations in these areas and as a consequence, I do not have the rich data many other anthropologists interested in forms of Islam might have.

More serious were the problems raised by the sense of inauthenticity or hypocrisy I sometimes experienced because I was only partially what and who I said I was. This came up in my description of the experiences I had in the summer of 1985. What had bothered me most during fieldwork was that I initially felt that my relationship with the people with whom I lived was not symmetrical. I do not mean this in the usual sense of a power or wealth differential in the anthropologist's favor since, as I will discuss below, I was a dependent and daughter with nothing to offer but my company. Rather, I was asking them to be honest and was trying to find out what their lives were like, but was unwilling to reveal much about myself. I was presenting them with a persona. They knew nothing of my life in the U.S.—my friends, family, university, apartment—in short, much of what I considered part of my identity. I felt compelled to lie to them about some aspects of this life, simply because they could not have helped judging it and me in their own terms. In that scheme, my reputation as a young woman would have suffered. So I doctored my descriptions, and changed the subject when they asked about me, but I felt uncomfortable doing so. For instance, because an unmarried woman could not possibly live alone in their society, I found myself having to leave them with the impression that Harvard University was in Chicago because they knew I was a Harvard student but never imagined that I did not live in my father's household, which was, they knew, in Chicago.

Unlike other anthropologists who not only can present themselves as different, but can use the difference as a way of stimulating comparative discussion, I had to disassociate myself as much as possible from Americans. With my Arab identity, I dared not say: "Where I come from, they do such and such." What bits they heard about life in America were sufficient to make them doubt my father's wisdom in choosing to live and bring up his children among non-Muslims. To have become associated with Americans, as a woman, would not have meant being modern, wealthy, or powerful, but immoral and "fallen."

How ethical was it to present myself in a way that could be interpreted as false, to pretend that I shared their values and lived as they did even when I was away from them? I felt compelled to do this because my father had presented me as his daughter and they had accepted me on the grounds that I was an Arab and Muslim. They included me in their moral community, a position that imposed a set of imperatives and constraints on me. I wanted to be accepted, and I also felt that I *was* a moral person—it was just that I did not define morality by some of the terms they used, particularly for women. Gradually my sense of inauthenticity subsided. As I participated more fully in the community, loosened my ties to my other life, and as we came to share a common history and set of experiences on which we could build our relationships, I *became* the person that I was with them. Although there always remained an asymmetry in the fact that I was writing about them, and observing perhaps a bit more closely than they were, for the most part I felt that our interactions were genuine.

The consequences for my research of being included in the Bedouins' moral community, in particular with regard to their expectations of daughters, will be explored below. Before that, I want to consider another aspect of the way they perceived and incorporated me into their social world. Perhaps because I did not claim and was not accorded superior class privilege or special power, I was rarely treated as an honorary male as are many women anthropologists. On the contrary, as their anxious questioning about my reproductive status during my return visit indicates, they saw me as a female.

### In the Women's World

By accompanying me, my father had shown those with whom I would be living and those on whose good opinion and generosity my life and work would depend, that I was a daughter of a good family whose male kin were concerned about her and wanted to protect her, even when pursuit of education forced her into potentially compromising positions. The Haj and his relatives took seriously their obligation to my father who had entrusted them with my care. Although the Haj understood that I was there to find out about their customs and traditions ('adat wtaqalid), and in our initial chat even assured me that I must feel free to go anywhere that my study required so long as I informed him of my whereabouts, I soon discovered that this was not to be the case. Through subtle cues by tactful but determined adults, I came to understand that I was free to go anywhere within the camp, but that to step beyond the bounds of the community, particularly alone, was not appropriate.

The restrictions on my movements had several motives. As the Haj explained to me in an exasperated moment, they feared for my safety. They would be responsible if anything happened to me, and they did not relish the idea of becoming embroiled in vengeance matters. Also, by living with them, I was automatically identified as a member of their family. Perceived by all as one of the women in the Haj's kin group, my actions reflected on them and affected their reputations. They had to make sure that I did nothing that could compromise them by insuring that, as far as possible, I conformed to the same standards of propriety their women did. This meant that I was restricted in where I could go, by whom I could be seen, and with whom I could speak.

As a woman, I found myself confronted with difficulties not faced by male researchers, but also advantages of access and the unexpected pleasures of intimacy in the women's world. In my first few weeks I tried to move back and forth between the men's and women's worlds. Then I realized that I would have to declare my loyalties firmly in order to be accepted in either. With the exception of the Haj, whom I got to know very well through almost daily conversations and occasional long car rides to Cairo, I found visits with the men boring because of the limited range of topics we could politely cover. So I opted for the women's world, where relations were more informal, refusing with increasing frequency the men's call to leave the women's company and join them. My polite refusals met with silent approbation from the women and girls, and so I was gradually incorporated into their worlds, involved in their activities and made privy to their secrets.

Although the extreme sex segregation characteristic of certain settled or urban groups, where there is a rigid division between public and private worlds, does not characterize Bedouin social life, there is little doubt that the extent to which these men and women live separate lives has increased with sedentarization. The social avoidance between certain categories of men and women, necessary to the moral code of honor and modesty, has ossified with the move from tents to houses.[6] When Awlad Ali lived in tents, a blanket suspended in the middle of the tent separated male and female domains if men other than close kin were present. Unlike walls, the blankets were both temporary and permeable, allowing the flow of conversation and information. Now that most Bedouins live in houses (even though they pitch their tents next to them), they build a separate men's room for receiving guests, set apart from the rest of the rooms, each of which belongs to one woman and her children. Greater involvement in the market economy has led to an increasing confinement of women to the household and camp as their traditional tasks of gathering firewood and milking the sheep become less necessary. By contrast, men's mobility and social contacts have widened. Still, it must be recalled that the Bedouin world is defined primarily by kinship, which links both men and women, and their code of modesty prescribes formality between unrelated men and women and between women and older men.

Some might consider my concentration on the women's world a limitation. In many ways, however, my access to both worlds was more balanced than a man's would be.[7] Except in rare instances, male researchers in sex-segregated societies have far less access to women than I had to men. Not only was my host an extremely articulate and generous informant about himself and his culture, but his younger brother, sons, and nephews, as well as the men of client status, were all frequent visitors in the women's world with whom I could speak relatively freely. Furthermore, the structure of information flow between the men's and women's worlds was not symmetrical. Because of the pattern of hierarchy, men spoke to one another in the presence of women, while the reverse was not true. In addition, young and low-status men served as informants on men's affairs to mothers, aunts, grandmothers, and wives, whereas no one brought news to the adult men. As I and others working in sex-segregated Arab societies have shown, a conspiracy of silence excludes men from the women's world (cf. Dwyer 1978; Makhlouf 1979; Abu-Lughod 1985a).

Furthermore, I would argue that not only is there no need to apologize for choosing to participate in the women's world, but that the choice entails numerous positive gains. The epistemological issues raised by careful reflection on the relationship between gender and ethnography are profound and complex. I consider ways in which gender shaped my analysis of Bedouin social life in the conclusion and reflect on more general issues elsewhere (Abu-Lughod 1984). Here I will only briefly note three consequences of participation in the women's world. First, an obvious point: since women constitute half of society, a study that focuses on their lives, treats them as actors, subjects rather than objects in social life, presents a no less partial picture of a society and culture than a study focusing on men. Second, the extent to which in a sexually dichotomous society, women's interests, concerns and even experiences of the central institutions of social life might differ from that of men, can be discovered through investigations in this women's world. To explore how social "reality" is structured by social experience as determined by social position is an important new enterprise. In my case, concentrating on the women led me to discover the importance of a genre of personal poetry that revealed aspects of interpersonal relations never mentioned in other studies of the Bedouins. Finally, the very human rewards of being able to have close personal encounters cannot be ignored. In a sex-segregated society, to expect this between members of the opposite sex is foolish. The Bedouin women I knew had a keen sense of what they assumed were the universal pains and pleasures of womanhood and they included me in their world. When I returned later for my summer visit, they all wanted to fill me in on what to them were among the most exciting events—the weddings that had taken place since I had left. They did this by recounting the songs that had been sung at each of the weddings involving members of "our" community. More moving, however, was what happened one afternoon when I asked the Haj's senior wife to sing a few songs so that I could tape-record them. As she sang, her oldest daughter began to cry. I was bewildered. Later the girl explained that it was because her mother was singing songs about my sad fate in love. Her mother had pitied me, empathized, and found traditional Bedouin poem-songs that described my predicament. Hearing about her "sister's" troubles saddened the daughter. They felt that they had understood me, and I was touched that they cared.

### A Dutiful Daughter

In Bedouin society, one can hardly talk about "women" in general. Every woman is a sister, daughter, wife, mother, or aunt and it is the role and relationship that usually determines how she will be perceived and treated. Having been introduced to the community as my father's daughter and being fairly young, unmarried, and childless, I was assigned and took the role of an adoptive daughter.[8] My protection and restriction were entailments of this relationship, but so was my participation in the household, my identification with the kin group, and the process by which I learned about the culture, a sort of socialization to the role.

Although I never completely lost my status as a guest in the Haj's household, my role as daughter superseded it. This caused some hardships. The choice pieces of meat the women initially set aside for me were later offered to other guests instead. I became part of the backstage when we had company, found myself contributing to household work more than I wished, and had my own chores. Men occasionally shouted commands at me, and felt free, even at night, to get me up, along with the girls who shared my room, to prepare tea for visitors.

In the first months, even as I appreciated the warm acceptance I received, I chafed at the restrictions of my role and position in the community. It was difficult being so dependent and powerless. Also, although I enjoyed living in the Haj's household and felt initially comfortable around the people I knew best, I had a fixed idea of the way anthropologists went about their work. I worried that I should be going door to door, meeting everyone in the vicinity, and conducting surveys. I did not think it appropriate to confine my contacts to one kin group or community. And yet to defy my hosts would have been insulting and would have seriously jeopardized my relations with them. They, after all, had undertaken to protect and care for me. My obligation as a dependent was to respect their wishes. My role as a daughter, like that of Jean Briggs among the Eskimos (1970), made defiance especially inappropriate.

I should not give the impression that this dutiful daughter role was forced on me. I was a willing collaborator for a number of reasons. First, it suited my temperament and my interests to be confined to a small group whose members I could come to know intimately. As I became more familiar with the people with whom I lived, I felt less interested in meeting strangers. I found tedious the superficial conversations possible with them and quickly tired of answering questions about whether they have sheep in *amrika*, and what they grow there. Second, I realized that in a society where kinship defined most relationships, it was important to have a role as a fictive kinsperson in order to participate. Since I was interested in the complexities of interpersonal relations, especially in the intimate sphere, and in the concepts by which Awlad Ali individuals understood their social world, I needed to be able to get to know people well.

I also collaborated in a more fundamental sense. The role my Bedouin family assigned me interacted with my own upbringing as a female and experience as the daughter of an Arab. The first aspect made me socially sensitive, eager to please and relatively unassertive. The people I lived with did not see me as a "researcher" with important work to do. They had no category "anthropologist participant-observer," as may some well-studied groups, and I found it hard to act as one. I was treated as a family member, long-term guest and dependent. I was unwilling to tear the fabric of social life they wove around me by acting in ways that were so much less gracious and human than theirs. It was hard for me to assert myself to demand things like privacy, or to put my work, say taking field notes, above the requirements of polite social interactions and the needs of the household. If I was writing and my "father" called me, I had to drop what I was doing and come.

I was especially grateful to the women in my household. Although I was not that much of an extra burden, I felt uncomfortable being idle when the women and the girls worked so hard. When the Haj's senior wife was ill and before her co-wife joined her, she was trying to run the household with only the help of one adolescent daughter. I had to assist them. Also during her difficult pregnancy, I spent much of my time with her, massaging her and worrying about her health, trying to take over what little of her work I was competent to do. During these periods, as I filled water containers, collected straw for the oven, carried trays of bread, peeled endless zucchinis and potatoes for dinner, I would worry that time was passing and I was not filling my notebook with information. If I was occasionally resentful, mostly I felt that my personal responsibilities came first.

Having been socialized partly at home and certainly with my relatives in Jordan to be a dutiful Arab daughter, or at least to know what one was, I found it hard to resist the unspoken expectations of my hosts that I conform in a multitude of specific ways. I was sensitive to subtle pressures to obey and be deferential to my "father" and "uncles" and even to serve elder women, my "grandmothers." I had a second sense about when it was inappropriate for me to be present in certain groups. All this could be summed up as the pressure to act modestly. Considered a member of the moral community, I had few special privileges besides the very important freedom to leave for Cairo.[9] With adults, who were more lenient, I always had to anticipate how things I said would reflect on my image and that of my family. But the adolescent girls in my household took it upon themselves to correct me when they felt I had erred. They probably identified with me, and they were most conscious of and rigid about matters of modesty, since this was the period in their lives when the issue of respectability or reputation was crucial. I had several difficult run-ins with one of the most outspoken girls in the camp. She criticized me for sitting with men and occasionally scolded me harshly for what she perceived as my immodesty, once accusing me of having my eyes twinkle too much when I spoke with her uncle. Five years later she apologized for having been so critical, explaining that she had never seen an educated woman and did not understand that it was possible to associate with men and be respectable. She was now in high school, the first girl in the community to reach that level of education, and she treated me with respect. She was even a bit possessive.

The surprising extent to which playing the role of a dutiful daughter led me to internalize the values of modesty can be seen in an incident that occurred not many months after I had begun living in this community. Women from most of the neighboring households in the hamlet had gathered at our household to help prepare a feast. In the courtyard behind the house we were all working frantically to get a massive meal of rice and fresh slaughtered lamb ready for two hundred or so guests (all male), who had come to show their support for my host, involved in an intertribal altercation. I had been bending over a large tray of rice, intent on my task of cleaning it, when I sensed a stillness. I looked up and saw that all the women had covered their faces with their black veils. Without thinking, I turned toward the house to see why. I found myself face to face with a dignified old man, not a relative, whom I had never seen before. We stared at each other, I blushed deeply, and ran into the nearest doorway. There I found myself surrounded by the adolescent girls who must have done what I had just done a few minutes earlier.

It was at this moment, when I felt naked before an Arab elder because I could not veil, that I understood viscerally that women veil not because anyone tells them to or because they would be punished if they did not, but because they feel extremely uncomfortable in the presence of certain categories of men. Veiling becomes an automatic response to embarrassment, both a sign of it and a way of coping with it. This and my other experiences trying to live as a modest daughter were, as I show below, essential to the development of my analysis of modesty and women's veiling.[10]

I think that I was especially vulnerable to expectations and sensitive to cues not just because I was living in a household, cut off from my old ways and ties, but because I was passing for an insider without really having the assurance that comes from belonging. This may have led me to conform more strictly than Arab women doing fieldwork in this part of the world. I remember being surprised when one young woman I knew well explained to another that I was more modest than they were. I had probably gone overboard in embodying what I assumed were their standards. For me, these standards had the rigidity of notions fixed in childhood and bolstered by informants' abstract statements about cultural ideals. For Bedouin women, or women brought up in other Arab societies, these ideals probably serve as flexible guidelines, not rigid rules. My insecurity about my Arab identity prevented me from considering the possibility that I might choose from alternatives within the system or reject aspects of it.

My vulnerability to the views of the community, the intensity of my desire to belong, and my sense that the Bedouin world had become perfectly ordinary and natural, are epitomized in the way I responded to one eventful day in the second year of my stay. I was awakened in the morning by one of the Haj's daughters who ran into my room with the good news that our neighbor had returned from the pilgrimage. We had feared him dead or imprisoned because he had been caught without a passport during the seizure of the Haram Mosque in Mecca and had not been heard from.[11] His wife had been weeping and worrying for weeks.

I hurried to ready myself to attend the feast welcoming him home. I dressed in my best clothes. What to wear in the field had been a difficult problem to solve. When I had first arrived, I wore long-sleeved blouses and ankle-length skirts and covered my hair with a kerchief. The girls had criticized me for not wearing a belt, since, as I later discovered, it is considered indecent for a girl over puberty to go without a kerchief tied around her waist or a married woman to go without a wide red woolen belt.[12] Furthermore, the women all thought my clothes were ugly because they were so drab—my skirts were navy blue and khaki. Eventually I had some dresses like theirs made, and I always wore a kerchief around my waist.[13] The women advised me to wear my own clothes when we went to visit people in other communities and I always wore them when I set off for Cairo, but within the community I preferred to wear my comfortable Bedouin-style dresses.

On this particular day, as we set off, I realized how proud I was that I finally had the proper items: a new dress given to me by my hosts at the last wedding, made of colorful synthetic that was the latest in Bedouin fashion, a red belt and a black shawl to wear on my head. I knew that my new sweater (worn *under* my dress), brightly colored and interwoven with metallic threads, would be much admired. My shiny new plastic bead necklace, a gift from my friend the seamstress, would also cause comment. I was able to see myself as I would be seen by others and I took pleasure in knowing that they would approve—even perhaps envy. I was also prepared to cover my face with my black shawl as we passed in sight of the men's tent, en route to the women's section. By this point, I knew how uncomfortable I would have been had I not been able to veil in front of that large group of strange men.

Upon entering the tent crowded with women, I knew exactly which cluster to join—the group of "our" relatives. They welcomed me naturally and proceeded to gossip conspiratorially with me about the others present. This sense of us versus them, so central in their social interactions, had become part of mine and I felt pleased that I belonged to an "us." Later, when there was a shortage of help in preparing tea for the guests, I assisted, assuming the proper part of a close neighbor.

I left the festivities with a few of the women from our community and spent the rest of the day going from household to household, visiting, catching up, listening to different sides of the story of the latest crisis in the camp. At one point a few of the adolescent girls came to find me, urging me to come with them while they collected firewood from an olive orchard being pruned nearby. I hurried off with them, it being a beautiful day, welcoming the chance to be outside. We hauled branches and twigs and loaded them onto donkey carts. As the sun sank, we started for home. A donkey cart driven by two young men from our camp passed us. The two women, three girls, and one toddler with whom I was walking, flagged them down begging for a ride. The young men were in a hurry and tried to wave us aside, no longer treating me as a guest to be pampered. But we chased them and jumped onto the moving cart, laughing wildly and exchanging joking insults with them.

That evening as we sat around the kerosene lantern, talking about the celebration we had attended, swapping bits of information we had gathered, and feeling happy because we had eaten meat, I became aware of how comfortable I felt, knowing everyone being discussed, offering my own tidbits and interpretations, and bearing easily the weight of the child who had fallen asleep on my lap as I sat cross-legged on the ground. It was only that night, when I dated the page in my journal, that I realized that it was only a few days until Christmas—a holiday that seemed part of some distant world.

However much I felt at home and however much people included me in their community, there was never any doubt that my identity as a daughter was fictive. This was clearest in my relationships with men. No one had the authority to control me, as they do their own young women, and I did have the freedom to leave. All the men in our community treated me with respect and protective feelings appropriate to a kinswoman, never hinting of even the slightest recognition of my identity as a sexual being.[14] Even Bedouin taxi drivers, who occasionally delivered me to my home when I was returning on my own from Cairo, treated me kindly and politely as the Haj's kinswoman as soon as I mentioned by destination. But I occasionally had to invoke and stress my social identity as a daughter deliberately, to negotiate potentially awkward relationships. Sometimes when I went visiting with the Haj, going to communities or households where he had no kin and which our women had never visited, I could not be guaranteed this invisibility as an attractive young woman. The result of one of these visits was that an old man composed a verse of poetry about me, a verse the Haj later recited to me and all the women in the community insisted on hearing and memorizing themselves. The Haj then composed a verse in response, taking up the theme of the first, stock images from Bedouin love poetry such as piercing eyes, rosy cheeks, and wounds of unfulfilled love. I was flattered but also extremely embarrassed. I could see from this that although I might be treated as a daughter in many ways, this was after all a polite fiction. Or perhaps it was that someone's daughter is always just a woman to everyone else. At times like this, I would find myself subtly asserting my daughterly status within the Haj's household. The Haj respected this, both of us knowing full well that this was a rhetorical move; but it was also proper. The dilemmas women, and perhaps men, face in managing the emotional intensity that can develop in such close opposite-sex interactions in the field are probably among the most difficult aspects of fieldwork, although they are rarely mentioned.

## Conclusion

From what I have described, it should be apparent what sorts of constraints and advantages my particular position in the community created for my ethnographic project. If my hosts' assumption that I was part of their moral community, not a foreigner with immunity, placed restrictions on me, it also allowed me to participate in a way that I could not have otherwise. By living in a social world with the same boundaries as those of members of the community, I was able to grasp in a more immediate sense how they experienced it. But my perspective was more that of a woman than a man in Bedouin society. Being a daughter forced me to learn the standards for women's behavior from the inside, as much through a process of socialization as observation.

In this final section, I want to touch on a few of the ways in which the three aspects of my identity—that I was female, a "powerless" daughter, and a partial insider—critically shaped not my fieldwork but my analysis of Bedouin life. Being a female made it difficult for me to assume a non-situated perspective on the society, or rather to mistake a situated perspective for an "objective" one.[15] Since every member of a society experiences life from a particular vantage point, it could be argued that a picture of a society that claims generality is a fiction. While my presentation of Bedouin society is partial, no presentation could be complete. One consequence of taking the female perspective was that I was led to consider how the politics of personal life, particularly relations between the sexes and generations within the family and lineage, intersects with the segmentary politics of tribal life, which dominates male discourse and is the usual focus of studies of Bedouin society (e.g., Evans-Pritchard 1949; Peters 1960, 1967; Meeker 1979; Lancaster 1981; Sowayan 1985). Related to this was the realization of the centrality and cultural and personal meaning of a genre of poem-song called the *ghinnawa*, which deals with intimate life. All other studies of Arab tribal poetry (Meeker 1979; Caton 1984; Sowayan 1985) focus on men's heroic poetry and its link to tribal politics. I analyze elsewhere (Abu-Lughod 1985b, 1986) how and why Bedouin individuals express in these personal poems sentiments that contradict those they express in ordinary conversation, showing how the code of honor and modesty by which people live only partially determines their experiences and actions, especially in situations of love and loss.

My position of powerlessness in the community prevented me from coercing people into discussions in which they had no interest. Nor had I any desire to do so. I appreciated the fact that they perceived me as different from those researchers they had previously encountered. I heard stories of the "exams" these researchers had given them (questionnaires) and the hilariously wild tales the Bedouins had fed them. The result of my non-directive approach was that while I was limited in the extent to which I could study some matters systematically, I was led to form my inquiry around matters found most interesting and central by those I knew well. If I had not been a deferent daughter, I perhaps would have been blind to the significance of poetry, and I might not have elicited the terms in which people conceive their social lives. This would have hindered my efforts to uncover the relationship between modesty and honor in the social ideology of the Bedouins, an important problem that has long puzzled analysts of Arab society.

Finally, the tension between being an insider and an outsider is reflected in a certain tension in the way I came to analyze the Bedouin ideology of honor and modesty, the basis of the system of morality in Bedouin and other Arab cultures. In the early stages of writing, I had the myopic vision of one immersed in a process of interpreting in order to act within a particular world. To some extent, I shared this vision with the Bedouins with whom I lived, avoiding what Bourdieu argues may be the most pernicious distortion of anthropology. The outside observer, "excluded from the real play of social activities is condemned to adopt unwittingly for his own use the representation of action which is forced on agents or groups when they lack practical mastery of a highly valued competence" (Bourdieu 1977:1-2). This outsider's representation is too often mistaken for the insider's experience of social life. I perceived my task to be one of describing as faithfully as possible how those participating in the system understood it, and making explicit and systematic what generated their actions, and even my own with regard to propriety.

One way of thinking about what I was doing in writing is in terms of my relationship to my parents. Initially, I was taking the systematic and defensive attitude of someone who had just begun to understand who her Arab father was and needed to explain it to her American mother. But as time elapsed, and the distance grew between myself and the Bedouins, and perhaps between myself and my parents, something new was added to my analysis. In rewriting my dissertation for publication, just before I returned to Egypt, I began to view the system of morality not only in the terms of those who believe in it and act according to its principles, but in terms that only an outsider might use: as an essential part of an ideology that serves to reproduce and maintain a system of domination in which elder males have power. Was I becoming my mother's daughter?

I am reminded of one lazy afternoon in the Western Desert. I was sitting with the Haj and his wife. Their two-year-old daughter, delighted to have them both there, restlessly moved back and forth from her father's lap to her mother's. She giggled and buried her head in the folds of her mother's dress when her father playfully reached for her, teasing her again and again by asking: "Whose daughter are you? Your father's daughter or your mother's?" In the five years since fieldwork, I had been discovering how complicated it was to be both.

### Acknowledgments

Parts of this essay were adapted from my book *Veiled Sentiments: Honor and Poetry in a Bedouin Society* (University of California Press, 1986). My initial research was supported by grants from the National Institute of Mental Health and the American Association of University Women. A small grant from the Program on African and Middle Eastern Studies at Williams College enabled me to return to the field in the summer of 1985. I want to thank Timothy Mitchell, Catherine Lutz, and the editors of this volume for helpful comments on a draft of this paper. I am also grateful to my Bedouin hosts for taking me into their lives in ways I only partially describe here.

## Notes

1. For a more detailed discussion of the psychological processes involved in returning from the field and writing ethnography, see Crapanzano (1977).

2. My host, who along with his brothers had had long conversations with her about Islam, insisted that she seemed very close to converting to Islam. I think this was the only way he could justify to himself how much he had enjoyed talking with her.

3. I explore the relationship between *asl* and morality in chapters two and three in Abu-Lughod (1986).

4. For discussions of these issues, see Messerschmidt (1981) and Fahim (1982a). Aguilar (1981) summarizes the debate on the value of insider versus outsider research.

5. The entailments of the Awlad Ali honor code are explored in chapters three and four of Abu-Lughod (1986).

6. For an extended discussion of the pattern of sexual segregation among Awlad Ali, see Abu-Lughod (1985a; 1986: 103–167).

7. Schrijvers (1979:103) makes a similar argument.

8. Being unmarried yet far older than the unmarried Bedouin girls placed me in an ambiguous position. The problems of the unmarried status have been noted by two Arab women trained as anthropologists in the West who returned to do fieldwork in Arab communities (Abu Zahra 1978; Altorki 1986).

9. Whenever I wished to go, however, I had to persuade my host to take me to Alexandria, where I could catch a train or bus, or wait until he was planning to go there.

10. See especially chapter four of Abu-Lughod (1986).

11. This refers to the two-week siege of the Grand Mosque in Mecca by Muslim fundamentalists in 1979.

12. I argue in Abu-Lughod (1986) that the symbolic significance of the red belt lies in its association with fertility, life, and reproduction.

13. I found the kerchief convenient for wrapping up the flea collar that I wore around my waist for a while as a tactic in my futile battle against fleas.

14. Laura Nader (1970:111) mentions a similar lack of trouble doing fieldwork in a Lebanese village.

15. Critiques of the appeal to "objectivity" in ethnographic writing and fieldwork have proliferated recently. For examples just from anthropologists who have worked in the Middle East, see Bourdieu (1977); Crapanzano (1977, 1980); Rabinow (1977); Dwyer (1982). An important new collection that takes up the problematics of the politics and poetics of ethnography is Clifford and Marcus (1986). For a perceptive exploration of the ways in which objectivity has been historically associated with masculinity in our thinking about science, see Keller (1978), and for a provocative denunciation of objectivity as masculine, see MacKinnon (1982). For a thorough treatment of the issue of "standpoint epistemologies" in feminist theory see Harding (1986). I explore the issues of gender and ethnography in Abu-Lughod (1984).

# References

Abbott, S. 1983. " 'In the end you will carry me in your car': Sexual Politics in the Field," in N. Scheper-Hughes, ed., "Confronting Bias in Feminist Anthropology," *Women's Studies* 10(1): 161–78 (special issue).

Abdel Malek, A. 1963. "Orientalism in Crisis." *Diogenes* 44: 107–8.

Abercrombie, N. 1980. *Class Structure and Knowledge.* London: Basil Blackwell.

Abidi, A. H. 1965. *Jordan: A Political Study 1948–1957.* Bombay: Asia Publishing House.

Ablon, J. 1977. "Field Methods in Working with Middle Class Americans: New Issues of Values, Personality and Reciprocity." *Human Organization* 36(1): 69–72.

Abu-Lughod, I. and B. Abu-Laban, eds. 1972. *Settler Regimes in Africa and the Arab World.* Illinois: The Medina University Press International.

Abu-Lughod, L. 1984. "Bedouin Ethnography 'In a Different Voice'." Paper presented at the 18th Annual Meeting of the Middle East Studies Association, San Francisco.

———. 1985a. "A Community of Secrets: The Separate World of Bedouin Women." *Signs* 10(4): 637–57.

———. 1985b. "Honor and Sentiments of Loss in a Bedouin Society." *American Ethnologist* 12 (2): 245–61.

———. 1986. *Veiled Sentiments: Honor and Poetry in a Bedouin Society.* Berkeley: University of California Press.

Abu Zahra, N. 1970. "On the Modesty of Women in Arab Muslim Villages: A Reply." *American Anthropologist* 72(5): 1079–88.

———. 1978. "Baraka, Material Power, Honour and Women in Tunisia." *Revue d'histoire maghrébine* 10–11: 5–24 (Tunis).

———. 1982. *Sidi Ameur: A Tunisian Village.* London: Ithaca Press.

Agar, M. 1973. *Ripping and Running.* New York: Seminar Press.

———. 1980. *The Professional Stranger.* New York: Academic Press.

Aguilar, J. 1981. "Insider Research: An Ethnography of a Debate," in D. A. Messerschmidt, ed., *Anthropologists at Home in North America: Methods and Issues in the Study of One's Own Society.* Cambridge: Cambridge University Press.

Altorki, S. 1973. "Religion and Social Organization of Elite Families in Urban Saudi Arabia." University of California, Berkeley, Ph.D. Thesis.

———. 1977. "Family Organization and Women's Power in Urban Saudi Society." *Journal of Anthropological Research* 33(3): 277–87.

———. 1982. "Anthropologist in the Field: A Case of 'Indigenous Anthropology' from Saudi Arabia," in H. Fahim, ed., *Indigenous Anthropology in Non-Western Countries.* Durham: Carolina Academic Press.

———. 1986. *Women in Saudi Arabia: Ideology and Behavior Among the Elite.* New York: Columbia University Press.

Antoun, R. 1968. "On the Modesty of Women in Arab Muslim Villages: A Study in the Accomodation of Traditions." *American Anthropologist* 70(4): 671–97.

Archer, J. and B. Lloyd. 1982. *Sex and Gender.* London: Penguin Press.

Aruri, N. H. 1972. *Jordan: A Study in Political Development 1921–1968.* The Hague: Martinus Nijhoff.

Asad, T. 1973. *Anthropology and the Colonial Encounter.* New Jersey: Humanities Press.

———. 1982. "A Comment on the Idea of Non-Western Anthropology," in H. Fahim, ed., *Indigenous Anthropology in Non-Western Countries.* Durham: Carolina Academic Press.

Asad, T. and R. Owen, eds. 1983. *Sociology of "Developing Societies": The Middle East.* London: Macmillan Press.

Aswad, B. 1967. "Key and Peripheral Roles of Noble Women in a Middle Eastern Plains Village." *Anthropological Quarterly* 40(3): 139–53.

Badri, H. n.d. *The Egyptian Fellah on Iraqi Soil* (fellah misr 'ala ard al-'iraq). Baghdad: General Union of Peasants' Cooperative Societies.

Baffoun, A. 1977. "Femmes et Développement dans le Maghreb Arabe: Socio-analyse des Origines de l' Inégalité." Unpublished manuscript submitted at Seminar on Decolonizing Research. Sponsored by Centre de Recherche pour le Développement International (Dakar, Senegal).

Bannoune, M. 1985. "What does it Mean to be a Third World Anthropologist?" *Dialectical Anthropology* 9(1–4): 357–64.

Barnes, B. 1980. *Scientific Knowledge and Sociological Theory.* London: Routledge and Kegan Paul.

Barnes, J. 1967. "Some Ethical Problems in Modern Fieldwork," in D. G. Jongmans and P. C. W. Gutkind, eds., *Anthropologists in the Field.* New York: Humanities Press.

———. 1977. *The Ethics of Social Enquiry: Three Lectures.* New Delhi: Oxford University Press.

Beck, L. and N. Keddie, eds. 1978. *Women in the Muslim World.* Cambridge: Harvard University Press.

Berger, M. 1962. *The Arab World Today.* New York: Doubleday.

Berkok, I. 1958. *The Caucasus in History* (Turkish). Istanbul: Istanbul Matbaasi.

Bernard, H. R. et al. 1984. "The Problem of Informant Accuracy: The Validity of Retrospective Data." *Annual Review of Anthropology* 13: 495–517.

Berreman. G. D. and K. M. Zaretsky, eds. 1981. *Social Inequality: Comparative and Developmental Approaches.* New York: Academic Press.

Birks, J. S. et al. 1983. "The Demand for Egyptian Labour Abroad," in A. Richards and P. Martin, eds., *Migration, Mechanization and Agricultural Labour Markets in Egypt.* Cairo: The American University in Cairo Press.

Blackman, W. 1977. *The Fellahin of Upper Egypt: Their Religion, Social and Industrial Life, With Special Reference to Ancient Times.* London: Frank Cass & Co. Ltd. (first published in 1927).

Boas, F. 1973. "Scientists as Spies," in T. Weaver, ed., *To See Ourselves: Anthropology and Modern Social Issues.* Glenview, Ill.: Scott, Foresman and Company.

Bourdieu, P. 1977. *Outline of a Theory of Practice.* Cambridge: Cambridge University Press.

Briggs, J. 1970. "Kapluna Daughter," in P. Golde, ed., *Women in the Field.* Chicago: Aldine Publishing Company.

Brown, H. and E. Hutchings, eds. 1972. *Are Our Descendants Doomed? Change and Population Growth.* New York: Harper & Row.

Bujra, J. 1975. "Women and Fieldwork," in R. Rohrlich-Leavitt, ed., *Women Cross-Culturally: Change and Challenge.* The Hague: Mouton.

Burton, Sir R. 1885. *A Personal Narrative of Al-Madinah and Meccah.* New York: Dover Books (reprinted 1964).

Cassell, J. 1977. "The Relationship of Observer to Observed in Peer Group Research." *Human Organization* 36(4): 412–16.

Caton, S. 1984. "Tribal Poetry as Political Rethoric from Khawlan At-Tiyal, Yemen Arab Republic." University of Chicago, Ph.D. Thesis.

Caufield, M. D. 1981. "Equality, Sex and Mode of Production," in G. D. Berreman and K. M. Zaretsky, eds., *Social Inequality: Comparative and Developmental Approaches.* New York: Academic Press.

Cesara, M. 1982. *Reflections of a Woman Anthropologist: No Place to Hide.* New York: Academic Press.

Churchill, C. 1967. "The Arab World," in R. Patai, ed., *Women in the Modern World.* New York: Free Press.

Clark, M. H. 1983. "Variations on Themes of Male and Female: Reflections on Gender Bias in Fieldwork in Rural Greece," in N. Scheper-Hughes, ed., "Confronting Problems of Bias in Feminist Anthropology." *Women's Studies* 10(1): 116–33 (special issue).

Clifford, J. 1986. "Introduction: Partial Truths," in J. Clifford and G. E. Marcus, eds., *Writing Culture: The Poetics and Politics of Ethnography.* Berkeley: University of California Press.

Clifford, J. and G. E. Marcus, eds. 1986. *Writing Culture: The Poetics and Politics of Ethnography.* Berkeley: University of California Press.

Colfax, D. 1966. "Pressure Towards Distortion and Involvement in Studying a Civil Rights Organization." *Human Organization* 25(2): 140–49.

Colson, E. 1982. "Anthropological Dilemmas in the Late Twentieth Century," in H. Fahim, ed., *Indigenous Anthropology in Non-Western Countries.* Durham: Carolina Academic Press.

Copans, J., ed. 1975. *Anthropologie et Imperialism.* Paris: François Maspero.

Crapanzano, V. 1977. "On the Writing of Ethnography." *Dialectical Anthropology* 2(1): 69–73.

———. 1980. *Tuhami: Portrait of a Moroccan.* Chicago: University of Chicago Press.

Critchfield, R. 1978. *Shahhat: An Egyptian.* Syracuse: Syracuse University Press.

Cunnison, I. 1966. *The Baggara Arabs: Power and Lineage in a Sudanese Nomad Tribe.* Oxford: Clarendon Press.

Davis, S. 1983. *Patience and Power.* Cambridge, Mass.: Schenkman Publishing Company.

De Josselin de Jong, P. E. 1967. "The Participants' View of their Culture," in D. G. Jongmans and P. C. Gutkind, eds., *Anthropologists in the Field.* New York: Humanities Press.

Dessouki, A. 1977. "Arab Intellectuals and Al-Nakba: The Search for Fundamentalism," in S. E. Ibrahim and N. S. Hopkins, eds., *Arab Society in Transition.* Cairo: The American University of Cairo Press.

Devons, E. and M. Gluckman. 1964. "Conclusion: Modes and Consequences of Limiting a Field Study," in M. Gluckman, ed., *Closed Systems and Open Minds: The Limits of Naivety in Social Anthropology.* Chicago: Aldine Publishing Company.

Diamond, N. 1970. "Fieldwork in a Complex Society: Taiwan," in G. Spindler, ed., *Being an Anthropologist.* New York: Holt, Rinehart & Winston Inc.

Diamond, S. 1974. *In Search of the Primitive.* New Brunswick: Transaction Books.

Dillman, C. M. 1977. "Ethical Problems in Social Science Research Peculiar to Participant Observation." *Human Organization* 36(4): 405–7.

Dua, V. 1979. "A Woman's Encounter with Arya Samaj and Untouchables," in M. N. Srinivas et al., *The Fieldworker and the Field*. Delhi: Oxford University Press.

Du Boulay, J. 1974. *Portrait of a Greek Village*. Oxford: Clarendon Press.

Durkheim, E. 1948. *The Elementary Forms of Religious Life*, translated by J. W. Swain, 1915. London: George Allen & Unwin Ltd.

Dwyer, D. 1978. *Images and Self-Images: Male and Female in Morocco*. New York: Columbia University Press.

Dwyer, K. 1982. *Moroccan Dialogues: Anthropology in Question*. Baltimore, Maryland: The Johns Hopkins Press.

Eickelman, C. 1984. *Women and Community in Oman*. New York: New York University Press.

Eickelman, D. 1981. *The Middle East: An Anthropological Approach*. Englewood Cliffs, N.J.: Prentice Hall, Inc.

El-Hamamsy, L. 1972. "Belief Systems and Family Planning in Peasant Societies," in H. Brown & E. Hutchings, eds., *Are Our Descendants Doomed? Change and Population Growth*. New York: Harper & Row.

_____. n.d. "The Daya of Egypt: Survival in a Modernizing Society," in *Caltech Population Progress Occasional Papers Series*, reprinted by Social Research Center, American University in Cairo.

El-Kinz, A. 1986. "The Theoretical and Political Problematic of Arab Social Science" (al-mas'ala al-nadhariyya wal-siyasiyya li 'ilm al-ijtima' al-'arabi). *Al-Mustaqbal al-Arabi* 84(2): 29–39 (Beirut, Lebanon).

El-Messiri, S. 1978. "Self-Images of Traditional Urban Women in Cairo," in L. Beck and N. Keddie, eds., *Women in the Muslim World*. Cambridge, Mass.: Harvard University Press.

El-Saadawi, N. 1979. *The Hidden Face of Eve: Women in the Arab World*. London: Zed Press.

_____. 1983. *Woman at Point Zero*. London: Zed Press.

Eren, A. C. 1966. *Problems of Migration and Immigrants in Turkey* (Turkish). Istanbul: Nugok Matbaasi.

Etienne, M. and E. Leacock, eds. 1980. *Women and Colonization: Anthropological Perspectives*. New York: Praeger.

Evans-Pritchard, E. E. 1949. *The Sanusi of Cyrenaica*. Oxford: Clarendon Press.

Fahim, H. 1977. "Foreign and Indigenous Anthropology: The Perspective of an Egyptian Anthropologist." *Human Organization* 36(1): 80–86.

_____. ed. 1982a. *Indigenous Anthropology in Non-Western Countries*. Durham: Carolina Academic Press.

_____. 1982b. "Communication Among Anthropologists Across Non-Western Countries," in H. Fahim, ed., *Indigenous Anthropology in Non-Western Countries*. Durham: Carolina Academic Press.

Fahim, H. and K. Helman. 1980. "Indigenous Anthropology in Non-Western Countries: A Further Note." *Current Anthropology* 21(5): 644–63.

Farrag, A. 1971. "Social Control Among the Mzabite of Beni-Isguen." *Middle Eastern Studies* 7(3): 317–27.

Fawzi El-Solh, C. 1984. "Egyptian Migrant Peasants in Iraq: A Case-Study of the Settlement Community in Khalsa." University of London, Ph.D. Thesis.

_____. 1985. "Migration and the Selectivity of Change: Egyptian Peasant Women in Iraq," in "Migrations et Méditerranée." *Peuples Méditerranéens* 31–32: 243–58 (Paris).

Fernea, E. W. 1965. *Guests of the Sheikh*. New York: Doubleday Press.

_____, ed. 1985. *Women and the Family in the Middle East: New Voices of Change*. Austin: University of Texas Press.

Fernea, E. W. and B. Q. Bezirgan, eds. 1977. *Middle Eastern Muslim Women Speak*. Austin: University of Texas Press.

Fluehr-Lobban, C. 1973. "Sudanese Women's Struggle," in *Women in the Middle East*. Cambridge, Mass.: Women's Middle East Collective.

Fluehr-Lobban, C. and R. A. Lobban. 1986. "Families, Gender and Methodology in the Sudan," in T. L. Whitehead and M. E. Connoway, eds., *Self, Sex, and Gender in Cross-Cultural Fieldwork*. Urbana and Chicago: University of Illinois Press.

Frank, A. G. 1975. "Anthropology = Ideology, Applied Anthropology = Politics." *Race and Class* 17(1): 57–68.

Freilich, M., ed. 1977. *Marginal Natives: Anthropologists at Work*. New York: Harper & Row.

Friedl, E. 1967. "The Position of Women: Appearance and Reality." *Anthropological Quarterly* 40(3): 97–108.

_____. 1970. "Fieldwork in a Greek Village," in P. Golde, ed., *Women in the Field*. Chicago: Aldine Publishing Company.

_____. 1975. *Women and Men: An Anthropologist's View*. New York: Holt, Rinehart and Winston.

Fuller, A. 1961. *Buarej: Portrait of a Lebanese Village*. Cambridge, Mass.: Harvard University Press.

Gans, H. J. 1962. *The Urban Villagers: Group and Class in the Life of Italian-Americans*. New York: Free Press.

Gilligan, C. 1982. *In a Different Voice: Psychological Theory and Women's Development*. Cambridge, Mass.: Harvard University Press.

Gluckman, M., ed. 1964. *Closed Systems and Open Minds: The Limits of Naivety in Social Anthropology*, Chicago: Aldine Publishing Company.

Golde, P., ed. 1970. *Women in the Field*. Chicago: Aldine Publishing Company.

_____. 1970a. "Introduction," in P. Golde, ed., *Women in the Field*. Chicago: Aldine Publishing Company.

_____. 1970b. "Odyssey of Encounter," in P. Golde, ed., *Women in the Field*. Chicago: Aldine Publishing Company.

Gonzalez, N. 1986. "The Anthropologist as Female Head of Household," in T. L. Whitehead and M. E. Connoway, eds., *Self, Sex, and Gender in Cross-Cultural Fieldwork*. Urbana and Chicago: University of Illinois Press.

Goodale, J. 1971. *Tiwi Wives: A Study of the Women of Melville Island*. Seattle: Washington University Press.

Goonatilake, S. 1984. *Aborted Discovery: Science and Creativity in the Third World*. London: Zed Press.

Gran, J. 1977. "Impact of the World Market on Egyptian Women." *Merip Reports* 58: 3–7.

Granqvist, H. 1935. *Marriage Conditions in a Palestinian Village*. Helsingfors: Soderstorm Forlagsaktiebolag.

Gregory, J. R. 1984. "The Myth of the Male Ethnographer and the Woman's World." *American Anthropologist* 86(2): 316–27.

Gupta, K. A. 1979. "Travails of a Woman Fieldworker," in M. N. Srinivas et al., *The Fieldworker and the Field*. Delhi: Oxford University Press.

Hacker, J. 1960. "Modern Amman: A Social Study," in *Research Papers Series*. Durham: University of Durham, England.

Hamady, S. 1960. *Temperament and Character of the Arabs*. New York: Twayne Publishers.

Harding, S. 1986. *The Science Question in Feminism*. Ithaca: Cornell University Press.

Hatfield, C. 1973. "Fieldwork: Towards a Model of Mutual Exploitation." *Anthropological Quarterly* 46(1): 15–29.

Henry, F. 1966. "The Role of the Fieldworker in an Explosive Political Situation." *Current Anthropology* 7(5): 552–59.

Honigman, J. L., ed. 1973. *Handbook of Social and Cultural Anthropology*. Chicago: Rand McNally & Company.

Hopkins, N. S. 1985. "The Political Economy of an Upper Egyptian Village." Unpublished manuscript, Anthropology/ Sociology/ Psychology Department, American University in Cairo.

Hsu, F. 1973. "Prejudice and Intellectual Effect in American Anthropology: An Ethnographic Report." *American Anthropologist* 75(1): 1–19.

Huizer, G. and B. Mannheim. 1979. *The Politics of Anthropology*. The Hague: Mouton.

Hunt, J. 1984. "The Development of Rapport Through the Negotiation of Gender in Field Work Among Police." *Human Organization* 43(4): 283–96.

Hurgrouje, S. 1970. *Mekka in the Later Part of Nineteenth Century 1885–1889*. Leiden: E. J. Brill (reprint translated by J. H. Monahan).

Husain, A. H. 1970. "Social Change in the New Wadi: An Anthropological Study of the Kharga Oasis" (al-taghayyur al-ijtima'i fi al-wadi al jadid: dirasa antropolojiyya 'an wahat al-kharga). University of Alexandria, Egypt, Ph.D. thesis.

Hymes, D., ed. 1974. *Reinventing Anthropology.* New York: Random House.

Ibrahim, F. M. 1979. "Cognitive Methods in the Study of Women: A Comparative Anthropological Study" (al-uslub al-ma'refi li dirasat al-mar'a: dirasa antropolojiyya muqarna). University of Alexandria, Egypt, Ph.D. Thesis.

Ibrahim, S. E. and N. S. Hopkins, eds. 1977. *Arab Society in Transition.* Cairo: The American University in Cairo Press.

Jenkins, R. 1984. "Bringing it all Back Home: An Anthropologist in Belfast," in *Social Researching, Politics, Problems, Practice.* London: Routledge and Kegan Paul.

Johnson, N. B. 1984. "Sex, Color and Rites of Passage in Ethnographic Research." *Human Organization* 43(2): 108–20.

Jones, D. 1973. "Culture Fatigue: The Result of Role-Playing in Anthropological Research." *Anthropological Quarterly* 46(1): 30–37.

Jongmans, D. J. and P. C. Gutkind, eds. 1967. *Anthropologists in the Field.* New York: Humanities Press.

Jordan, B. 1981. "Studying Childbirth: The Experiences and Methods of a Woman Anthropologist," in S. Romalis, ed., *Child-birth: Alternatives to Medical Control.* Austin: University of Texas Press.

Joseph, S. 1975. "Urban Poor Women in Lebanon: Does Poverty Have Public and Private Domains?" Paper presented at the Association of Arab-American University Graduates' Meetings, Chicago.

_____. 1976a. "Women and Community Formation in an Urban Working Class Lebanese Neighborhood." Paper presented at the New School for Social Research. Forum on Anthropological Studies of Women.

_____. 1976b. "Institutions or Counter-Institutions. The Role of Women in Community Formation in Urban Lower Class Neighborhoods." Paper presented at the Women and Development Conference, Wellesley College, Wellesley, Mass.

_____. 1977. "Zaynab: An Urban Working Class Lebanese Woman," in E. W. Fernea and B. Q. Bezirgan, eds., *Middle Eastern Muslim Women Speak.* Austin: University of Texas Press.

_____. 1978a. "Women and the Neighborhood Street in Borj Hammoud, Lebanon", in L. Beck and N. Keddie, eds., *Women in the Muslim World.* Cambridge, Mass.: Harvard University Press.

_____. 1978b. "Women in Lebanon and the World Capitalist System: A Perspective." University of California, Davis. Women's Resources and Research Center. Paper presented at the Conference on Women, Culture and Society.

_____. 1978c. "Effects of Capitalist Penetration on Urban Working Class Women in Lebanon." University of California, Los Angeles. Paper presented at the Women's Studies Program Lecture Series.

_____. 1979a. "The Political Context of Women in Borj Hammoud, Lebanon." Paper presented at the Najda: Women Concerned About the Middle East, Berkeley.

_____. 1979b. "Women, Power and Local Community in Lebanon." Sacramento Anthropology Society and Department of Anthropology. Paper presented at the Annual Conference on Women in Anthropology.

_____. 1979c. "Women and Patronage in Lebanon." Paper presented at the Alternative Middle East Studies Seminar, New York.

_____. 1982. "The Mobilization of Iraqi Women into the Wage Labor Force," in "Women and Politics in Twentieth Century Africa and Asia." *Studies in Third World Societies* 16.

_____. 1983. "Working Class Women's Networks in a Sectarian State: A Political Paradox." *American Ethnologist* 10(1): 1–22.

Kandiyoti, D. 1984. "Emancipated but Unliberated? Reflections on the Turkish Case." Paper presented at the Middle East Studies Association Meetings, San Francisco.

Kaplan, A. 1984. "Philosophy of Science in Anthropology." *Annual Review of Anthropology* 13: 25–39.

Karpat, K. 1972. "Ottoman Immigration Policies and Settlement in Palestine," in I. Abu-Lughod and B. Abu-Laban, eds., *Settler Regimes in Africa and the Arab World*. Illinois: The Medina University Press International.

Keiser, L. 1969. *The Vice Lords: Warriors of the Streets*. New York: Holt, Rinehart & Winston.

Keller, E. F. 1978. "Gender and Science." *Psychoanalysis and Contemporary Thought* 1(3): 409–33.

_____. 1983. "Feminism as a Tool for the Study of Science." *Academe* (Journal of the American Association of University Professors) 69(5): 15–21.

Khalifa, A., et al. 1984. *Problems of the Social Sciences in the Arab World* (ishkaliat al-'ulum al-ijtima'iyya fi al-watan al-'arabi). Cairo: Dar al-Tanwir lil-Tiba'a wal-Nashr.

Kloos, P. 1969. "Role Conflicts in Social Fieldwork." *Current Anthropology* 10(5): 509–23.

Koch, K., et al. 1977. "Ritual Conciliation and the Obviation of Grievances: A Comparative Study in the Ethnography of Law." *Ethnology* 16: 269–84.

Koptiuch, K. 1985. "Fieldwork in the Postmodern World: Notes on Ethnography in an Expanded Field." Paper presented at the 84th Annual Meeting of the American Anthropological Association, Washington, D.C.

Krieger, L. 1986. "Negotiating Gender Role Expectations in Cairo," in T. L. Whitehead and M. E. Connoway, eds., *Self, Sex, and Gender in Cross-Cultural Fieldwork*. Urbana and Chicago: University of Illinois Press.

Kuhn, S. 1970. *The Structure of Scientific Revolutions.* Chicago: University of Chicago Press.

Lancaster, W. 1981. *The Rwala Bedouin Today.* Cambridge: Cambridge University Press.

Leacock, L. 1974. "Review of the Inevitability of Patriarchy by Steven Goldberg." *American Anthropologist* 76(2): 363–65.

――――. 1981. *Myths of Male Dominance: Collected Articles Cross-Culturally.* New York: Monthly Review Press.

――――. 1982. "Marxism and Anthropology", in *The Left Academy: Scholarship on American Campuses.* New York: McGraw Hill.

Lewis, D. 1973. "Anthropology and Colonialism." *Current Anthropology* 14(12): 581–602.

Liebow, E. 1967. *Tally's Corner.* Boston: Little, Brown & Company.

Lukacs, G. 1922. *History and Class Consciousness.* London: Merlin Press Ltd. (reprint).

Lynd, R. S. and H. M. Lynd 1929. *Middletown: A Study in Contemporary American Culture.* New York: Harcourt, Brace & Company.

MacKinnon, C. 1982. "Feminism, Marxism, Method and the State: An Agenda for Theory." *Signs* 7(3): 515–44.

Madan, T. N. 1982. "Indigenous Anthropology in Non-Western Countries: An Overview," in H. Fahim, ed., *Indigenous Anthropology in Non-Western Countries.* Durham: Carolina Academic Press.

Makhlouf, C. 1979. *Changing Veils: Women and Modernization in North Yemen.* London: Croom Helm.

Mannheim, K. 1976. *Ideology and Utopia.* London: Routledge & Kegan Paul (reprint, first published in 1936).

Maquet, J. J. 1964. "Objectivity in Anthropology." *Current Anthropology* 5(1): 47–55.

Marshall, G. 1970. "In a World of Women: Field Work in a Yoruba Community," in P. Golde, ed., *Women in the Field.* Chicago: Aldine Publishing Company.

Marx, K. 1971. *A Contribution to the Critique of Political Economy.* London: Lawrence & Wishart. With an introduction by M. Dobb (first published in German in 1859; English translation by N. I. Stone, 1909).

Massialas, B. G. and S. A. Jarrar. 1983. *Education in the Arab World.* New York: Praeger.

Mathiasson, C., ed. 1974. *Many Sisters: Women in Cross Cultural Perspective.* New York: Free Press.

Mayfield, J. 1971. *Rural Politics in Nasser's Egypt: A Quest for Legitimacy.* Austin: University of Texas Press.

Meeker, M. 1979. *Literature and Violence in North Arabia.* Cambridge: Cambridge University Press.

Mernissi, F. 1975. *Beyond the Veil: Male-Female Dynamics in a Modern Muslim Society.* Cambridge, Mass.: Schenkman Publishing Company, Inc.

Merton, R. 1974. *The Sociology of Science.* Chicago: University of Chicago Press.

Messerschmidt, D. A., ed. 1981. *Anthropologists at Home in North America: Methods and Issues in the Study of Ones's Own Society.* Cambridge: Cambridge University Press.

Mohsen, S. 1967. "Legal Status of Women Among Awlad Ali." *Anthropological Quarterly* 40(3): 153–66.

_____. 1974. "The Egyptian Woman: Between Modernity and Tradition," in C. Mathiasson, ed., *Many Sisters: Women in Cross-Cultural Perspective.* New York: Free Press.

_____. 1985. "New Images, Old Reflections: Working Middle-Class Women in Egypt," in E. W. Fernea, ed., *Women and the Family in the Middle East: New Voices of Change.* Austin: University of Texas Press.

Mokhtar, A. 1974. "The Problematic Relationship Between Ideology and the Social Sciences" (ishkaliat al-'ilaqa beyn al-ideolojiyya wal-'ulum al-ijtima 'iyya), in A. Khalifa et al., *Problems of the Social Sciences in the Arab World* (ishkaliat al-'ulum al-ijtima'iyya fi al-watan al-'arabi). Cairo: Dar al-Tanwir lil-Tiba 'a wal-Nashr.

Morgan, S. 1983. "Towards a Politics of Feelings: Beyond the Dialectic of Thought and Action," in N. Scheper-Hughes, ed., "Confronting Problems of Bias in Feminist Anthropology." *Women's Studies* 10(1): 203–24 (special issue).

Morsy, S. 1978. "Sex Roles, Power and Illness in an Egyptian Village." *American Ethnologist* 5(1): 137–50.

_____. 1983. "Zionist Ideology as Anthropology: An Analysis of Joseph Ginat's 'Women in Muslim Rural Society'." *Arab Studies Quarterly* 5(4): 362–79.

_____. 1986a. *Reflections on the Politics of Health* (ta'mullat siyasiyya fi al-mas'ala al-sihiyya). Cairo: Dar al-Tali 'a 2: 49–59.

_____. 1986b. " 'Indigenous' Anthropology in the Context of Intellectual Dependency." Paper presented at the Annual Central States Meetings of the American Anthropological Association, Chicago, Illinois.

Mulkay, M. 1980. *Science and Sociology.* London: George Allen & Unwin Ltd.

Murphy, R. 1972. *The Dialectics of Social Life: Alarms and Excursions in Anthropological Theory.* London: George Allen & Unwin Ltd.

Musry, A. 1969. *An Arab Common Market: A Study in Inter-Arab Trade Relations 1928–1967.* Washington: Praeger.

Nader, L. 1969. "Up the Anthropologist—Perspectives Gained From Studying Up," in D. Hymes, ed., *Reinventing Anthropology.* New York: Random House.

_____. 1970. "From Anguish to Exultation," in P. Golde, ed., *Women in the Field.* Chicago: Aldine Publishing Company.

Nader, L. and T. W. Maretzki 1973. "Cultural Illness and Health: Essays in Human Adaptation." *Anthropological Studies* 9. Washington, D.C.: American Anthropological Association.

Nagel, E. 1961. *The Structure of Science*. New York: Harcourt, Brace & World.

Nakhleh, K. 1979. "On Being a Native Anthropologist," in G. Huizer and B. Mannheim, eds., *The Politics of Anthropology*. The Hague: Mouton.

Nash, D. 1963. "The Ethnologist as Stranger: An Essay in the Sociology of Knowledge." *Southwestern Journal of Anthropology* 19(2): 149–67.

Nash, J. 1978. "The Aztecs and the Ideology of Male Dominance." *Signs* 4(2): 349–62.

Nelson, C. n.d. "An Anthropologist's Dilemma: Fieldwork and Interpretative Inquiry." Unpublished paper, Anthropology/ Sociology/ Psychology Department, American University in Cairo.

_____. ed. 1973a. *The Desert and the Sown*. University of California, Berkeley: Institute of International Studies.

_____. 1973b. "Women and Power in Nomadic Societies in the Middle East," in C. Nelson, ed., *The Desert and the Sown*. University of California, Berkeley: Institute of International Studies.

_____. 1974. "Public and Private Politics: Women in the Middle Eastern World." *American Ethnologist*. 1(3): 551–63.

_____. 1986. "Old Wine, New Bottles: Reflections and Projections Concerning Research on 'Women in Middle Eastern Studies'." Unpublished manuscript, Anthropology/ Sociology/ Psychology Department, American University in Cairo.

Nelson, C. and V. Olesen 1977. "Veil of Illusion: A Critique of the Concept 'Equality' in Western Feminist Thought," in C. Nelson and V. Olesen, eds., "Feminist Thought". *Catalyst* 10–11: 8–36.

Niblock, T., ed. 1982. *Iraq: The Contemporary State*. London: Croom Helm.

Oakley, A. 1981. "Interviewing Women: A Contradiction in Terms," in H. Roberts, ed., *Doing Feminist Research*. London: Routledge & Kegan Paul.

Ortner, S. 1974. "Is Female to Male as Nature is to Culture?" In M. Z. Rosaldo and L. Lamphere, eds., *Women, Culture and Society*. Stanford: Stanford University Press.

Owusu, M. 1978. "Ethnography of Africa: The Usefulness of the Useless." *American Anthropologist* 80(2): 310–34.

Papanek, H. 1964. "The Woman Fieldworker in Purdah Society." *Human Organization* 23(2): 160–63.

Passmore Sanderson, L. 1981. *Against the Mutilation of Women: The Struggle Against Unnecessary Suffering*. London: Ithaca Press.

Pastner, C. 1982. "Rethinking the Role of the Woman Fieldworker in Purdah Societies." *Human Organization* 41(3): 262–64.

Patai, R. 1955. "The Dynamics of Westernization in the Middle East." *Middle East Journal* 9(1): 1–16.

_____. 1967. *Women in the Modern World.* New York: Free Press.

Pelto, P. and G. Pelto. 1973. "Ethnography: The Fieldwork Enterprise," in J. L. Honigmann, ed., *Handbook of Social and Cultural Anthropology.* Chicago: Rand McNally & Company.

Peters, E. 1960. "The Proliferation of Segments in the Lineage of the Bedouin of Cyrenaica." *Journal of the Royal Anthropological Society of Great Britain* 90: 29–53.

_____. 1967. "Some Structural Aspects of the Feud among the Camel-Herding Bedouin of Cyrenaica." *Africa* 37: 261–82.

Pettigrew, J. 1981. "Reminiscences of Fieldwork Among the Sikhs," in H. Roberts, ed., *Doing Feminist Research.* London: Routledge & Kegan Paul.

Powdermaker, H. 1967. *Stranger and Friend: The Way of an Anthropologist.* London: Martin Seiker & Warburg Ltd.

Rabinow, P. 1977. *Reflections on Fieldwork in Morocco.* Berkeley: University of California Press.

Rassam, A. 1974. "French Colonialism as Reflected in the Male-Female Interaction in Morocco." *Transactions of the New York Academy of Sciences* 36(2): 192–99.

_____. 1980. "Women and Domestic Power in Morocco." *International Journal of Middle East Studies* 12(2): 171–79.

_____. 1982. "Revolution Within the Revolution? Women and the State in Iraq," in T. Niblock, ed., *Iraq: The Contemporary State.* London: Croom Helm.

Reiter, R. 1975. *Towards an Anthropology of Women.* New York: Monthly Review Press.

Richards, A. and P. Martin, eds. 1983. *Migration, Mechanization and Agricultural Labour Markets in Egypt.* Cairo: The American University in Cairo Press.

Roberts, H., ed. 1981. *Doing Feminist Research.* London: Routledge & Kegan Paul.

Rogers, S. 1975. "Female Forms of Power and the Myth of Male Dominance: A Model of Female/Male Interaction in Peasant Society." *American Ethnologist* 2(4): 727–56.

Rohrlich-Leavitt, R. 1975. *Women Cross Culturally: Change and Challenge.* The Hague: Mouton.

Romalis, S., ed. 1981. *Childbirth: Alternatives to Medical Control.* Austin: University of Texas Press.

Rosaldo, M. Z. and L. Lamphere, eds. 1974. *Women, Culture and Society.* Stanford: Stanford University Press.

Rugh, A. 1985. *Family in Contemporary Egypt.* Cairo: The American University in Cairo Press.

Rynkewich, M. A. and J. P. Spradley, 1976. *Ethics and Anthropology: Dilemmas in Fieldwork.* New York: John Wiley & Sons.

Sabbah, F. 1984. *Women in the Muslim Unconscious.* New York: Pergamon Press.

Sacks, K. 1974. "Engels Revisited: Woman, the Organization of Production and Private Property," in M. Z. Rosaldo and L. Lamphere, eds., *Woman, Culture, and Society*. Stanford: Stanford University Press.

Said, E. 1978. *Orientalism*. New York: Pantheon Books.

Scheper-Hughes, N., ed. 1983a. "Confronting Problems of Bias in Feminist Anthropology." *Women's Studies*. 10(1): (special issue).

_____. 1983b. "Introduction: The Problem of Bias in Androcentric and Feminist Anthropology," in N. Scheper-Hughes, ed., "Confronting Problems of Bias in Feminist Anthropology." *Women's Studies* 10(1): 109–16 (special issue).

_____. 1983c. "From Anxiety to Analysis: Rethinking Irish Sexuality and Sex Roles," in N. Scheper-Hughes, ed., "Confronting Problems of Bias in Feminist Anthropology." *Women's Studies* 10(1): 147–60 (special issue).

Schrijvers, J. 1979. "Vivicentrism and Anthropology," in G. Huizer and B. Mannheim, eds., *The Politics of Anthropology*. Berkeley: University of California Press.

Schuetz, A. 1944. "The Stranger: An Essay in Social Psychology." *American Journal of Sociology* 49: 499–507.

Schwartz, M. and C. Schwartz. 1955. "Problems in Participant Observation." *American Journal of Sociology* 60: 343–53.

Shami, S. 1982. "Ethnicity and Leadership: The Circassians in Jordan." University of California, Berkeley, Ph.D. Thesis.

Shukri, G. 1985. "Conceptual Problems on the Arab Road Towards a Sociology of Knowledge" (min al-ishkaliyya al-manhajiyya fi al-tariq al-'arabi ila 'ilm ijtima' al-ma'refa). *Al-Mustaqbal al-Arabi* 77(7): 126–36 (Beirut, Lebanon).

Sowayan, S. A. 1985. *Nabati Poetry: The Oral Poetry of Arabia*. Berkeley: University of California Press.

Spindler, G., ed. 1970. *Being an Anthropologist*. New York: Holt, Rinehart & Winston Inc.

Spradley, J. P. 1970. *You Owe Yourself a Drunk*. Boston: Little, Brown & Company.

_____. 1979. *The Ethnographic Interview*. New York: Holt, Rinehart & Winston.

Spradley, J. P. and D. W. McCurdy. 1972. *The Cultural Experience*. Chicago: Science Research Associates.

Srinivas, M. N. et al. 1979. *The Fieldworker and the Field*. Delhi: Oxford University Press.

Stavenhagen, R. 1971. "Decolonizing Applied Anthropology." *Human Organization* 30(4): 333–43.

Stein, H. F. 1976. "A Dialectical Model of Health and Illness: Attitudes and Behavior Among Slovak-Americans." *International Journal of Mental Health* 5(2): 117–37.

Stephenson, J. B. and L. S. Greer. 1981. "Ethnographers in their own Cultures: Two Appalachian Cases." *Human Organization* 40(2): 123–30.

Sukkary-Stolba, S. 1985. "Roles of Women in Egypt's Newly Reclaimed Lands." *Anthropological Quarterly* 58(4): 182–89.

Sweet, L. 1960. *Tell Toqaan: A Syrian Village*. Ann Arbor: University of Michigan Press.

_____. 1967. "The Women of Ain ad Dair." *Anthropological Quarterly* 40(3): 167–83.

_____. 1974. "In Reality: Some Middle Eastern Women," in M. Mathiasson, ed., *Many Sisters*. New York: The Free Press.

Tillion, G. 1983. *The Republic of Cousins: Women's Oppression in Mediterranean Society*. London: Al Saqi Books.

Tucker, J. 1983. "Problems in the Historiography of Women in the Middle East: The Case of Nineteenth Century Egypt." *International Journal of Middle Eastern Studies* 15(3): 321–36.

van Baal, J. 1975. *Reciprocity and the Position of Women: Anthropological Papers*. Assen/Amsterdam: Van Gorcum.

Van Spijk, M. 1982a. *Remember to be Firm: Life Histories of Three Egyptian Women*. Cairo/Leiden: Research Centre Women and Development, State University of Leiden.

_____. 1982b. *Eager to Learn: An Anthropological Study of the Needs of Egyptian Village Women*. Cairo/Leiden: Research Centre Women and Development, State University of Leiden.

_____. 1982c. *Who Cares for her Health? An Anthropological Study of Women's Health Care in a Village in Upper Egypt*. Cairo/Leiden: Research Centre Women and Development, State University of Leiden.

Warner, W. L., et al. 1949. *Democracy in Jonesville*. New York: Harper.

Wax, R. H. 1952. "Field Methods and Techniques: Reciprocity as a Field Technique." *Human Organization* 11(3): 34–37.

_____. 1971. *Doing Fieldwork: Warnings and Advice*. Chicago: University of Chicago Press.

_____. 1986. "Gender and Age in Fieldwork and Fieldwork Education: 'Not Any Good Thing is Done by One Man Alone'," in T. L. Whitehead and M. E. Connoway, eds., *Self, Sex, and Gender in Cross-Cultural Fieldwork*. Urbana and Chicago: University of Illinois Press.

Weaver, T., ed. 1973. *To See Ourselves: Anthropology and Modern Social Issues*. Glenview, Ill.: Scott, Foresman and Company.

Whitehead, T. L. and M. E. Connoway, eds. 1986. *Self, Sex, and Gender in Cross-Cultural Fieldwork*. Urbana and Chicago: University of Illinois Press.

Wolcott, H. 1981. "Home and Away: Personal Contrasts in Ethnographic Style," in D. A. Messerschmidt, ed., *Anthropologists at Home in North America: Methods and Issues in the Study of One's Own Society*. Cambridge: Cambridge University Press.

Wolf, E. 1982. *Europe and the People Without History.* Berkeley: University of California Press.

Zimmermann, S. 1982. *The Women of Kafr Al-Bahr: A Research into the Working Conditions of Women in an Egyptian Village.* Cairo/Leiden: Research Centre Women and Development, State University of Leiden.

# Index

ARAB WOMEN IN THE FIELD

was composed in 10¹/₂ on 12 Goudy Old Style on a Quadex 5000 and Compugraphic 8400
by BookMasters;
with display type provided by Dix Type, Inc.;
printed by sheet-fed offset on 60-pound, acid-free Glatfelter Natural Hi Bulk,
Smyth-sewn and bound over binder's boards in Joanna Arrestox B,
also adhesive bound with paper covers printed in two colors
by Braun-Brumfield, Inc.;
and published by

SYRACUSE UNIVERSITY PRESS

Syracuse, New York 13244-5160